MW00576364

ROOSEVELT AND CHURCHILL: THE ATLANTIC CHARTER

ROOSEVELT AND CHURCHILL: THE ATLANTIC CHARTER

A RISKY MEETING AT SEA THAT SAVED DEMOCRACY

Michael Kluger and Richard Evans

FRONTLINE
BOOKS

First published in Great Britain in 2020 by

FRONTLINE BOOKS
an imprint of Pen & Sword Books Ltd,
47 Church Street, Barnsley, S.Yorkshire, S70 2AS

ISBN: 9781526786302

For more information on our books, please visit
www.frontline-books.com, email info@frontline-books.com
or write to us at the above address.

Printed and bound by TJ Books Limited, Padstow, Cornwall
Typeset by Concept, Huddersfield, West Yorkshire

Pen & Sword Books Ltd incorporates the imprints of Pen & Sword
Archaeology, Atlas, Aviation, Battleground, Discovery,
Family History, History, Maritime, Military, Naval, Politics,
Social History, Transport, True Crime, Claymore Press,
Frontline Books, Praetorian Press,
Seaforth Publishing and White Owl

For a complete list of Pen and Sword titles please contact
PEN & SWORD LTD
47 Church Street, Barnsley, South Yorkshire, S70 2AS, England
E-mail: enquiries@pen-and-sword.co.uk

Or

PEN AND SWORD BOOKS
1950 Lawrence Rd, Havertown, PA 19083, USA
E-mail: Uspen-and-sword@casematepublishers.com

Contents

Dedication

Michael Kluger: For my mother: Eleanor Kluger.
Richard Evans: For my sister: Margot Melville.

List of Illustrations

11. A portrait of Sumner Welles, circa 1940. (Library of Congress)
12. A portrait of Harry Hopkins, circa 1940. (Library of Congress)
13. The original draft of the eight-point Atlantic Charter showing Winston Churchill's handwritten changes. (Randolph Churchill)
14. Edwina Sandys called this painting of her grandfather painting 'Brush with History'. (Copyright: Edwina Sandys 2016)

Acknowledgments

The authors would like to pay special thanks to members of the Churchill family in the telling of this story, in particular, two of Sir Winston's granddaughters, Edwina and Celia Sandys, and great-grandson Randolph Churchill. We are also in debt to the keeper of the Churchill Archives, Allen Packwood, at Churchill College, Cambridge.

In addition our thanks to Robert and Mary Simses, Donald Barrett, Julia Brimelow, Charles Johnson, August Kluger, Geoffrey Leonard and to Owen Williams for bringing us together.

In this virtual moment of history, working across the Atlantic seemed normal and our thanks for the co-operation of John Grehan, Stephen Chumbley, Lisa Hoosan and all the team at Pen & Sword in the UK.'

Introduction

It wasn't planned. It wasn't signed. And when President Franklin D. Roosevelt was asked to produce a copy, he didn't have one. 'You would probably have to ask the radio operators on the *Augusta* or the *Prince of Wales*,' was the best suggestion of the man who, with a visitor, had sketched out an eight-point plan by which civilized nations would continue to conduct their affairs from that pivotal moment in history in 1941.

The visitor, appearing out of the mists of a grey Atlantic morning off the coast of Newfoundland, was, of course, Winston Churchill. Personally, they barely knew each other, but the minds of these two vastly different characters had already established an intimate understanding of one another's thoughts and goals by letter, often handwritten, and cable.

There were those who thought the meeting, which required the British Prime Minister to make a desperate dash across the U-boat-infested Atlantic on the unescorted battleship *Prince of Wales*, foolhardy, to say the least. The Canadian Prime Minister, Mackenzie King, put it bluntly: 'I feel he [Churchill] is taking a gambler's risk, with large stakes, appalling losses, even to that of an Empire, should some disaster overtake the gamble. It is a matter of vanity. There is no need for any meeting. Everything essential can be done better by cable communications.'

It was hard to argue with King. His appraisal of the meeting's circumstances was accurate. But buried in his assertions was a false claim. The essence of everything these two leaders would achieve together in the coming years would, in fact, stem from the irreplaceable act of personal contact: the look in the eye; the toast at dinner; the cigar and the cigarette late at night; the sizing up of the other man's mood, fears and ambitions. Face to face.

Of course, Churchill's journey had been foolhardy – wildly so. He took with him senior members of his armed services, and one torpedo from a U-boat could have sent them all to the bottom. Britain, standing alone against Hitler in Europe, would have been left leaderless. And leaderless in a sense that subsequent generations may find difficult to understand. Yes, he would have been replaced by his deputy in the Coalition Government – a shrewd if somewhat uninspiring Labour Party leader called Clement Atlee – but, at that moment in history it is possible to say that Winston S. Churchill was irreplaceable.

What had kept Britain going as troops were grabbed from the beaches of Dunkirk and bombs rained down on every industrial town in the country, night after night after night? The voice. The jut of the jaw. The look of ultimate defiance. 'We shall never surrender!' Through their radios, the British people heard it and read it in their newspapers and believed it.

Churchill, abused and scorned in Parliament as a warmonger, had become the only possible choice to replace the frail and discredited Neville Chamberlain once war was actually declared. And, accepting the King's call to take over the governance of a besieged and lonely nation in May 1940, he knew that his moment of destiny had arrived.

> As I went to bed at about 3.00 a.m., I was conscious of a profound sense of relief. At last I had the authority to give directions over the whole scene. I felt as if I was walking with destiny, and that all my past life had been but a preparation for this hour and for this trial. I was sure I would not fail. Therefore, although impatient for the morning, I slept soundly and had no need for cheering dreams.

From the miserable, hopeless 15-year-old who had written pleading letters to his mother to rescue him from Harrow, one of England's most prestigious schools, where he was known as a troublemaker who was quite good at history and fencing but useless at everything else, Churchill had, in an extraordinarily short span of time, turned himself into a young Army officer known for his bravado and risk-taking. Willingly, he sought action in Cuba, at the Battle of Omdurman in September 1898, and in the Boer War a year later before attaining high political office. This had been the preparation and, with the handshake of destiny in his grasp, it enabled to him to 'sleep soundly' on the eve of assuming responsibilities for a nation, an Empire and its peoples that would have left most men buried face down in their pillow.

But Churchill rose with a message for the country that bristled with all the defiance and, most importantly, all the honesty that his imperilled people needed to hear. He told a nervous and still sceptical House of Commons:

I would say to the House, as I have said to those who have joined the government, that I have nothing to offer but blood, toil, tears and sweat. We have before us an ordeal of the most grievous kind . . . You ask, what is our policy? I will say: It is to wage war, by land, sea and air, with all our might and with all the strength that God can give us: to wage war against a monstrous tyranny, never surpassed in the dark, lamentable catalogue of human crime. That is our policy. You ask: what is our aim? I can answer in one word: It is victory, victory at all costs, victory in spite of all terror, victory, however long and hard the road may be; for without victory there is no survival.

You want a leader who gives it to you straight? Churchill was your man. He knew the country needed to be rallied and reassured and that British citizens would react with cynicism to any hint of false promises. The great cartoonist David Low, whose left-leaning views had often mocked Churchill in the past, picked up on the tone set with such high oratory by the new Prime Minister and published a memorable drawing in the *Evening Standard*. It depicted Churchill with jutting jaw, his sleeves rolled up, marching at the head of a pack of politicians of all political stripes – Attlee, Chamberlain, Bevin, Halifax, Eden – also attired in shirtsleeves with a mass of supporters behind them. The caption read 'All behind you, Winston!'

And they were. Suddenly they realized he had been right all along. Throughout the 1930s, Churchill had issued warnings about the Nazi threat of massive rearmament. However, the impact of the Great War, to a far greater extent than in America, had decimated an entire generation of Britain's youth, leaving both the populace and Parliament with their hands over their ears. They hid behind the falsehood that Churchill was a warmonger and, time and time again, the Commons shouted him down.

No longer. After a brief spell in his old First World War position as First Lord of the Admiralty, Churchill was offered the job the country so desperately needed him to do, and he was ready. Overnight, No. 10. Downing Street became occupied by a very different leader.

Across the Atlantic, from his desk in the Oval Office, refusing to allow paralysis from polio to impair his own remarkable leadership qualities, Franklin Roosevelt read the cables and listened to the speeches as they crackled across the ocean, and realized that before he could entertain the thought of taking America into war against Germany, he would need the partnership of the British Empire – a term and concept that this avowed

Democrat found somewhat indigestible – as well as the British Bulldog who was leading it.

Roosevelt had already reconciled himself to the inevitability of war with Germany – and even, possibly, with Japan – at some stage, but he was careful to keep it to himself and his closest advisers. He, too, had an isolationist mood to deal with in Congress, and he knew he could not carry the country on the back of a gung-ho message of joining Britain in war. But Roosevelt, to a far greater extent than Churchill, who wore his emotions on his sleeve, was a master at camouflage.

Those around him discovered the longer they knew him, the less they knew him. Robert E. Sherwood, the playwright who was taken on as one of three speechwriters in the White House, found himself unable to penetrate what he described as FDR's 'heavily forested interior'. The President used the English language with skill but in a very different way than his new English friend – less oratorical, less forthright and frequently, and quite deliberately, confusing.

But the document that Roosevelt and Churchill worked on together over the four days they spent conferring aboard their respective navy vessels at Placentia Bay was the opposite. It was brief and clear and left nothing open to negotiation. It had been obvious to FDR and Churchill right back at the beginning of 1941 that, to defeat the Nazi evil and sort out issues relating to a possible war with Japan, the two countries would need a partnership, a partnership based on military cooperation and procurement. While envoys and advisers could meet, send cables, establish plans and carry them out, the leadership at the top needed to know and trust each other.

The document they pieced together was briefly referred to as a Declaration until the *Daily Herald*, a heavily left-leaning British newspaper that, with great irony, was the mouthpiece of the socialist Labour Party, came up with a name that better reflected its importance: the Atlantic Charter.

The informality of its creation and the bizarre circumstances under which the two leaders who would save the free world met and agreed on a template for proper relations between their nations remains one of the most extraordinary and unlikely happenings in history.

Stretching back to the Middle Ages, King John of England, pressured by his barons, had agreed to the creation of the Magna Carta in June 1215; in 1776 the fledgling states that would become the United States of America had created the Declaration of Independence and, with considerably less illustrious results, the end of the First World War produced the Treaty of Versailles in 1919.

Anyone with a peripheral knowledge of history would be able to point to these documents as having had an indelible impact on the way nations have conducted themselves in peace and war. But the Atlantic Charter? Today, like the mists that shroud Placentia Bay, a vagueness comes into the eye when people are asked about it. Yet the two great minds that forged this vision knew precisely what they wanted to achieve: keep it simple; keep it short; stick to the basic principles of morality and fairness without particular reference to religious mores. Attempts to disparage it came from all quarters, especially when a rambling Presidential press conference left reporters confused as to Roosevelt's exact intentions.

Although it would be an exaggeration to suggest – as did a *Christian Century* editorial – that the Atlantic Charter had been scrawled out on 'the backs of a couple of old laundry slips', the President did admit to 'scraps of paper' having been used as he and Churchill first put their thoughts in writing.

As the *Prince of Wales* and the *Augusta* rolled gently at anchor on the Atlantic swell of Placentia Bay at Newfoundland, it fell to Patrick Kinna, Churchill's young stenographer, to make sense of the scraps of paper and to decipher these musings which had morphed into the Eight Points which would form the Charter. It could be said that the densely inscribed Magna Carta might have been easier to read today had it not been written in medieval Latin but, even in English, the Charter proved no easy task for Kinna who was assigned to lending some coherence to the material thrust before him. Kinna, who died in Brighton at the age of 95 in 2009, was growing up in a different age, and had only one of those old bulky black typewriters to work with and did his best.

In the very first introductory lines there was an uncorrected typo – the intended word 'lift' being typed as 'loft' – and then, as is clear when one examines the document at the Archive Centre of Churchill College in Cambridge, Churchill went to work with his red pen. The small writing has blurred with time, and the red ink is smudged in places, but it is possible to verify that virtually all Winston's corrections went into the final document.

It would be nice to argue that each and every word of the Charter has been adhered to in the intervening decades. Obviously vicious eruptions of violence in places like Korea, Vietnam, Cambodia, Bosnia and Syria, externally or internally, have made that impossible. International trade has been another area of abuse and contention, while the arms race has barely been contained.

But the fact remains that the Atlantic Charter stands as a guide to principles that all men of integrity and decency can abide by. And, despite their moments of bombast and deviousness, of wrong turns during the course of long careers in positions of immense power and, in Churchill's case, of well-intentioned decisions that went cruelly wrong, Franklin D. Roosevelt and Winston S. Churchill strove, through the most challenging of times, to care for their peoples and ensure that hope always flickered through the darkest hours.

Writing now at the end of the second decade of the twenty-first century as the United States and democracies plough their way through the upheavals created by populism and instant communication, one can only hope that leaders approaching the stature of Roosevelt and Churchill re-emerge to guide us.

In returning to a story already well told many times over, we felt it would be helpful, at this moment in time, to throw additional light on an age of extreme danger and heroic deeds; of leaders of honour and decency who strove beyond the limitations of the average man, despite their age and infirmity, to preserve the rights of men and women across the globe so that they might live without fear in peace and freedom.

It was a seemingly impossible task of awesome complexity but, on scraps of paper off a desolate island in the Atlantic, they wrote history – and did their best.

PART I: THE ACTION

Chapter 1

Atlantic Voyage

Harry Hopkins, President Roosevelt's emissary to London, travelled down to Dover with Churchill in 1940 to inspect the front line of Britain's defences. From the vantage point of the famous White Cliffs, they could see the distant outline of the French coast where Hitler's battalions lay, champing at the bit.

They were passing some workmen, grappling with more barbed wire, when Hopkins overheard one of them look up and say to a pal, 'There goes the bloody British Empire!' Churchill smiled with delight when Hopkins relayed the remark to him. Given what we know of Churchill's level of realism and self-confidence, it is likely he did not think it too much of an exaggeration.

So it was even more incredible that a matter of months later 'The British Empire' was to be found setting forth on a 'Catch me if you can' journey of such foolhardy daring and such unjustified optimism as to leave historians gasping at its audacity several decades later.

Answering the call of the man he knew he must woo and befriend like no other, Churchill had embarked on this headlong dash across the North Atlantic on 9 August 1941, to meet with President Roosevelt off the coast of Newfoundland. Obviously, the Prime Minister felt the risk worthwhile but let no one be in any doubt that the undertaking appealed greatly to his schoolboy sense of adventure that remained undiminished at the age of 67.

Every effort had been made to keep the journey secret – easier in the days before the Internet – but the odds of the Germans not getting wind of it before Churchill was safely returned to 10 Downing Street were slim. Sooner or later the U-boat packs would be alerted to the fact that the biggest fish in the sea was swimming within reach. And those German submarines were everywhere.

Even a man with as stout a heart as Churchill must have had some forebodings about undertaking such a journey. In the month of June alone, U-boats sank seventy British or neutral ships in the Atlantic. A total of 329,000 tons of shipping went to the bottom of the ocean. By the time the Battle of the Atlantic was over, Hitler had lost 783 U-boats, but, in a relentless hunt and destroy operation, the German submarines had sunk 3,500 merchant ships and 175 naval vessels. Even before Roosevelt offered support by signing the Lend-Lease Act in March 1941, supplies had been getting through, but at crippling cost. Lend-Lease was a lifeline, but it alone would not suffice. So, despite the less than favourable odds of which, as a former First Sea Lord, he was well aware, Churchill felt he had no option but to accept Roosevelt's invitation for a meeting. He knew that, unless the relationship with President Roosevelt he had built by letter – signing as 'A Former Naval Person' – could be elevated to a full-blown alliance based on mutual and personal friendship, with all the full force of military might it would engender, Britain would lose the war. Equipment and armaments were Britain's most vital need. Ammunition, guns, tanks, food and auxiliary supplies: without these the lopsided nature of the conflict would tilt Britain into defeat.

Unless the United States became a fully-fledged military partner of the Allies against Germany, the heroics of the young British, Polish and Commonwealth pilots in their Spitfires and Hurricanes as they pitted their slightly faster and more manoeuvrable machines against the Luftwaffe's Messerschmitts would count for nothing. Creating crazy vapour trails over the Sussex Downs and the gardens of Kent in the hot summer of 1940, their victorious dogfights had made a fool of the boastful Reichsmarschall Hermann Göring and put his Luftwaffe to flight. By winning the Battle of Britain, the RAF had halted Hitler's plans for invasion in its tracks and altered the course of the war. Given the odds they had faced, it was no wonder the RAF fighter pilots inspired one of Churchill's most famous accolades: 'Never in the field of human conflict was so much owed by so many to so few.'

Those fighter pilots, often teenagers straight out of school with a few weeks' training, had been forced into the skies to defend Britain's island fortress as casualties mounted. They had made the ultimate sacrifice a hundred times over, and Churchill was not going to allow them to have died in vain.

The subject of a meeting between the President and the Prime Minister had been raised on several occasions during Harry Hopkins's frequent visits to London. By happy chance, the opinionated Englishman and the clever American diplomat had struck up an easy relationship that soon turned into one of the most vital friendships of the war. So Hopkins was already feeling at home in Downing Street in July 1941 when Churchill invited him into the little walled garden, which backs onto Horse Guards Parade from the rear of the house, to relay Roosevelt's latest and increasingly urgent wish for a meeting. 'I need to explain things to him face to face', was the message Hopkins had been told relay to the Prime Minister by a President who was walking a tightrope between the growing inevitability of joining the war against Hitler and keeping Congress, with its large isolationist factions, off his back. Acceptance was a huge gamble but, once he had received Cabinet approval, as well that as that of King George VI, Churchill set off in a mood of high optimism. Of course, there was danger, but both politically and militarily, danger had been Churchill's lifelong companion.

The journey itself was probably too far-fetched for the theme of a modern-day video game. From the moment of its inception the project had been a cloak-and-dagger operation of the utmost secrecy. The small, carefully selected cadre of British officers who gathered, at very short notice, on Platform 4 of Marylebone Station on Sunday, 3 August 1941, were wearing puzzled expressions. For the previous 24 hours, they had been sworn to such secrecy that they had barely dared to say hello to friends at their Whitehall offices. Who was going? Who was not? Until they congregated on the platform, no one knew. Even as the train chugged north, no one, except Churchill, Hopkins and a handful of very senior officers, had the slightest idea of where they were going, how they were going or why.

To be able to relate the story as it unfolded, we are indebted to *Atlantic Meeting*, the splendidly descriptive book written by H.V. Morton, a leading travel writer of the time who, with the novelist Howard Spring, author of the bestselling *My Son, My Son*, had been invited along to record the historic mission. Poor Spring, summoned to London from his home in the West Country, found himself answering the call without his teeth, which he had had extracted about week before. The new dentures were at his dentist's. Royal Navy steaks were not meant to be chewed on raw gums.

There was just time for lunch (probably soup for Spring) to be taken in the restaurant car before the train slowed to a halt at Wendover, a station just north of London. By then, given the subterfuge and unanswered questions, it was probably not so much of a surprise for the party on board to see, standing on the platform, wearing a blue suit, yachting cap and a wicked smile, the figure of the Prime Minister. And, of course, he was smoking a cigar.

A short while later, Morton and Spring were let in on the secret. 'No point in keeping it from you any longer,' said Colonel Hollis from the Ministry of Defence. 'We are going to Newfoundland to meet the President of the United States. We are to cross the Atlantic in the *Prince of Wales*.' Colonel Hollis added that it had been the best-kept secret that he could remember in Whitehall: 'Only one or two men in London know that he is really leaving England.' When asked about the Prime Minister's mood, the Colonel replied, 'He's rather like a schoolboy who's been left out of school suddenly. He says it's the only holiday he's had since the war.' For Churchill, it was an adventure and, to an amazing degree, he treated it as such.

An equal level of subterfuge was being conducted across the Atlantic with, it must be said, an equal dose of boyish enthusiasm. President Roosevelt was also a man of the sea, and, when he had time for a vacation, he liked nothing better than to sail on his official yacht, the SS *Potomac*. So what could be more natural than for him to announce to reporters that he would be taking a cruise up the coast to Maine 'to get some cool nights' during the hot and humid Washington summer?

Roosevelt even went so far as to exclude his wife Eleanor from the secret. The President's relationships with women close to him was complex. Respect, rather than any deep love, lay at the root of his marriage. He actually saw more of his cousin, Daisy Suckley, a dog-loving spinster, who spent time with him whenever his visited his country estate at Hyde Park in upstate New York. From all accounts, there was no romance but, even so, FDR evidently felt more inclined to confide in Daisy than he did his wife. Writing to Daisy on the eve of the Newfoundland adventure, Roosevelt let his true feelings be known:

'Even at my ripe old age,' he wrote, 'I feel a thrill in making a getaway – especially from the American press!'

In fact, the President went a step further than escaping the press. He escaped his own Secret Service too! After travelling by train from Washington to New London, Connecticut, from where he boarded the *Potomac*, a veil of secrecy and subterfuge was dropped over the whole adventure. On Monday, 4 August, much was made of the President welcoming a royal party on board consisting of Princess Martha of Norway and her three children so that they could all go fishing in Buzzard's Bay. This meeting was reported in the evening papers, and there were long-distance photos taken from the shore of the President relaxing on the yacht's deck. Except it wasn't the President.

With a quick sleight of hand, FDR, along with a small group of aides, had been whisked away to the *Augusta* anchored nearby, while the *Potomac*'s crew had been told to switch from uniform into 'holiday mode' civilian clothes. One crewmember, wearing rimless glasses and waving around a long cigarette holder, stood in for FDR. Secret Service agents, stationed along the Cape Cod Canal leading out to sea, were completely taken in. The President was thrilled that his ruse had worked so well. Leading people down the wrong canal, figuratively and in this case literally, had always appealed to his devious nature.

Staying in touch with the White House via naval radio, Roosevelt also ordered a bulletin to be issued to the press in a couple of days along the lines of 'All members of the party showing signs of sunning. Fishing luck good. No destination announced.' It worked for a while but, even before the President reached Newfoundland, the rumours were flying.

However, the secret held fast for a little longer in Britain. Having travelled the length of the country, Churchill's party left the train at Thurso, the northernmost mainland town, to be greeted by a chilly summer mist which hung low over the little harbour side houses. Men in oilskins took care of the luggage, while the Prime Minister was driven to the sea wall and thence, via a small craft, to the destroyer HMS *Oribi*. The new ship was named after a South African antelope, and, with the proud crew wanting to show her off to the Prime Minister, she fairly pranced across the narrow, heaving stretch of water – no more than eight miles wide – that separates the Atlantic from the North Sea.

It was a short run to Scapa Flow, the wide expanse of water a few miles to the north that was surrounded by small islands and served as the Royal Navy's base in both world wars. Shrouded in mist, the impressive outline of the battleship HMS *Prince of Wales* lay in wait. With Captain Leach clasping his telescope on the bridge; the band of the Royal Marines playing and many of the ship's 1,500 crew lining the decks as the *Oribi* drew alongside, H.V. Morton noticed sailors turning to each other and mouthing 'It's Winston!' as the bulky figure in naval uniform and his peaked cap crossed the gangway from ship to ship.

The *Prince of Wales* had been only recently commissioned but, in a matter of days, had seen action as one of the ships involved in the sinking of the *Bismarck*. Proof that this had not been a simple matter was offered to Morton when he was shown his cabin. There was a slight swelling of the floor. 'That's where a *Bismarck* shell came in,' explained Lieutenant Dyer-Smith, whose cabin Morton was requisitioning. 'It didn't do much damage but it left a bump, as you can see.'

The bump was the least of Morton's worries. His new quarters were over the propeller shaft. 'I was appalled at the thought of living there for the next three weeks,' he wrote. 'I knew I would never get used to it. The revolving shaft thundered below . . . and the vibration was almost worse than the noise. Small objects were given a life of their own . . .

Pennies, a book, a pencil all dancing out of time . . . falling one by one on the cabin floor.'

But worse was to come. The first night out, the *Prince of Wales* ran into an Atlantic gale. It was an epic storm, furious enough in its intensity for Winston Churchill, who had been in a few storms in his time, to rise uncertainly from his bed in the admiral's suite and order to be taken up to the captain's sea cabin on the bridge. The young officer charged with this task recalled the Prime Minister advancing towards him like 'an enraged cherub'. The lieutenant could understand why. With the propellers coming out of the water as the mighty ship reached the crest of another gigantic wave, the noise was, he said, 'quite hellish'.

So were conditions throughout the ship. Morton wrote vividly of what it was like:

> The monstrous plunges of a great battleship are so deliberate and slow as to be unlike the movement of any other ship; indeed, they are not like the movement of a ship at all. It is as though some vast steel works were flying unsteadily through the air. Almost as alarming as the movement are the sounds of a battleship in a storm; sounds to which the landsman can give no name and for which he can find no explanation: sudden bumps and bangs of ferocious power, as if the ship had a struck a rock or had been kicked by a passing leviathan, followed by an uneasy silence in which metallic objects fall with a crash and men are heard far away running in heavy boots on steel decks.

At 1:15 in the morning the decision had been made to forget about the three-destroyer escort, which simply could not keep up in such conditions, and to increase speed from 18 knots to near the ship's maximum of almost 30. 'Full steam ahead,' was the cry, an order and an attitude of mind with which Churchill, unsurprisingly, fully concurred. Happily, the raging storm was a hindrance to U-boats as well and, although one was reported to be directly ahead at one stage, necessitating a change in course, the *Prince of Wales*, with its irreplaceable cargo, ploughed on through 40-foot waves and howling winds.

It was at about this time that Churchill decided to change cabins, from a lower deck to one of the highest in the ship. In daytime on a calm sea, this would require no small physical effort. But at night in a gale? No wonder the young officer felt the task to which he had been assigned – getting a considerably overweight man in his late sixties, who just happened to be Prime Minister – from one end of the battleship to the other, was a nightmare that had never entered his dreams. Fighting the *Bismarck* was one thing, but this?

The inside of a battleship is a mass of steps, ladders and small staircases encased in a world of metal abutments protruding at nasty angles. It makes for an awkward journey at any time, but, in the dead of night with the rolling, bucking ship blacked out and nothing but the officer's torch for illumination, the odds of an elderly gentleman's hand missing a supporting rail were considerable. So when it came to a particularly tall and awkward staircase, the officer put a helping hand on the Prime Minister's arm.

'Young man! Do you imagine that I have never climbed a ladder in my life?'

Speechless, the officer shrank back, dropping his torch momentarily and when he could see again, he was presented with the sight of this large figure clad in a siren suite making good headway, ever upwards, to the captain's cabin. Once there, Churchill elected to stay put and quartered himself in these smaller but more convenient surroundings for the rest of the voyage. Captain Leach did not complain.

The storm ebbed, but the danger did not. As dawn broke, a rumour began circulating that Churchill's Atlantic dash had become known in Germany. No one seemed the least worried by this news, which Morton and Spring found slightly disconcerting. One officer, casually flipping through the satirical magazine *Punch* in the comfort of a wardroom chair, remarked that the *Prince of Wales* might have to fight her way home.

Some reported that the Prime Minister, on hearing that the cat was out of the bag, 'chuckled and twinkled and had been immensely amused'. The general opinion seemed to be that Winston would like nothing better than a bit of action and that keeping him below the armour plate, as the rules dictated, would not be easy.

'Well, that may be the rule,' one of the officers laughed. 'But I wouldn't like to be the man who ordered him to go down there. I know where he WOULD be during action – on the bridge!'

A routine quickly developed every evening, which included Churchill selecting a favourite movie to be shown in the wardroom. *Pimpernel Smith*, starring Leslie Howard, had been the first choice. On the second night, there was a quick change in the programme. Unexpectedly, the room full of officers found themselves watching a newsreel showing snippets of Harry Hopkins on his travels to Russia.

'Ah, there you are Harry!' Churchill exclaimed, obviously delighted by the gift of caviar the American had brought with him. During the intervals, while reels were being changed, he asked if anyone had a recording of Noel Coward's famous song 'Mad Dogs and Englishman Go Out in the Midday Sun.' It seemed highly appropriate, and when it was produced, the old Sea Dog proved he knew the words and the tune by singing along.

On the other side of the large 78 record, was the tune 'To England' from Coward's musical *Cavalcade*. When the last words were spoken, referring to the hope that England should live in dignity and peace, there was no sound in the wardroom until Churchill said, 'Hear, hear' with deep emotion. When the show was over, the Prime Minister, smoking a cigar evaluated by a gunnery officer to be a 'fifteen-incher', bowed gracefully and retired, as Morton put it, 'on a tidal wave of benevolence'. The whole scene would have driven Hitler nuts.

Chapter 2

Arrival in Newfoundland

He was up with the dawn, eager and impatient. While most of the battleship's crew lay in their bunks, the Prime Minister stood in his siren suit, savouring the day's first cigar, on the outside platform of the admiral's bridge. The Prime Minister was scanning the horizon, not for glimpses of a U-boat's conning tower, for that danger had momentarily passed, but for signs of the American fleet.

H.V. Morton, restless like any good reporter with a story unfolding before him, was the only other person to emerge that early on Saturday, 9 August 1941. We will let him describe the scene:

> Just out of bed, his sandy hair still ruffled from the pillow, he stood watching the sea that stretched to the New World . . . The War had provided no picture quite like this. We had seen the Dictators (Hitler and Mussolini) stepping from their armoured trains in the Brenner Pass, marching stiffly in military uniforms, their faces set in calculated scowls, but here was England's leader at the end of a hazardous voyage – which he had treated as if it were a pleasure cruise – alone, unspectacular, wearing the garment he had worn through London's most hideous nights.
>
> I had no idea what was to be discussed or decided between Roosevelt and Churchill, but I had no doubt that it would be one of the most significant meetings in history, and I thought I should always remember the picture of Churchill just out of bed that morning, anxious to be the first to greet the American Navy.

Churchill's anxiety to get the meeting with the President of the United States underway would have been clear to anyone who truly understood Britain's predicament that summer. The RAF might have helped save Britain from invasion, but Göring's bombers were setting the nation's industrial heartlands aflame every night, causing death and destruction on a scale never before seen in any war. The nation's women, wearing their headscarves, their sleeves rolled up, were working the assembly lines at factories, feverishly building aircraft, tanks and munitions. Their men were at war, but so were they. And so many died.

King George VI, ignoring pleas to flee to Canada, stayed put at Buckingham Palace, which did not escape the bombs. The nation as a whole was ready to heed Churchill's call to fight on the landing grounds, to fight on the beaches, to fight in the streets, but oratory would only take them so far, and reality was closing in. Britain stood alone, and only one person in the world had the capability to come to her aide. But did he have the will? That was what Churchill was so desperate to find out.

A few miles away, President Roosevelt, aboard the cruiser *Augusta*, was pondering his own reasons for having called for the meeting, with all the political and military dangers it involved. There is little doubt that the President saw it as a method of edging the deeply sceptical American people towards an unpalatable reality: that war with Germany was inevitable, sooner or later.

His methods would, of course, be the precise opposite to that of the British Bulldog. Straight answers, unequivocally enunciated, might, of necessity, have worked for the British Prime Minister in his darkest hour, but those were not the tools with which Roosevelt, with his soothing tones and radio fireside chats, drew the American people to his way of thinking. One could liken him to a poker player with a smiling countenance but, in conversation with his Secretary of the Treasury, Henry Morgenthau, he used another, even more revealing, description.

'I am a juggler,' he had said. 'I never let my right hand know what my left hand does. I may have one policy for Europe and one diametrically opposed for North and South America. I may be entirely inconsistent, and, furthermore I am perfectly willing to mislead and tell untruths if it will help win the war.'

But he did it with – as historians Douglas Brinkley and David R. Facey-Crowther put it – the infectious smile, the ebullient wave, the gift of phrasing lofty sentiments in unaffected language. It earned him the nickname of 'Snake Charmer' and, despite vociferous opposition, he kept the majority of the American people under his spell through four elections over two decades.

The fact that the *Prince of Wales* arrived far too early at Placentia Bay, the huge harbour where the two navies would be anchored for the next four days, was not on account of Prime Ministerial eagerness. Someone had miscalculated the time difference! The meeting had been set for 9:00 a.m., but the *Prince of Wales* arrived at 7:30 and steamed off along the coast for a while, peering at the mist hanging over low-lying hills which formed the edge of this heavily-indented island with its shores offering one bay after another. Placentia, 55 miles across at its mouth, was one of the largest anchorages in the world. Its water penetrated 19 miles inland.

Eventually, nearer the appointed time, Captain Leach, on the bridge with his telescope and the Prime Minister at his side, was able to make out the US Navy destroyers as they turned into the bay, guarding, as they had done all the way up the East Coast, the cruiser *Augusta*, with President Roosevelt aboard, the battleship *Arkansas* and the cruiser *Tuscaloosa*. Overhead, American seaplanes circled above this impressive rendezvous of what, Churchill so fervently hoped, could soon be called Allied sea power.

Shortly, the *Augusta* and the *Prince of Wales* would draw alongside each other and, as the Royal Marines band erupted into the 'Star Spangled Banner,' so the strains of 'God Save the King' would be heard drifting across the water. Churchill had already doffed his cap and was soon able to make out a tall, easily recognizable figure, standing under an awning and leaning on the arm of his son Elliott Roosevelt, who was then serving in the United States Army Air Forces. Elliot, like his brother Ensign Franklin Roosevelt Jr, had been summoned by their military superiors at the request of the President for this task, so that both leaders could be standing when they greeted each other or needed to move about during the Conference. The President wore a Homberg hat and was dressed in a light grey suit. For the first time since their brief and less than favourable encounter in London in 1918, the two leaders of the beleaguered Western World were about to meet.

The expressions on the faces of the sailors from both ships were full of curiosity. They shared a profession but, as of that moment, their experiences had been a literal ocean apart. The *Prince of Wales*, guns protruding from its turrets, was camouflaged, and its crew already hardened by combat. The American ships, by contrast, were painted in virgin, peacetime grey; their smiling sailors waving happily, still innocent of what lay ahead.

That they were about to witness something unique was no longer in doubt. Soon, the Admiral's barge appeared at the foot of the gangway and, as the bosun's pipe shrilled, the Prime Minister stepped aboard with a genial wave of the hand, before being whisked across the short strip of water to the President's cruiser.

He was seen emerging under the awning, bowing slightly as he handed President Roosevelt a letter from King George. There the formalities ended, as both leaders smiled and grasped each other's hands. Out came a Churchill cigar, and Roosevelt was soon reaching for his cigarette holder.

13

It was a scene that would be played out in many venues over the next four fraught years.

Watching from the *Prince of Wales*, Morton pondered as to whether he was actually watching History or, as he put it, one of History's understudies. Later, he wrote, 'It had that touch of drama and romance that enlivens every history book: the secret rendezvous, the guessing world, the swift voyage across seas open to the enemy; and as I leaned on the guard-rail, looking at the placid hills and assembled ships, I wondered if in years to come children will be taught the date – "Council of Placentia, August ninth, 1941".' Looking back over the decades, the answer to Morton would probably have to be, 'Not often enough'.

Lunch finally allowed the two leaders to interact face to face. There had been a warmth to their initial exchange, and it continued throughout the meal despite one awkward moment when Churchill appeared to forget their brief meeting in 1918. When Roosevelt referred to it – quite diplomatically considering how offended he had been at the time by the Englishman's imperious attitude – Churchill looked momentarily perplexed but recovered quickly and the conversation moved on to more urgent topics.

The Former Naval Person was, if not exactly at sea, then certainly anchored in more ways than one to the business of consummating a relationship that, in the space of four days, enabled two men to evaluate each other and come to trust each other to such an extent that, in tandem, they wrote the unfolding history of the world.

On that first day of meetings, Churchill, having taken his nap back on the *Prince of Wales*, returned to the *Augusta* for dinner with his new friend. He may have been as surprised as Morton and Spring to see all the ships at anchor ablaze with light, including the Royal Navy battleship. An officer explained that it had been decided to lift the normal wartime blackout as she rode at anchor amidst the US Navy because, from the air, a lone large dark vessel might have looked suspicious. 'It's unlikely the Germans will send over long range bombers because they would never make it home,' said the officer, adding cheerily, 'Still you never know . . .'

Had an enemy reconnaissance aircraft made it that far the next morning, its crew would have gazed down on an even more memorable scene. During the crossing, Churchill had decided to hold a Sunday prayer service for both crews on the deck of the *Prince of Wales*. The President had thought it a fine idea and, as if in agreement, the sun burst through the clouds for the very first time since Churchill's party had left Scapa Flow.

Small boatloads of American sailors converged on the British battleship from all over the bay and were greeted warmly as they swarmed over the side, mingling immediately with their counterparts, as the Prime Minister had insisted on no formality. Soon the President came aboard, walking stiffly and painfully on the arm of his other son, Captain Elliott Roosevelt of the American Air Corps. The two leaders were seated side by side with the vast gathering of over 1,500 seamen crowding the quarterdeck behind them.

'We have a grand day for a church parade,' Churchill had remarked to Morton beforehand, 'And I have chosen some grand hymns.'

Before the singing, a prayer was offered for King George VI by the British chaplain, who followed it with one for the oppressed countries of Europe:

'Let us pray for the invaded countries in the grief and havoc of oppression; for the upholding of their courage; and the hope for the speedy restoration of their freedom.'

Then, with voices uplifted to sunny skies over a silent bay, came the lusty rendition of 'O God, Our Help in Ages Past' and, unsurprisingly, Churchill's handkerchief was soon emerging from his pocket.

Lieutenant Colonel Ian Jacob, one of the senior officers in the Prime Minister's entourage, had reported that Harry Hopkins arrived from Moscow laden with vodka and caviar when he had joined them at Scapa Flow. Much of the caviar had probably been consumed by the time Captain Leach was able to invite the *Augusta*'s officers into his wardroom at Placentia Bay. But the vodka was still flowing along with all the other beer and spirits that are never allowed on US Navy ships. There was much comradery and swopping of sea-going tales and Lieutenant Colonel Jacob was able to come to some pertinent conclusions about the different attitudes about the war.

Like H.V. Morton, Jacob kept a diary of the voyage, but he was not a journalist, and most of what he wrote has never been published. Thanks to Allen Packwood at Churchill College, we are able to delve into his report and quote some of it here.

After pointing out that US naval officers seemed primarily concerned that as little as possible of the US Fleet should be drawn into the Pacific theatre – an irony that was not lost on Jacob when the United States was attacked at Pearl Harbor before the end of the year – Jacob wrote, 'They seem to think that the war can be won by simply winning the Battle of the Atlantic. General Marshall, on the other hand, favours reinforcing the Philippines so as to constitute a serious check to Japanese southward expansion.'

Even if General Marshall's advice had been heeded, it is doubtful whether it would have prevented Pearl Harbor, but Jacob's observation suggests that Marshall was one of Roosevelt's most perceptive and imaginative advisers. George Marshall went on, of course, to conceive the Marshall Plan, which, with financial aid totalling the equivalent of $140 billion in 2018 money, saved Europe economically after the war and helped reconstruct Germany.

Observing from the point of view of a British officer who had already been involved in the war for two years, Jacob analysed the differing attitudes to a possible conflict amongst the various members of the American forces whom he met.

'Their Navy is further ahead than their Army both in thought and resources,' he wrote.

> Both are standing like reluctant bathers on the brink, but the Navy are being forced to dip a toe into shark-infested waters. Their ideas have not got beyond how to avoid being bitten. They have not got beyond how to get rid of the sharks. The President and his entourage are far ahead and intend to keep pushing forward until the time comes when the Germans can no longer disregard American provocation.

And there was provocation, no matter how subtle to begin with, such as the very fact of a meeting with Churchill, but more obviously a short while later when Roosevelt agreed to get his navy more involved by offering to protect British convoys off Iceland, a favourite hunting ground for German U-boats. The question remained as to just how far the President was prepared to go. It was the question that hung in the air through all the lunches and dinners, intermingling with Churchill's cigar smoke throughout the four days that the great ships were anchored at Placentia Bay. Whenever he thought he saw an opening, a chance for something more concrete, Churchill would scrawl an idea on the back of a menu and try to push it past the silver cutlery and candelabra of the boardroom table towards the President. Hawk-like, despite his gaunt looks and barely functioning stomach, Harry Hopkins would grab it, stuffing it in his pocket before it reached its destination. Hopkins understood full well the Prime Minister's desires, but he also knew how and when to guard the President. No matter how ill Hopkins looked or felt, his guard never dropped; ever the umpire trying to ensure a balanced playing field, a formidable task when stuck between two heavyweights – particularly so on a literally rolling deck.

Churchill's greatest hope, of course, was for Roosevelt to declare war on Germany, but that was never going to happen while Congress, checking and perhaps misreading the shifting attitudes of the American public, feared a political backlash. Roosevelt was listening to Churchill and felt his anguish, but in August of 1941, he continued to play the juggler with both his political and military balls still in the air. Having just finished an agreeable lunch on the Tuesday, FDR would have been forgiven had he dropped both those balls in shock when news reached the *Augusta* of a frighteningly close vote in the House of Representatives on whether to expand the Selective Service Act of 1940. The Act initially required all men aged 21 to 45 to register so they could be notified in case they were drafted for a period of one year of service in the armed forces. The extension vote taken in the House of Representatives on 12 August 1941 extended the period of service from one year to two and a half years. The margin was one vote – 203 to 202.[1] The numbers offered stark evidence of the stubborn refusal of the isolationist, anti-war lobby in Congress. Of all the meetings that took place between the two principals and their top advisers, two stood out. On Saturday evening, Hopkins was able to get everyone's ear with a report on his visit to the inner sanctums of the Kremlin. The question of how much aid to offer the Soviets was still unanswered and depended very much on the information Hopkins had been able to bring back from Moscow. He was able to offer fresh news on the state of play on the Russian front, estimates of their military strength and, in particular, their attitude towards the threat of Japan. Hopkins was able to tell of Stalin's concern, relayed to him through Foreign Minister Molotov. They realized how tempting it would be for Japan to invade Siberia. As an act of dissuasion, Molotov wanted the United States to issue a strongly worded statement, vowing to come to the aid of the Soviet Union in the event of a Japanese attack. In some respects, it mirrored what Churchill was asking or FDR. The issue was settled a few months later by Pearl Harbor.

After dinner the tables were cleared, and those officers who had not dined with the top brass were invited in to hear Churchill talk. Curious, Roosevelt had wanted to let everyone have a first-hand experience of the British leader in full flow. He would not, of course, allow himself to be swayed by anything specific Churchill had to say, but he wanted to hear the oratory, to give himself a better understanding of the way in which Churchill was able to use words to combat the enemy at his doorstep and maintain the morale of his people.

---

1. Davis, p. 273.

The Prime Minister did not disappoint. Even Elliott Roosevelt, who could be bitingly Anglophobic, found it impossible not to be swept up in the moment. Later he would write: 'Churchill reared back in his chair; slewed his cigar around from cheek to cheek and, always at a jaunty angle, his hands slashed the air, his eyes flashed. He held the floor that evening and he talked. He held us enthralled that evening even when we were inclined to disagree with him.'

In other words, it was a classic Churchillian performance and, for once, Roosevelt was prepared to sit back and listen, silent throughout, ceding centre stage in a manner that few had ever seen him do before. But, typically, he kept his thoughts closeted in that 'forested interior' as Churchill unleashed his vision of the world. The Prime Minister focused on the need for reinforcements in Middle East, where he felt the Germans were vulnerable, ramming home his point because he knew the Americans were unconvinced. Turning to the Pacific region, Churchill called, not for the first time, for a joint warning to be sent to Japan and pointed to Singapore as a base that needed to be strengthened. (It never was and Singapore was overrun the following year as Japanese forces hacked their way through the jungle down the Malay Peninsula.)

Roosevelt's prime interest lay in what Churchill felt was required of America to win the war. It was not, the British leader emphasized, a war to be waged in trenches, requiring vast land armies, but a mobile war on land, sea and air. What was needed, he insisted, were squadrons of heavy bombers. Strategic bombing would slow Hitler's ability to replenish his armaments and also affect the morale of his people. 'Heavy bombing will bring home to the Germans the horrors of war, just as the Germans have brought it home to the British,' he said. Of the assembled Americans in the audience, only Hopkins, who had been in London during the Blitz, had seen it and felt it and could fully understand what the defiant Prime Minister was talking about.

Reaching for a high note, Churchill finished with a peek into the future, urging that 'when this disturbed condition in Europe was over' the United States and Great Britain could lead the way in forming a new League of Nations in an attempt to ensure that there would be no recurrence of 'the terrible tragedies we are now witnessing'.

There was a silence as Churchill, flicking away his cigar ash, subsided back into his chair. Roosevelt, perhaps wearied by the lateness of the hour, quickly retired to bed. He had seen it now, in close up, the full impact of Churchill's personality, and he must have understood the imperative of working with this formidable force of nature if Britain was to survive.

18

Generally, the meetings between the two principals and their senior staff officers had gone well, although General Marshall and his colleagues still felt they had not convinced the British of the impossibility of some of their demands. And, of course, the exact wording of the Atlantic Charter had not passed without argument.

Meanwhile, the elfin-like figure of Lord Beaverbrook had flown in and was soon in deep confab with the Prime Minister, sometimes pacing up and down the deck of the *Prince of Wales* as they discussed Britain's needs. An irascible and brilliant Canadian who had become a British newspaper tycoon when he bought the *Daily Express* in 1916, Beaverbrook had been called into Churchill's Cabinet and tasked with the formidable job of upping the output of the planes, tanks and ammunition Britain needed to survive.[2] But whatever numbers he managed to produce, it was never going to be enough, and he soon disappeared back down to Washington to negotiate for more assistance from the Pentagon.

---

2. Known to friend and foe alike as the Beaver, the Canadian certainly lived up to his name and played a major part in the war effort. Later, in retirement, Churchill was a regular visitor to his villa in Cap d'Ail where to this day, you can get off the bus heading for Monaco at the stop called Beaverbrook.

Chapter 3

The Atlantic Charter

For Roosevelt, it was clear that some form of joint declaration should come out of his meeting with Churchill. Whether FDR was aware that this document would, ultimately, provide a stepping-stone to something far broader and more permanent, namely the United Nations, is unclear. But the similarities in objectives are unarguable. Churchill admitted he had hardly set foot on the *Augusta*'s deck before the 'idea of laying down some broad principles that should guide our policies along the same road' came up. From this it is clear that the idea of the Charter had emanated from the American side.

However, FDR was quick to pick up on the fact that any American-driven document would almost certainly challenge the British Empire by critiquing colonialism and trade protectionism. Having realized that the concept of empire was a non-negotiable issue with Churchill, he decided to let the Prime Minister work from the 'bits of scrap paper' and come up with something that sounded sufficiently impressive and meaningful to attract attention while remaining vague enough so that areas of possible disagreement were not seriously impinged upon. Hopkins was told to give the message to the Prime Minister: start writing! Churchill immediately retired to his cabin, grateful that he was given the opportunity to produce the first draft. Recording the moment later, Churchill stated, 'considering all the tales of my reactionary, Old World outlook, and the pain this is said to have caused the President, I am glad that it should be on record that the substance and spirit of what came to be called "The Atlantic Charter" was, in its first draft, a British production cast in my own words'.

In achieving the required balancing act, vagueness probably won out, but the final document was still met with scorn by Roosevelt's isolationist critics who, rightly, regarded it as taking the United States and Britain a step closer to uniting in war. The isolationists' intent was to play down the whole affair, deriding the necessity of secret meetings at sea with battleships, cruisers, seaplanes and all the panoply of war.

Peace or principle? It is the everlasting question that haunts all leaders who know the difference between right and wrong and will not bow to the bully. It was the need to lay down the parameters of principle and the requirements thereof that inspired Roosevelt and Churchill to produce eight principles by which they felt nations needed to live in a post-war world. Given its almost immediate acceptance as a historic declaration, is birth was far from orderly.

As Brinkley and Facey-Crowther write: 'Initiated for immediate political purposes and conceived in haste and confusion, the Atlantic Charter ultimately achieved the status of a defining moment in the evolution of a post-war international order.'

Working through the night was, of course, no great problem for Churchill and the next morning he was able to present Sir Alexander Cadogan and Sumner Welles, the two prime members of the supporting cast, with his first draft. Having perused this initial effort, Welles went off to present it to Roosevelt.

Welles thought the first three articles of the Charter draft prepared by Churchill to be 'essential in their import and admirable in their clarity'. Welles was particularly pleased to see that the third point of the Charter recognized the 'right of all peoples to choose the form of government under which they live'. The concern, which had been discussed among the attendees, was that in 1941 Britain still had an extensive empire and was very sensitive to statements that might impact public thinking in India and other Commonwealth countries. It is a measure of Churchill's deep desire to gain American support for the war effort that he allowed the third article in his first draft. Welles did, however, find issue with several of the other points. One of his concerns was that the first draft contained a 'pledge that the United States would 'defend the rights and freedom of speech and thought whose rights were [then] abrogated in every Axis country'. Welles also found the Churchill first draft lacking in its support for free trade. The United States had been leading an 'effort to eliminate all such fatal impediments to international trade' such as 'high protectionist tariffs'.[1] Welles rewrote the draft with this and other issues in mind and then met with FDR to discuss it. Welles reported that the President considered and analysed every word. FDR then asked Welles to prepare a revised draft.

---

1. Sumner Welles, pp. 7–8.

22

The President and Welles presented their revised draft to Churchill and Cadogan at a meeting on the *Augusta* at 11.00 a.m. on the morning of 11 August. Harry Hopkins also attended the meeting. According to Welles, 'We sat around informally in the admiral's quarters, which the president used as his study as well as his messroom. The president was dressed in a grey suit with shirt open at the collar. The prime minister was dressed, as he was throughout the meetings, in his uniform. The bright sunlight streamed in through the open portholes.'[2] Welles reports that Churchill raised the topic of the joint statement by the President and himself at the conclusion of the Atlantic Conference. FDR proposed that an 'identic' statement be made in London and the United States with a suggested release date of 14 August. FDR was careful to not have the statement go beyond the provisions and commitments contained in the Lend-Lease Act. Churchill worried that if the joint statement said there were no further commitments made by the Conference it would be demoralizing to his countrymen and others around the world fighting Nazism. The parties agreed to have the joint communication reaffirm the commitments made under Lend-Lease rather than saying that nothing else had been agreed. The parties then turned to discussing the Charter.

The two parties were in essential agreement on the first three articles. However, Welles had inserted into Article Three the phrase 'people would have the right to self government'. Churchill advocated that this should be broadened to read 'that people would have their sovereign rights and self-government restored'. In Article Four, Roosevelt and Welles had focused on their concerns about free trade. The Americans wanted Article Four to make clear that 'all peoples had access without discrimination and on equal terms, to the markets and raw materials . . . needed for their economic prosperity'.[3] Churchill was concerned that Britain was bound by agreements such as the Ottawa Agreement which governed trade among the Dominions, knowing that he didn't have the authority to supersede. At best, Churchill felt he would need a week to gain necessary approvals.

Hopkins was horrified at the thought of a declaration of this importance being held up by the details embedded in a trade agreement and suggested that Welles and Cadogan rework the phraseology. But it was the Prime Minister who found the key, he suggested, '. . . with due respect to their existing obligations . . .' and that was the phrase

---

2. Sumner Welles, p. 11.
3. Ibid.

that did the trick. With that smoothed over, Churchill said he was in 'entire accord' with the fifth and sixth articles but an argument arose over the seventh, in which there was no reference to an effective international organization, as had been included in Churchill's original draft. Roosevelt, worried by 'suspicions and opposition' at home, was prejudiced against any revival of a new League of Nations and only wanted to deal with the reality – that, during any period of transition after the war was over, the United States and Britain would police the world. Who would argue? If those two nations had virtually all the ships and all the aircraft, opposition to the concept would be futile.

And so it was done, points conceded, arguments acknowledged but generally set aside to achieve a document that, only later, would become known as The Atlantic Charter. By the time Churchill had returned to the *Augusta* on Monday evening for a much more relaxed and convivial dinner with the President, he had wired the Declaration, as it was being called, to his deputy Clement Attlee in London. It was received at 2:00 a.m. Big Ben time but luckily that did not present a problem to Attlee. 'I was still up', he recalled later, 'I never got to bed early.'

That was probably not the case for the other members of the Cabinet who were roused from slumber just before 3:00 a.m. Working with a speed that amazed the Americans, Attlee had his colleagues read through the document, make a few comments, and then had it telegraphed back to the *Prince of Wales* by 4:00 a.m.

And so, the text below was agreed, but, as we have noted, never signed.

The Atlantic Charter

The President of THE UNITED STATES OF AMERICA, and the Prime Minister, Mr. *Churchill*, representing HIS MAJESTY'S GOVERNMENT IN THE UNITED KINGDOM, being met together, deem it right to make known certain common principles in the national policies of their respective countries on which they base their hopes for a better future for the world.

1. Their countries seek no aggrandizement, territorial or otherwise.
2. They desire to see no territorial changes that do not accord with the freely expressed wishes of the peoples concerned.
3. They respect the right of all peoples to choose the form of government under which they will live, and they wish to see

24

sovereign rights restored to those who have been forcibly deprived of them.

4. They will endeavour, with due respect for their existing obligations, to further the enjoyment by all States, great or small, victor or vanquished, of access, on equal terms, to the trade and the raw materials of the world which are needed for their economic prosperity.

5. They desire to bring about the fullest collaboration between all nations in the economic field with the object of securing, for all, improved labor standards, economic advancement and social security.

6. After the final destruction of the Nazi tyranny, they hope to see established a peace which will afford to all nations the means of dwelling in safety within their own boundaries, and which will afford assurance that all the men in all the lands may live out their lives in freedom from fear and want.

7. Such a peace should enable all men to traverse the high seas and oceans without hindrance.

8. They believe that all of the nations of the world, for realistic as well as spiritual reasons, must come to the abandonment of the use of force. Since no future peace can be maintained if land, sea or air armaments continue to be employed by nations which threaten, or may threaten, aggression outside of their frontiers, they believe, pending the establishment of a wider and permanent system of general security, that the disarmament of such nations is essential. They will likewise aid and encourage all other practicable measures which will lighten for peace-loving peoples the crushing burden of armaments.

Franklin D. Roosevelt
Winston S. Churchill
August 14, 1941

The public first heard of it when Attlee read it out loud on the BBC Radio the following day. It was well received but not ecstatically so. Especially in Britain, the people wanted tougher language and some hint that President Roosevelt was going to bring America into the war. Long before the end of the four days off Newfoundland, Churchill had reconciled himself to the fact that the timing was still not right. He took what he could get and, importantly for the future of the war and indeed for the future of mankind, worked carefully and cleverly on establishing a personal as well as working relationship with the man whose support he needed above all others.

The relationship between the two men may have been in its infancy but such was the almost instantaneous rapport that sprung up between them, they were able to leave us a charter which reflected the common goals and values of two nations at a moment of utmost peril.

Chapter 4

On The Waves – Homeward Bound

The two civilians, H.V. Morton and Howard Spring, viewed the return journey with trepidation. The President had steamed away on the *Augusta* and they were left to contemplate the message that had been relayed to everyone aboard the *Prince of Wales* that Hitler's navy was now fully appraised of the fact that their prize target was loose on the ocean and that the U-boats would be hunting in packs. 'The danger of a submarine attack must be considered imminent,' said Captain Leach over the loudspeaker. 'And, as we approach home, the danger of air attack must not be overlooked.'

Morton's response was to practise inflating his lifejacket in his cabin and, having done so, admitted to feeling unusually buoyant as he joined everyone for dinner. The Prime Minister, despite having just recovered from a cold, was rarely less than buoyant and was in full form as the battleship ploughed through the waves at full speed with its escort of four Royal Navy destroyers able on this occasion to keep up. But one of his greatest wishes had, as yet, not been granted. He wanted to see a convoy.

So on Friday, 15 August, as they were approaching Iceland, the captain managed to steer a course that would enable the *Prince of Wales* to catch up with a convoy of no less than seventy-two ships, carrying supplies to Britain. But below decks there was a problem. The signals officer, instructed to send the convoy the message 'The Prime Minister wishes you the best of luck' couldn't find the correct signal for Prime Minister. It didn't exist. Morton came to his rescue by suggesting he split the words 'Church' and 'Hill' preceded by 'Good Voyage'. So the problem was solved by the time Morton was called out onto the quarterdeck to see the convoy.

He wrote:

> I ran out and saw an amazing sight. We were racing through
> the middle of the convoy. There were tramps, tankers, liners
> and whalers, salty old tubs and cargo boats of every type, age
> and size on each side of us, the nearest only two hundred yards
> away, the crews clustered on decks and fo'c'sles, waving their
> caps and cheering like mad into the wind.

Morton felt sure they were yelling, 'Good old Winnie!' which would have
been appropriate as the man himself was up on the Captain's Bridge,
making his famous V sign and cheering back, as madly as any of them.
What he saw from that elevated position was the convoy spread out over
miles of ocean in six columns; ships with aeroplanes tied to their decks;
cargo-boats wallowing to the Plimsoll line with food and munitions;
liners deep in the water laden with every kind of war material and
tankers heavy with petrol. And they were headed for England! What a
heartening sight for a leader of an island at war.

Churchill could not get enough of it and ensured that he was not
denied. To everyone's surprise, when the *Prince of Wales* reached the
head of the convoy, leaving the leaders tossing in the tidal wave of their
wash, she turned full circle and raced back, beyond the last ship. With
his schoolboy's enthusiasm unquenched, 'Winnie' wanted to do it all
again and so they did, the great battleship speeding through the lanes
of the convoy at 28 knots, passing ships doing a quarter that speed,
with everyone cheering and waving all over again.

After the second run, he watched the convoy fade in growing
dusk and they disappeared, leaving only a smudge of smoke and the
knowledge that seventy-two ships were heading home to England.
Churchill watched them until he could see no more. 'A delectable sight,'
he said.

There was more to be said once the Prime Minister had disembarked
at Scapa Flow on Monday 18 August, and boarded the destroyer which
would ferry him to Thurso where his splendid train was waiting for him.
The restaurant car attendant in his brown uniform stepped forward to
greet him, asking if he had enjoyed a pleasant trip, as if he had been sun-
bathing in Florida.

When he addressed Parliament six days later, it became clear the
voyage had been a little more serious than that. 'This was a meeting,'
the Prime Minister began in those measured tones that the House had

been missed for three long weeks as a rapt chamber hung on his every word,

> which marks forever in the pages of history the taking-up by the English speaking nations amid all this peril, tumult and confusion, of the guidance of fortunes of broad, toiling masses in all continents, and our loyal effort, without any clog of selfish interest, to lead them forward out of the miseries into which they have been plunged back to the broad high road of freedom and justice. This is the highest honour and the most glorious opportunity which could ever come to any branch of the human race.

With that, ensconced once again at No. 10 Downing Street, the Prime Minister set about achieving the aim of which he had spoken previously. Victory.

PART II: THE ACTORS

Chapter 5

The Young Roosevelt

For two months, following his birthday on 30 January 1882, the 32nd President of the United States remained unnamed.

It was not a question of his parents, James and Sara Roosevelt, being short of options. Rather, there were too many. Both sides of the family could trace their roots to the very beginning of the fledgling nation and beyond – almost back to the *Mayflower* in 1602.

Franklin's ancestor, Claes van Rosenvelt, was a Dutchman who arrived in the 1650s. He worked as a miller in New York and had one son, Nickolas. One of Claes's grandsons, Jacobus – or James in English – founded the side of the family through which Theodore Roosevelt, the 26th President of the United States, traced his ancestors. They had settled in the Hudson River Valley and it is with James's son, Isaac, that we can find the first stirrings of involvement in public affairs.

Isaac was Theodore's great-great-grandfather. A sugar refiner by trade, Isaac supported the Revolutionary cause and helped draft New York State's first constitution. His influence was such that he rose to become the first President of the Bank of New York. So Isaac must have been on the list of possible names for the baby boy.

But then there was Franklin's mother, Sara Delano. Her family came from a long line of seafaring merchants, also dating all the way back to the *Mayflower*. In many ways, the Delanos were more established and wealthier than the Roosevelts. Sara's grandfather, Warren Delano, went to sea as a young man, became a merchant captain, and ended his career in the whaling industry in New Bedford, Massachusetts. Sara's father, also named Warren, was born in 1809 and, at the age of 24, sailed on the clipper *Commerce* to Canton, China, where he stayed for 12 years. Joining a company overseeing trading operations in Macao, Canton and Hong Kong, Warren became a partner of the Russell Company, the largest American trading firm in China. While amassing a fortune of more than $1 million, Warren was able to return to the United States for some leave during which time he met and married Sara's mother, Catherine Robbins Lyman. The newlyweds went back to China for several more years and eventually returned home in 1846 to settle in New York. Warren did not waste his wealth either. Grabbing the burgeoning opportunities of the new industrial age, he made shrewd investments in real estate, railroads and a mining operation in Tennessee. Meanwhile Catherine was busy producing eleven children. The seventh, Sara, Franklin's mother, was born on 21 September 1854.

So, apart from Isaac, Warren must have come into the reckoning as a name for the future President. But there was another contender. Warren had a younger brother named Franklin Delano who Sara grew up calling 'Uncle Frank'. Settling on a child's name can be a contentious issue, and while we do not know what arguments ensued in naming this particular baby, if any, it is clear that Sara's wishes carried the day. She must have been fond of her uncle, because, two months into a life that would guide the history of the world, the baby became Franklin Delano Roosevelt.

Unsurprisingly, this seemed to please Uncle Frank, the baby's great-uncle, and, writing of the new arrival, he said the baby was 'a beautiful little fellow – well and strong and well behaved with a good shaped head of a Delano type'. Franklin Jr. had plenty of opportunity to grow stronger still as the family spent almost all their holidays and family events at Algonac, a 60-acre estate which Warren Delano had built on the west side of the Hudson River near Newburgh to allow them to escape the confines of New York City.

Not surprisingly for a youth of his relatively affluent means, Franklin was home schooled until he went off to Groton School at the age of 14. While home schooling might have deprived him of social interaction, his educational path was superior. He rose early each morning and had a full day of study. He began learning German at the age of six and shortly thereafter studied French. There was a set recreational period in the afternoons before returning to more studies. While Franklin didn't have school companions, he did have an abundant supply of cousins and neighbours, many of whom became lifelong friends. There was also a half-brother called Rosy, who was his father's son from a previous marriage but Rosy was 26, hardly a playmate sibling.

All in all, it was an idyllic upbringing with his doting mother, Sara, playing a constant role in the young boy's life. Franklin saw less of his father, who was well into his fifties at the time of his birth. James Roosevelt was born in 1828 and, after attending Union College and Harvard Law School, from which he graduated in 1851, he began practising law in New York City. However, the profession obviously did not hold his interest. Upon coming into his inheritance, which included the family estate, Mount Hope, as well as considerable funds, James decided to quit the law and devote himself to maintaining the large estate where his own father, Isaac, had spent much of his life raising exotic plants and breeding horses.

James had been married 23 years when his wife, Rebecca Brien Howland, died suddenly of heart failure at the age of 41. James was 48 and it was four years before he met the future mother of Franklin Roosevelt. For James, it was love at first sight, but Sara viewed the relationship more cautiously. Not only was she two inches taller than her future husband and considerably younger – 26 to his 52 – but there had been a man in her life. In her early twenties, the architect Stanford White had courted her. At the time, White was far from becoming one of the leading architects in the United States and hadn't yet reached any level of financial security. As a result, Sara's father was adamantly opposed to the relationship. Forced to give up the only man she really loved, according to her friends, Sara started to become more amenable to James Roosevelt's advances. It was said that she eventually agreed to marry him because she feared ending up as 'old Miss Delano'.

The couple were wed at Algonac on 7 October 1880 and spent their first month together at Springwood, a home James had bought some time earlier which sat in 110 acres with a spectacular view of the Hudson River Valley at Hyde Park. They then embarked on a lengthy European honeymoon, designed, one might assume, to get Stanford White out of Sara's mind.

Sara was a devoted mother, and her children became her central focus as she endeavoured to create a loving home for the son who would go on to become America's longest-serving President. Inevitably, after home schooling and so much personal attention, the transition to Groton School in Massachusetts wasn't easy for young Franklin. He was 14 when he matriculated but many of his classmates, having enrolled at age 12, had long since formed strong relationships by the time Franklin arrived. He had never been away from his parents before, and his early letters to them contain elements of homesickness, although nothing compared to the desperate, pleading letters Winston Churchill fired off to his mother from Harrow at about the same age. Franklin confined himself to such guarded comments as 'thanks very much for your letters, the more the better'. But, as we have seen, he was never as direct as his future comrade-in-arms.

Franklin was tall for his age, but he wasn't a high-achieving athlete. He did excel at tennis and golf, but those were not the sports that helped gain status and respect among his classmates. He never played team sports and was somewhat of an initial loss athletically. Franklin also grew up in the age of the gentleman C, and, while he was a competent student, he was far from top of his class. Churchill, bottom in everything but history, would have sympathized, perhaps a little enviously.

An early report card shows a B in Latin, Greek, English and Composition, and a C in Physics. Still, in his time at Groton, Franklin comported himself well. He was polite and on time and, in his last year, he was awarded a prize in Latin, became a dormitory prefect and won a letter as equipment manager of the baseball team. No budding Babe Ruth, but at least he was involved.

At Groton he had matured into a fine young man with a growing sense of confidence. He had learned to get along with his classmates and formed several lasting friendships. In 1900, he graduated and was accepted to Harvard that coming autumn. But his new life was interrupted within a few weeks by the death of his father. James's health had been failing for some time and he was staying at a New York apartment so as to be near various physicians when he passed away on 8 December that year.

Franklin was clearly upset by the loss of his father. They had spent happy times together at Springwood and travelling in Europe when Franklin was young, but they saw less of each other once Franklin went off to Groton and his father's health declined. Dutifully, Franklin attended the funeral and stayed with his mother throughout the holidays before returning to Harvard after the New Year.

Franklin may also have viewed attending Harvard itself as something of a duty. He had already fallen in love with the sea as a result of sailing on his father's boat *Half Moon*. When she was docked in New York, father and son used to enjoy sailing up the coast into Buzzard's Bay and the Gulf of Maine, all the way to the northernmost point of Maine where the family had a summer home on Campobello Island. Franklin was so taken with being a seaman that, during his third year at Groton, he considered enlisting in the US Navy when the Spanish-American War broke out. Had he been allowed to follow his instincts, he might have ended up in Cuba with Churchill, but he was under tighter parental control than the adventurous Englishman. James and Sara were adamant that he should pursue a career in law, so Harvard it was.

Life at Harvard was easier for Franklin than his time at Groton, as Jean Edward Smith writes about his living arrangements in the biography *FDR*:

> The University was rigidly stratified in those years. Students from socially prestigious families, most of whom had attended East Coast private schools, lived off campus in sumptuous resident halls . . . Roosevelt, together with his Groton classmate Lathrop Brown, took a three-room corner suite at Westmorly Court, the newest of the Gold Coast edifices, and, with Sara's help, furnished it in opulent style. He lived there for the next four years surrounded Grotonians and other preppies.

Socially and academically, Franklin found Harvard to be liberating. In addition to his comfortable living quarters, which allowed him to make friends more easily, he was able to select his own courses. In his last year at Groton, Franklin had taken the equivalent of a first-year required course load at Harvard. This freed him to choose his own classes and, if he preferred, to graduate in three years rather than four. Unlike many of his friends, who relied on money and connections to become successful in life, Franklin took his studies seriously and handled a full course load. But he was still selective. He chose to avoid philosophy and theory and stuck to history, government and economics courses where he felt more confident of doing well. At the end of his first year at Harvard, Franklin was elected to the editorial board of *The Harvard Crimson*, the college newspaper. That was an achievement in itself but, after three years, he was considered highly enough to be made editor-in-chief.

Franklin was obviously becoming a person of note on campus, which made his failure to win election for membership into the Porcellian Club all the more disappointing and mysterious. The Porcellian was deemed to be the most prestigious social club at Harvard, and membership was so closely guarded that it needed only one negative vote to ensure someone was blackballed. As Franklin's record at the university was without blemish, there was speculation that a relative was the cause of the problem. Franklin had a nephew who had married a dance hall girl from the Tenderloin district of Boston, a defiant act that had scandalized the social world in which the Roosevelts lived. If true, it was sad because Franklin would, on occasion, admit that being turned down by the Porcellian was the greatest disappointment of his life. And the reason for it seems to have been beyond his control.

Around the turn of the century, Franklin had been given a chance to become better acquainted with Theodore Roosevelt. Cousin Teddy had also attended Groton and had visited his old preparatory school while he was Governor of New York. The visit overlapped Franklin's time there, and the Governor was sufficiently impressed with his young cousin to invite him to a 4 July gathering at his home on Long Island.

Uncle Teddy had also attended Harvard, which gave the pair of them another bond. Once Theodore was elected President in 1901, it shouldn't surprise the reader to learn that Franklin visited his relative in the White House. The visit did nothing to dim the younger cousin's growing ambition to follow in Uncle Teddy's footsteps and, at some point in the future, to make 1600 Pennsylvania Avenue his residence, too.

Their lives had already been following uncannily similar paths. We have noted the educational similarities, which continued, since both attended Columbia Law School. Teddy had enrolled in 1880 but left after two years to begin serving in the New York State Assembly. Franklin attended Columbia Law in 1904, but he, too, chose not to graduate when he passed the New York Bar exam after his second year and began practising law at the New York firm of Carter, Ledyard & Milburn. Both Teddy and Franklin went on to serve in the New York State Legislature, as Assistant Secretary of the Navy, then Governor of New York and eventually ran as for the office of Vice-President and then President. These remarkably similar paths ensured that a Roosevelt had a dominant hand in the affairs of the United States of America for the better part of half a century.

Franklin was happy to follow in his cousin's footsteps but they were ultimately very different people. Teddy was a forceful and exciting politician. He obtained national prominence as the colonel who led the charge at the Battle of San Juan Hill during the Spanish-American War – a conflict which, of course, allowed an upstart British lieutenant to taste the thrill of war, if only briefly, in Cuba. It is interesting to speculate what Teddy and Winston would have made of each other had they met during the war, but differences in rank forbade that. They both defined the characteristics of a Big Personality.

Franklin, in contrast, differed totally in the way he moved his career forward. Charming, thoughtful, cautious and devious, Franklin mapped out his future with care. Considering how different they were, it is remarkable that they were able to follow such a similar path to the ultimate prize.

In 1910, after three years practising law, Franklin decided to run for public office. Spending his days behind a desk in New York had started to bore him, and he was drawn to the more active and stimulating life of a politician. While his cousin Teddy was a Republican, Franklin's social instincts drew him towards the Democratic Party, not least perhaps because his parents had always been role models of civic goodness. Although the Roosevelts lived in great comfort in the small village of Hyde Park in upstate New York, their home was not nearly as grand as that of the Vanderbilts, which was located just two miles north of the Roosevelts' Springwood estate. Nevertheless, they were considered among the leading citizens of Duchess County. One might argue almost a New World version of *noblesse oblige*. This sense of fairness and restraint was also emphasized in the rigour and simplicity of the life Franklin was forced to live his formative years at Groton.

His father, James, had been a lifelong Democrat and had taken him to meet President Grover Cleveland in the White House as a boy. Cleveland was a Democrat who worked for social reform and always tried to distance himself from party machines. Cleveland spoke out against patronage and favoured politicians who were honest and capable. Franklin admired the political dynamism of his cousin, whose platform did focus on progressivism but, in the end, Franklin registered as a Democrat. When the time came to run for political office, there was little doubt that he would do so as a member of the Democratic Party.

Franklin's first campaign was for the office of State Senator, representing the area around Duchess County. His skill in his newly chosen field became immediately apparent when he won in what had been a heavily Republican Senate District. The vote tallied was 15,708 for Roosevelt and 14,568 for his opponent, Stanley Weintraub.

Franklin served in the New York Senate for a little more than two years before accepting the appointment from the then President Woodrow Wilson as Assistant Secretary of the Navy in March 1913. So, in step as ever with Cousin Teddy, Franklin moved to Washington, where he could set about building himself a national reputation. Dealing with the sea and ships was greatly to Franklin's liking and he served with distinction in his first nationally-important role for eight years – right through the First World War.

On a personal level, behind the public figure, it is widely acknowledged that there were four women who impacted Franklin Roosevelt's life from birth to death. His mother, Sara Delano Roosevelt; his wife, Eleanor; the woman he loved, Lucy Mercer; and the woman who loved him, Missy LeHand.

Sara Roosevelt was the definition of a devoted mother. There may have been servants at her beck and call, but it was Sara who bathed and dressed Franklin. She breastfed him until he was one and didn't allow him to take a bath unattended until he was eight. As Sara's only child, Franklin had no rivals for her attention. Until the day she died, her son was the prime focus of her life, and the two of them were never far apart.

Sara was only 26 when she had Franklin, a young and vigorous woman who had no intention of pampering her son despite her devotion to him. She expected him to be strong and successful and was always on hand to ensure that he had everything he needed to fulfil her dreams as well as his own.

When Franklin's father died, Sara promptly moved to Boston to be near her son. Later, when Franklin was married and working as a lawyer in New York City, Sara purchased a house for her son and his bride at 49 East 65th Street and immediately bought a home for herself a short walk away. She was even more involved in the family home at Hyde Park, presiding over every aspect of the house, including furnishings. This included bedroom assignments. Whether Franklin liked it or not, his mother's bedroom was next to his, while his wife's was down the hall. This was the pattern throughout Franklin's life. When he became President, his ever-present mother moved into the White House, too.

Franklin's wife, Eleanor, was born a Roosevelt and her husband's cousin. Her father, Elliot Roosevelt, was a brother of President Theodore Roosevelt. Great family connections could not, however, compensate for the awful sadness that left her an orphan by the age of 10. Her father, mother and one of her two brothers all passed away before she reached her teens. As a result, Eleanor was sent to live with her maternal grandmother, who was not able to offer the comfort and love that the poor girl must have craved. Strict and cold, the grandmother packed Eleanor off to school in England at the age of 15.

The Allenswood Academy for Girls was not your average English school. For a start it was French, totally French. It was owned by a French woman called Marie Souvestre who, in her way, was even stricter than Eleanor's grandmother. All classes were taught in French, and not a word of English was allowed to be spoken. Punishment for breaking this or any of the other numerous rules resulted in having your bed stripped and the contents of your locker dumped on it. The girls were allowed three baths a week of exactly 10 minutes in duration. Exercise was mandatory and consisted of long walks on nearby Wimbledon Common.

The school was situated on Albert Road which, going downhill instead of up to the Common, is about fifteen-minute walk from what is now the All England Lawn Tennis Club. In Eleanor's day, that would have been a farm, as the tennis championships did not move from nearby Worple Road to the current site at Church Road until after the First World War.

The house, which acted as the school building, was part of Earl Spencer's estate, which was torn down in 1950, long before the family's most famous member, Diana, was born. An apartment block, still bearing the name Allenswood, was built in its place.

Eleanor seemed to enjoy her new life in England, despite the strict regime. In contrast to some of the other British and American students, she quickly became fluent in French and found herself stimulated by the boldly progressive, feminist views of Mlle. Souvestre. The pair actually became quite close, and Eleanor found herself being invited to accompany her teacher and mentor on trips to Europe during school breaks. At Allenswood, in many ways a female equivalent of Groton, Eleanor was taught social responsibility and personal independence. Students were encouraged to be women who thought for themselves and lived their lives for the betterment of society. They were expected to challenge the conventional norms and assert themselves to make the world a better place. It would be interesting to know how many of Mlle. Souvestre's young ladies went on to become suffragettes.

At the age of 17, Eleanor wanted to complete another year at Allenswood but was recalled to New York at the insistence of her grandmother for less intellectual reasons. Eleanor was to become a debutante, which meant joining in the endless parties that made up the social season on the East Coast – an activity designed, almost exclusively, for young ladies of a certain class to find a husband. Thinking for oneself was not high on the list of requirements.

Back on the East Coast, Eleanor was fortunate to move in circles that were far from vacuous. The Roosevelts, as a clan, met on numerous occasions during the year, especially at Christmas and, as cousins, Franklin and Eleanor became casually acquainted. But there was an attraction that blossomed quite quickly when they took a walk together one afternoon in 1903 as the woods along the Hudson were decorating the landscape with the glorious colours of fall. They talked, and no doubt Eleanor recounted her stories from Allenswood and the impression the progressive Mlle. Souvestre had made on her. Franklin was already a liberal thinker, and their commonality of purpose soon created a strong bond.

From that point on, Franklin and Eleanor were in constant contact, and, when they couldn't meet, Eleanor wrote Franklin almost every day. In September 1904, when Franklin enrolled at Columbia Law School, law was not the only thing on his mind. On 11 October, on the occasion of Eleanor's 20th birthday, Franklin presented her with a ring. Nothing was officially announced, however, until 1 December. With Sara no doubt working overtime, all the wedding plans were soon in place, and the young couple was married in New York City on 15 March 1905, with the recently inaugurated President Theodore Roosevelt presiding. Babies were very much on the agenda, and Franklin, who was three years older than his wife, soon found himself with five children, their third child, Franklin Jr., having died at one year old.

The Roosevelt's came of age during the early years of the twentieth century as the Victorian era began to fade into history. It was a time for new ideas on both sides of the Atlantic, and, stimulated by what she had learned in London, Eleanor found herself in step with her husband's progressive thinking. Franklin himself was influenced by the thoughts modern thinkers like Uncle Ted and the man who would succeed Theodore in the White House, Woodrow Wilson.

In New York, as in other major cities, the rich enjoyed grand lives, but the lower classes lived mostly in squalor and overcrowded slums. Jacob Riis's 1890 book, *How the Other Half Lives*, had documented their plight, but nothing much had been done. Slowly, a new generation of well off upper- and middle-class Americans began to pay attention to the needs of those less fortunate. It became an era of social reform and improved housing, and the Roosevelts wanted to play their part. It was also an era of 'muckraking' against entrenched political machines that governed not so much for the good of their citizens as to keep themselves in power.

This did not sit well with a person of Franklin's ethics although, as we shall see, it took a while for his liberal tendencies to kick in. Surprisingly for someone who would become beloved by huge swaths of the country over two decades as President, the young man who got himself elected to the New York State Senate in 1912 was not popular in Albany. According to Jean Edward Smith's *FDR*, most of his colleagues found him insufferable. Jean Edward Smith describes how he was viewed by several leading politicians and reformers. Al Smith, a four-time Governor of New York, thought him a dilettante; the great reformer Robert Wagner felt he was only after publicity, and even the genial Tim Sullivan, who was inclined to think well of most people, found him to be 'an awfully arrogant fellow'.

Frances Perkins, who would later become the longest-ever serving Secretary of Labor under FDR but was then fresh out of Colombia Graduate School, was more detailed in her criticism of the future President. Perkins, who moved in the same New York social circles, felt that no one would have thought Roosevelt could rise to the highest position in the land. Observing him on the floor of the New York Senate, she wrote of him: 'He was not particularly charming (that came later);

artificially serious face, rarely smiling, with an unfortunate habit of – so natural that he was unaware of it – throwing his head up. This, combined with his pince-nez and great height, gave him the appearance of looking down his nose at most people.'

Perkins got the impression that Roosevelt didn't like people very much and was afflicted with a youthful lack of humility – 'a streak of self-righteousness and a deafness to the hopes, fears and aspirations which are the common lot'.

If this evaluation flies in the face of the concerned politician Roosevelt became, Perkins had her own experience of FDR's early indifference. In 1911 a bill to limit the workweek of women and children to 54 hours was tabled. The measure stalled in committee, and the Democrats were divided. Perkins sought Roosevelt's help but was given short thrift. 'No, no. More important things. More important things. Can't do it now. Much more important things,' she quoted him as saying.

Roosevelt was also a bystander during debates about the devastating Triangle Shirtwaist factory fire, which had killed 146 people, mostly young women working in appalling conditions in a building in New York's Greenwich Village. Most fire exits had been blocked on high floors and many people jumped to their deaths. Rose Schneiderman of the Women's Trade Union League uttered sentiments many were scared to voice themselves when she told a rally at the Metropolitan Opera House, 'The life of men and women is so cheap and property so sacred, it matters little if one hundred and forty six of us are burned to death.'

The uproar gave rise to thirty-four bills addressing industrial reform throughout the nation being tabled which went some way to reducing fire hazards in poorly maintained buildings. Roosevelt, however, played no part in these proceedings.

Soon after being elected to the New York State Senate, Roosevelt aligned himself with the Democratic leaders from upstate New York who wanted to break the hold of New York Tammany Hall Democrats and Republicans. However, with his ambitions growing, Franklin soon realized just how difficult, if not impossible, it would be to overcome the deeply entrenched Tammany Hall power block and decided to look elsewhere.

So, one day in 1911, he crossed the Hudson River and paid a visit to the Governor of New Jersey, Woodrow Wilson, who was planning to run for President. He was with a group of Democrats who had travelled to Trenton to meet and discuss how to rustle up votes for Wilson in New York. In a move that would help shape his destiny, Roosevelt managed to get himself invited to travel back to Princeton, where Wilson lived, with the Governor. The dour, stern 55-year-old Presbyterian academic and the 29-year-old rookie New York State senator sat next to each other on the train. Wilson thought his young companion to be a little glib, a little too eager and pushy, but became impressed when Roosevelt gave an accurate report on the state of the potential delegate count in New York.

As a result, Roosevelt began trying to help Wilson in the run-up to the 1912 Presidential campaign. It was not an easy task because Wilson had angered Wall Street with his progressive agenda and was losing support. Roosevelt invited nearly a hundred delegates from upstate New York to attend a dinner at the Belmont Hotel in an effort to counterbalance to the antipathy in Manhattan. But only three showed up. If that was a crushing embarrassment, Roosevelt brushed it aside and continued to do what he could for Wilson's cause. When the 1912 Democratic Convention got under way, the New York state senator, getting his first taste of national politics, was working the city's hotel lobbies and restaurants, letting the charm that he had concealed in Albany burst forth. Although still patrician in manner, his height, good looks and quick repartee ensured that he was noticed – and listened to – as he extolled Wilson's virtues.

When the balloting started in a stifling convention hall, it was unclear how much effect Roosevelt and other Wilsonian supporters had had with their arm-twisting. Champ Clark led with 440 votes, Wilson was second with 324, and Judson Harmon, the conservative governor of Ohio, had 148. Waiting in the wings was Charles Murphy and his ninety-strong New York delegation. When it appeared Clark was gaining unstoppable strength, Murphy decided the moment had come and, announcing that New York would throw its votes behind Clark, reckoned he had made the decisive move. William Jennings Bryan, known as the Great Commoner from Nebraska who had led the Democrats to defeat on three previous occasions, decided he hadn't. Rising to address the Convention, Jennings Bryan intoned in a voice that had held so many previous gatherings spellbound that he would withdraw his support and vote for Wilson 'so long as the ninety wax figures of the New York delegation vote for Champ Clark'.

Chaos ensued and, with the heat rising literally and emotionally, one ballot followed another. On the thirtieth ballot, Indiana Governor Thomas R. Marshall switched his state's 31 votes to Wilson, who pulled ahead 460 to 455, still far away from the required 726 needed to nominate. Then, as the balloting entered its fourth day, Illinois succumbed to the Wilsonian momentum and, on the forty-sixth ballot, Wilson was nominated with a total of 990 votes.

It had been a hugely demanding process, taxing everyone's stamina and will, but the result was to have an extraordinary knock-on effect for the presidential history of the United States. Woodrow Wilson, who would bring Franklin Roosevelt to Washington as Assistant Secretary for the Navy, went on to win the Presidency in November after beating divided Republican opposition in one of the most confusing elections in history. William Taft, who had succeeded Theodore Roosevelt in 1908 when Roosevelt had elected not to run, suddenly found himself faced with his predecessor who had decided to return to the fray four years later. Unable to reach an agreement with Taft, Teddy Roosevelt formed what was known as the Bull Moose party and became a second Republican candidate or a third party candidate – depending on opposing viewpoints – in opposition to Wilson and the Democrats.

As was to be the case so much in 2000 and 2016, the Electoral College came into play and elected the candidate who lost the popular vote. Combined, Taft and Roosevelt earned 1.3 million more popular votes than Wilson, but the Democrat gained 435 Electoral College votes as opposed to Roosevelt's 88 and Taft's measly eight. The Wilson Presidency, carrying Franklin Roosevelt's destiny with it, was born.

In the meantime, FDR had been battling to retain his seat in the New York Senate, an exercise made all the more difficult by the handicap of being struck down with a serious attack of typhoid fever As a result, he was forced to spend the entire campaign in bed. The fact that he managed to win, despite a total absence from the hustings, was almost totally due to one man: Louis McHenry Howe.

For a man of such patrician appearance, the tendency to gather offbeat characters around him was a particularly Rooseveltian inclination. We see it much later in his career when, as President, he leant heavily on the advice of Harry Hopkins, who was far from being a traditional political aide. But he had no problem with that. He had been prepped in eccentricity by Louis Howe. The foul-smelling Sweet Caporal cigarette that hung permanently from his lips was the least of it – after all, everyone smoked. But Howe, a newspaperman writing mostly for *The New York Herald*, was 5ft tall, thin as a rail, with a scar on his face from a childhood bicycle accident. He was described as being rumpled beyond repair – the sort of man you could spend a fortune on at Brooks Brothers and have him walk out onto Madison Avenue still looking a mess. He seemed to take delight in his less than salubrious appearance, claiming to be one of the four ugliest men in New York. 'Children take one look at me on the street and run,' he said.

So what was Howe's appeal? He was a political mastermind, totally engrossed in the genre, and in search of a hero. Being permanently broke, he needed patronage and was not afraid to ask. Having helped

FDR during the Wilson's election, he fired off a desperate letter to the young State Senator. 'I'm in a hole. If you can connect me with a job during your campaign, for heaven's sake help me out.' Roosevelt listened, and a strange partnership was born.

From his sickbed in Manhattan, Roosevelt let Howe run his campaign. In truth, he didn't have much alternative, but he could hardly have found a more willing or energetic surrogate. By the time he had finished, Howe had mailed more than 11,000 letters with FDR's signature, most directed at specific groups like apple growers or farmers. Howe knew apple growers had a problem with being charged for oversized barrels, and he told them that FDR would fix that. This was his specific political genius: on such details are elections won.

The farm vote was vital, and Howe knew what made farmers mad: the middleman who pocketed the difference between what the farmers received and what the consumer paid. Howe pointed out that, if elected, FDR would become chairman of the Senate Agriculture Committee and would take care of the hated New York Commission merchants. Shad fisherman were also told they would pay less for licence fees on the Hudson.

As an example of how to hit voters where they live, it was a master class. Needless to say, Roosevelt loved it and even smiled when he received a letter like this from Howe: 'Here is your first [newspaper] ad. As I have pledged you in it I thought you might like to know casually what kind of mess I was getting you into . . . Your slave and servant, Howe.'

The 'slave' was incorrigible to an extraordinary degree. With FDR flat on his back at East 65th Street, never having set foot in his own district, Howe wrote a letter attacking the Republican opponent for not having visited Columbia County during the campaign! Somehow the media didn't pick up on it, as Howe began to display his ability to fool most of the people most of the time. When he went on to help FDR with his run for President of the United States, he managed to orchestrate public appearances with such care that many people remained unaware that Franklin Roosevelt, already stricken with polio, could not walk.

On a national level, the 1912 election reflected Roosevelt's local triumph, made all the more amazing by the fact that Howe had somehow managed to increase his man's margin of victory compared with two years before. He was just part of a Democratic sweep that saw Woodrow Wilson trounce his two opponents with the Electoral College. Immediately, FDR's thoughts turned to Washington although, by the time he was well enough to return to Albany, he did not seem capable of taking on any greater tasks. Pallid and drawn, his appearance worried

Eleanor and his mother Sara, but slowly he gathered enough strength to keep his ambitions in focus.

So much so that, when Wilson began choosing Cabinet appointments, Franklin and Eleanor checked into the Willard Hotel, a long-time watering hole for Washington politicians. They wanted to be seen, to make it obvious that FDR was around, available and healthy. On his first day in Washington, he ran into the incoming Secretary of the Treasury, William Gibbs McAdoo, whom he had gotten to know during the campaign. McAdoo suggested two plum jobs: either secretary or collector of customs at the Port of New York. FDR was grateful but did not commit himself. He knew what he wanted: the No. 2 job at Navy.

On the morning of the inauguration, FDR caught the fish he was angling for. Just a few days before, Wilson had chosen Joseph Daniels, the editor of a North Carolina newspaper, as his Secretary of the Navy. The fact that Daniels didn't know the difference between a bosun and a yardarm may have prompted him to offer FDR the job he craved almost on sight when they met in the Willard Hotel's vast lobby. He must have heard that Roosevelt was a sailor, as at comfortable at sea as on land, and would have been comforted by the thought of having an expert to turn to.

And anyway, first impressions were good. Daniels found FDR 'bubbling with enthusiasm' and not afraid to display his eagerness. 'Nothing would please me so much as to be with you in the Navy,' he said. 'All my life I have loved ships and been a student of the Navy.'

Having agreed to Roosevelt's immediate appointment, Daniels felt he should, out of courtesy, pay his respects to the Empire State's most senior senator, a Republican called Elihu Root who had served as Teddy Roosevelt's Secretary of State. Daniels remembered that a strange look came into Roots eye when he mentioned FDR. 'You know the Roosevelts, don't you?' Root asked. 'Whenever a Roosevelt rides, he wishes to ride in front.'

But evidently Daniels was a confident man, despite sailing into new waters. 'A chief who fears an assistant will outrank him is not fit to be chief,' he said.

Even if he didn't know much about seafaring, Daniels, with his journalistic background, did not need to be reminded that he was offering FDR the same position from which Theodore Roosevelt had launched his own presidential bid. Following in the family tradition did the young Roosevelt no harm at all.

Nor did having Louis Howe at his side. Having established himself as a political whizz-kid, Howe was an obvious choice for Roosevelt to take to Washington with him, and he quickly set about teaching the new Assistant Secretary a few vital details about how to deal with labour leaders during wage hearings. Howe's natural role was that of a troubleshooter and, at the first whiff of a strike, Little Louis was off to put out the fire. Roosevelt was not the only person to benefit from Howe's tactical acumen. By the end of his presidency, Wilson had gained a reputation as a strong friend of labour.

Roosevelt needed less coaching when it came to naval matters. Having battleships and destroyers at his disposal was nothing less than pure joy to this intrepid sailor, and he made the most of his new powers, enjoying a seventeen-gun salute – four more than a rear admiral! Not to be outdone on the flag front, FDR had his own flag designed so that it could be flown whenever he was aboard a navy warship.

All that might have been for show, but Roosevelt knew what he was doing when he asked to be allowed to take over the wheel of a destroyer and quickly gained the confidence of the naval officers whose company he kept. He was one of them, and the naval hierarchy were thrilled when he pushed for the enlargement of the navy just as Teddy Roosevelt had done from the same desk a decade before.

With the eruption of conflict in Europe in August 1914, Roosevelt emphasized the need for preparation within his own department and was more vociferous on the matter than Daniels. According to Frank Freidel in *Roosevelt*, FDR wrote to Eleanor, 'I am running the real work, although Josephus is here! He is bewildered by it all, very sweet but very sad!'

In 1914, as wholesale war flared in Europe, Roosevelt flirted with political danger by passing on naval details to Senator Henry Cabot Lodge, a Wilson foe, and being openly critical of the Navy's deficiencies when he testified before the House Naval Affairs Committee. At no little risk to himself, FDR was determined to let everyone know that America was unprepared. It gained him a lot of newspaper coverage, and Lodge's son-in-law, Congressman Augustus P. Gardner was quoted as saying, 'I admire the courage of Franklin Roosevelt.'

Interestingly, Daniels does not appear to have reprimanded his subordinate for any of this, despite personally toeing the President's more cautious line. However, by the fall of 1915, Wilson was starting to realize that some action was necessary and implemented a preparedness programme. It was a good thing he did so, because on 1 February 1917 Germany announced it was unleashing the full might of its submarine force in an effort to starve out Britain and France before the United States entered the war.

That Wilson would take that final step was becoming inevitable, but the snail-like pace at which he moved towards the inevitable decision frustrated Roosevelt. Desperate to keep the momentum going, FDR dug out of the government archives a piece of old legislation that allowed a President to authorize the arming of merchant vessels without any new Congressional approval. This enabled Wilson to ignore a Senate filibuster and do the Assistant Secretary's bidding, to an extent. When FDR went to him to urge that the whole fleet be moved and be prepared for war, the President refused. But just as an infuriated Roosevelt was about to leave the Oval Office, Wilson called him back and explained his reasons in words that FDR never forgot, especially when he found himself in a similarly agonizing situation in the early 1940s. Roosevelt, apparently speaking with great accuracy, reported Wilson as having said, 'I want history to show that not only that we have tried every diplomatic means to keep out of the war; to show that war has been forced on us deliberately by Germany; but also that we have come into the court of history with clean hands.'

When Wilson did, finally, call for a declaration of war against Germany in 1917, Roosevelt was like a man released from his bonds and threw himself into the task of making the American Navy as shipshape as possible for the coming conflict. He would later boast that, during the previous years, he had jigged and sidestepped conservative naval regulations like a running back in an effort to prepare for the inevitable and, allowing for some considerable exaggeration, it was true that he was the most dynamic and far-sighted member of Wilson's team when it came to waging war.

It must be emphasized, however, that no matter how frustrated FDR had become in his role as Daniels's No. 2, he bristled at any suggestion of disloyalty. When the media attacked some of Daniels's cautious decisions while finding little fault with his deputy, a friend of FDR's wrote suggesting that he should work to push his boss out of the way. Replying, Roosevelt said that he had 'no use for a man who, serving in a subordinate position, is continually contriving ways to step into his boss's shoes, and I detest nothing so much as that kind of disloyalty'.

Wilson's hand had been forced when three American ships had been sunk by U-boats in March, and the President knew he had no alternative but to put the proposal before his cabinet. Daniels was in tears when he made the vote for war unanimous. Later, facing Congress, the President, greeted by a standing ovation, said, 'A state of war has been thrust upon us. The world must be made safe for democracy.'

Such was FDR's reputation in Washington at the beginning of hostilities that 'See young Roosevelt about it!' became a catch phrase among those searching for some urgent task to be completed at full speed. The Assistant Secretary was in charge of the Navy's procurement and often he did not wait for Congress to appropriate the money before sending out contracts for huge amounts of materiel and equipment. Many things got done at his behest, not least the rapid construction of training centres and, more dramatically, the laying of a North Sea underwater mine barrage, stretching from the Orkney Islands to the coast of Norway, against the German U-boats. The original idea was not his, but FDR was the man who ensured that it happened.

Roosevelt was desperate to get into uniform himself but, despite urging from cousin Theodore, the President insisted he stay put in DC. In the summer of 1918, however, FDR was allowed to travel to Europe and got close enough to the front in Flanders to hear the guns blazing. He met with King George V, French Prime Minister Georges Clemenceau, whose energy at 77 impressed him immensely, and had a brief introduction to a snooty Winston Churchill who, occupied as he was as Minister of Munitions after his own brief foray in the trenches, gave the Assistant Secretary of the Navy short thrift. Roosevelt was not impressed but, happily for the outcome of the next war, he put the slight aside when the pair met properly off Newfoundland in 1941.

Roosevelt, who also visited Rome to meet with senior Italian naval officers, was thrilled with every aspect of his trip right up to the moment the frightful European flu epidemic of 1918 hit the crew and passengers of the USS *Leviathan* on the way home. Globally, the epidemic claimed 20 million lives and several of the passengers of the *Leviathan* were buried at sea. Roosevelt did not escape the disease and spent much of the voyage in his bunk, semi-conscious.

Eleanor went to get him when the ship docked at New York, but he was too weak to walk and, having been transported to his mother's East 65th Street house by ambulance, he had to be carried up the stairs by orderlies – an unhappy foretaste of things to come. In a week or two, FDR recovered but, after Eleanor found a bundle of love letters while unpacking his luggage, his marriage never did.

The letters were from Lucy Mercer, a young lady from an impoverished socialite background whom Eleanor had hired as a secretary to help her with the mail when the Roosevelts had moved to Washington in 1914. Once Eleanor started spending more time with the children at Hyde Park, FDR saw more of Lucy. Her smile captivated everyone, but no one more than the Assistant Secretary of the Navy. Inevitably, perhaps, they fell in love. The attraction was so strong that anyone spending time in their company could tell what was happening. Friends provided cover by acting as escorts for Lucy at dinners and others, such as Alice Longworth, offered safe houses where the pair could meet. Alice also offered an unnecessarily unkind observation. 'Franklin deserved a good time,' she said. 'He was married to Eleanor.'

For most of the war, the couple and their friends managed to keep the secret from Eleanor, who had become consumed with her involvement with the Red Cross, for whom she worked almost every day. But she felt increasingly isolated from her husband's Washington life and turned to his mother for comfort, writing to Sara several times a week. She craved some intimacy and did not hide her feelings from her mother-in-law: 'As I have grown older I have realized better all you do for us and all you mean to me, and the children especially, and you will never know how grateful I am and nor how much I love you, dear.' Happily, Sara responded with equal warmth, and the pair became increasingly close – an unlikely occurrence in many respects as there had been considerable friction between these two powerful personalities in the early years of Eleanor's marriage.

No one had a greater opportunity to witness how the two women related to each other than Curtis Roosevelt, FDR's grandson who grew up at the White House and Hyde Park during the 1930s. In his book *Too Close to the Sun* he wrote:

> My grandmother's ordinarily scrupulous politeness towards people seems to have been set aside whenever Granny [Sara] was the topic under consideration. She always looked down on her mother-in-law's 'vanities'. What she meant by this was Granny's unembarrassed practice of a life-style that was completely passé. My grandmother had a keen sense of the reforms needed in our society and, in her view, her mother-in-law was living in the past in a society where 'knowing your place' was the norm, a desirable value.

However, such differences melted away when Eleanor found herself in desperate need of someone close to turn to. Sara had been instrumental in refusing any thought of a divorce on the grounds that it would destroy her son's political career and, anyway, Lucy Mercer, as a Catholic, would have had great difficulty in marrying a divorced man. So, with Louis Howe acting as broker in the family crisis, an agreement was reached. FDR agreed never to consort with Lucy again – a pledge that lasted until clandestine meetings began again in 1941 – while Eleanor agreed to continue, outwardly, as the faithful, supportive wife. It could be said

51

that she remained supportive of his career but, personally, the bedroom door was locked. They never had personal relations again, which might well have been a relief to Eleanor who, divulging her thoughts about sex to her daughter Anna much later, admitted to never having enjoyed 'the act'.

That did not diminish the emotional blow she had suffered on reading Lucy's love letters. 'The bottom dropped out of my world,' she said later. But she was only relating to her personal world. Girding herself in true Roosevelt tradition, she flung herself into the list of good causes she espoused throughout her life and, once her husband became President, earned a thoroughly justified reputation as one of the most effective and best loved First Ladies in history.

As for the future President, FDR hid a broken heart with fortitude and remained unerringly protective of his wife's feelings, never allowing a critical word of her to be uttered in public. But inwardly he grieved, and it must have been difficult for him to accept Lucy's marriage in 1920 to Winthrop Rutherford, a hugely wealthy and respected member of East Coast society.

But no amount of personal grief was allowed to interfere with the sometimes startling way he went about his business as Assistant Secretary of the Navy. Edward Smith recounts an incident that illustrates just how decisive and daring Roosevelt was becoming with his newfound power. Towards the end of the war, the Navy Department had ordered the construction of two battleships for the Argentine government. They were built at the Fore River shipyard in Quincy, Massachusetts. The shipyard was run by Bethlehem Steel whose assistant manager at the time was none other than Joseph P. Kennedy, founding father of the Kennedy dynasty.

All went well until the Argentine government admitted it could not come up with the cash. Roosevelt, in a meeting with Kennedy in Washington, told him not to worry, as the State Department would take care of it. Kennedy, on the instruction of his boss, Charles Schwab, said that wasn't good enough and that the ships would remain in the yard at Quincy until they were paid for.

Roosevelt thought not. Less than a week later, four Navy tugboats were to be seen approaching up the Fore River, loaded with combat-ready Marines. As the shipyard workers looked on in amazement, the marines, bayonets at the ready, boarded the two battleships and had the tugboats tow them into the harbour where Argentine crews were waiting to receive them.

Kennedy was forced to stand by helplessly while this operation took place, and he admitted later that, 'Roosevelt was the hardest trader I'd ever run up against. I was so disappointed I broke down and cried.'

When the tears dried, Kennedy found himself politically in the Roosevelt camp and campaigned vigorously for FDR's re-election in 1936. As a result, he landed the plumb posting of Ambassador to the Court of St. James where, unhappily for his future political ambitions, he chose the wrong horse. Unable to conceal his anti-Semitic and fascist views, he championed Prime Minister Chamberlain's appeasement policy and found himself increasingly *persona non grata* in London society when Churchill came to power.

Chapter Six

President! Overcoming the Odds

The fact that Roosevelt had made an ill-judged pitch for a New York senate seat in 1914 – losing heavily to James W. Gerard, the US Ambassador to Berlin who had left his post to run on the Republican ticket – did not douse FDR's long-term political ambitions. He knew the journey had to be taken in stages, but there was never any doubt that the White House was his goal. Had he listened to his boss, Josephus Daniels, who had warned him it was not the right time for Democrats, he might have avoided the tripwire that the political climate presented. As it turned out, he lost by the embarrassing margin of 210,765 votes for Gerard to FDR's 76,888.

Roosevelt was hurt by the severity of his defeat but quickly put it behind him, storing away some political lessons for the future. It was six years before another chance presented itself, and FDR grabbed it in the most literal sense. At the 1920 Democratic Convention in San Francisco, a spontaneous, sentimental show of appreciation for President Wilson erupted as delegations from state after state poured into the aisles holding their standards aloft. Only New York, displaying their distaste for the outgoing President, remained seated. Seizing his chance, Roosevelt, with a wink from the delegation leader Charles Murphy, grabbed his state's standard and joined the parade. Hundreds cheered. FDR had been noticed.

More significantly, he was noticed again when he volunteered to give the speech seconding the nomination of Al Smith, whom Murphy would use as a stalking horse for whomever emerged as their favourite in early balloting. 'I love him as a friend,' said FDR of Smith. 'I look up to him as a man, I am with him as a Democrat . . .'

The speech was well received and not merely for the oratory. Frances Perkins, that stern critic of FDR during his early days at Albany, called him 'one of the stars of the show' and, with bitter irony considering what fate had in store, recalled how 'he displayed his athletic ability by vaulting over a row of chairs to get to the platform in a hurry'.

Al Smith survived seven ballots before Murphy switched most of New York's votes to James Cox, the solid but not terribly exciting Governor of Ohio. FDR and some colleagues from upstate New York preferred William Gibbs McAdoo, Wilson's son-in-law. The next four days saw the Convention dither between Cox, McAdoo and Wilson's Attorney General A. Mitchell Palmer. But Cox pulled ahead and clinched the nomination near midnight on Monday, 6 July.

What price a name? Not for the first or last time in American politics, James Cox offered an example of the value it carries. Stating his reason for choosing FDR as his running mate, Cox said, 'My choice is young Roosevelt. He's right geographically and his name is good . . .'

Backing Cox's decision the next day, Ohio's leader, Judge Timothy J. Ansberry, spoke from the podium to say, 'His name is a name to conjure with in American politics – Franklin D. Roosevelt.'

At that moment in history, even the most ardent FDR fan could not have envisioned the impact 'the young man,' who was already 38, would have on the future of his nation. A four-term President in the years ahead? No one could have envisioned with that.

On 6 August 1920, the pending star of Democratic politics resigned from his post at the Navy Department with the blessings of his boss ringing in his ears. 'It is of particular gratification,' said Josephus Daniels, 'that this Convention unanimously has chosen as candidate for Vice President that clear-headed and able executive and patriotic citizen of New York, the Assistant Secretary of the Navy, Franklin D. Roosevelt.'

So, spared of any reference to bayonet-wielding Marines in tugboats, FDR hit the campaign trail. By the end he could have done with more than a boatload of them. Louis Howe thought he was improving in eloquence on the stump, but a growing tendency to get carried away with his own (often highly exaggerated) achievements started to work against him. He had not, for instance, written the Haitian Constitution or 'run Santo Domingo for seven years'. Truth mattered, even in an age when facts were not as easily verified as in the modern age of Twitter and Google.

But these fibs were not the cause of the disaster that hit the Cox-Roosevelt ticket. The electorate was tired of Wilsonian politics and tired of his insistence on the formation of the League of Nations, and their boredom with the policies on which Cox and FDR were campaigning showed up dramatically on election day. In what became the Democrats' worse showing since the Civil War, Cox failed to win a single state outside the South, polled only 27 per cent in New York and lost the electoral college

404–127. Warren G. Harding, who was to die in office in August 1923, was elected President with a very comfortable 61 per cent of the vote.

Once again, however, it had not been a futile exercise. FDR would say many years later that running for the office of the Vice-Presidency had allowed him to forge relationships and become better known nationally, thus helping to lay the ground work for his Presidential triumph in 1932.

And the world was waiting for Franklin D Roosevelt to embrace it. He was young, handsome, audacious and as fit as could be. Then, in August 1921, it all changed. That year, the Roosevelts took their customary summer vacation on Campobello Island in Maine, where the family had a home. Shortly after arriving at Campobello, FDR went for a quick dip in the Bay of Fundy and then led his boys on a vigorous hike on the island. Finally, they took a swim in the slightly warmer waters of Lake Glen Severn. It was to be the last unencumbered physical exercise of his life.

Later that evening, FDR complained to Eleanor that he felt weak and had a chill. Rather than infecting the children with what he thought was a cold, he went to bed without eating dinner. The next morning Franklin's condition was worse. Campobello is a rural island off the coast of Maine and medical assistance took a long time coming. Eventually a qualified doctor was found, and a diagnosis of poliomyelitis was made. But the damage had been done. Despite retaining full bowel and bladder control as well as normal sexual function, the future President of the United States would be paralyzed from the waist down for the remainder of his life.

Initially, FDR was terribly weak and had trouble sitting up in bed, but by October, his arm and back muscles recovered, and he could pull himself out of bed and swing into a wheelchair. He continued a vigorous programme of rehabilitation for several years and even went so far as to buy a resort in rural Georgia called Warm Springs. At the time of the purchase, the resort was somewhat dilapidated and in need of refurbishment, but unlike his stricken body, that could be dealt with. Of more importance to Franklin were the magnesium-infused spring waters, warm and buoyant, in which he could bathe. For years, he sought a cure for his condition and viewed his Warm Springs resort as a centre for those like himself who were afflicted with the effects of polio.

His smiling, outward confidence masked an inner grimness to succeed, but no amount of willpower and arduous physical effort could repair the destroyed nerve tissue. It took an exceptional man to continue on towards his goal of becoming a major political figure. The fact he resolved to do so while knowing he would have to mask his handicap as much as was possible may have come more easily to FDR than some. He had always enjoyed a little subterfuge, if not outright deception, and now both, to a point, became a necessity. Obviously he was handicapped but, as Kenneth S. Davis points out in *FDR: The War President*, he actually managed, in some respects, to turn it to his advantage.

People had to come to him. And he received them, with all his charm and intellect, on his turf and in his surroundings. More often than not, he was playing at home, and no sports fan needs to be told what an advantage that can be. Davis writes of FDR's 'home turf' advantage:

> This was true even in situations where his actual need for their support was considerably greater than theirs for his. For since they came as invited guests into his house, or by his permission into his office, or onto other ground ruled by him, they came perforce under felt obligations and must assume in some degree, willy-nilly, a supplicatory attitude. By the manner of his welcome and greeting he could, and did, set the tone of every personal encounter and, having done so, could and did dominate the discussion.

As politics is all about persuasion, the manner in which Franklin Roosevelt was able to turn his affliction to his own advantage goes some way to explaining to how he beat the odds and rose to the highest office in the land.

Throughout the 1920s, Roosevelt spent considerable time and effort maintaining his contacts with New York politicians and voters while at the same time restoring his finances. He accepted the role of front man for Fidelity and Deposit Company of Maryland, which was owned by a very rich Democratic contributor who also owned the *Baltimore Sun*. For this, he was paid $25,000 a year, five times his salary at the Navy Department. His new position enabled Roosevelt to add Louis Howe to his staff and hire an attractive 23-year-old secretary called Marguerite LeHand who became known as Missie and would remain at his side until illness struck her down in 1941. Tall, charming and devoted, Missie had the ability to turn away those wanting some of FDR's time without giving offence and probably spent more time in his company than anyone, even Louis Howe. Most significantly, she did so with Eleanor's full approval. As we have seen, Eleanor had ceased to play the part of a loving wife some years before, and, possibly as a means of assuaging any guilt she might have felt, she was pleased that someone could offer her husband the full-time devotion she herself had withdrawn.

Along with FDR's black valet, LeRoy Jones, who bathed and dressed him every morning, Missie was ever-present during the early years of his attempted rehabilitation. Once he entered the White House, she learned how to write letters on his behalf and took dictation at his bedside every morning. She controlled access to him and acted as a *de facto* White House Chief of Staff. She became recognized as one of the most powerful people in Washington right up to the moment she collapsed at a dinner party in June 1941 and suffered a stroke shortly afterwards. She lost the power of speech and, after a time trying to recover at Warm Springs, she was forced to return home to Massachusetts, where she died in July 1944 at the age of 47.

No one seems to have come up with a definitive answer to the question of whether or not FDR and Missie were lovers. Miss LeHand's only biographer, Kathryn Smith, thought it unlikely as no one had ever caught them in compromising situations, despite the constant close attention of Secret Service agents and household staff. Even two of FDR's sons differed on the possibility of an affair. The eldest, James felt that they loved each other 'but it was not a physical love', while Elliott, in his book *The Untold Story*, wrote that FDR and Missie 'led a familiar life in all aspects'.

* * *

Despite earlier differences, Al Smith, four times elected Governor of New York, became a Roosevelt supporter. In 1924, Smith tried but failed to win the Democratic nomination for the Presidency. As the campaign heated up, Smith asked Roosevelt to be his campaign chairman and to give his nominating speech at that year's Democratic Convention, which was held at New York's Madison Square Garden. The second of three 'Gardens,' this one was situated on Eight Avenue at 48th Street.

FDR accepted the position of chairman to the campaign and, having agreed to make the nominating speech, made a dramatic entrance as he walked to the speaker's platform, unaided except for crutches and metal braces under his suit. He then delivered a rousing speech on Smith's behalf. It wasn't enough to win Smith the nomination as the Democratic candidate that year, but the energy FDR put into the delivery, coupled with that dramatic entrance, enhanced his reputation and national name recognition.

FDR and Al Smith were not cut from the same cloth. Smith was a working-class hero, and though the pair had little in common, that did not prevent Smith from recognizing his young colleague's talents. He became a powerful supporter, appointing Roosevelt to the Taconic State Park Commission. Smith tried again in 1928, and this time secured the Democratic nomination but still could not achieve his goal and lost badly to Herbert Hoover in the presidential race, even losing his home state of New York. In the meantime, Smith had vacated the New York governorship and, ironically, it was Roosevelt who nipped in and won the prestigious post by a slim margin.

The fact that FDR won at all was a surprise – not least because a tremendous physical effort was required to even try. Although Louis Howe used all his expertise to disguise the fact, Franklin Roosevelt was a cripple. It was only his iron will, coupled with the huge encouragement offered by Eleanor and Howe, that had enabled him to return to a seemingly normal life. But every day and every movement from one place to another required a painful effort that would have kept most people on their couch or, in Roosevelt's case, at Warm Springs, which is where he really wanted to be.

There was no escaping his physical dependence on others. Describing how one of his personal bodyguards, a former New York City cop called Gus Gennerich, needed all his strength to get him out of his car, Curtis Roosevelt, his grandson, wrote:

> On arrival at church, Papa could hitch himself forward, stretching to push out his legs, snapping their steel braces in place. Gus then opened the rear door, which was hinged from the back rather than the front to make it easier for my grandfather to get in and out. Gus would step partway into the car, putting his arm under his charge's outstretched arm. Together they lifted him up and – hey presto! – my grandfather was on his feet, a smile on his face, his hand reaching out, making greetings all round.

Putting a cane into his right hand, Gennerich never, for an instant, let go of FDR whose balance was so precarious that, according to Curtis, 'a strong gust of wind or a too-enthusiastic handshake could topple him'. As far as allowing his name to be placed in nomination for the governorship of New York was concerned, it was FDR's will that was wavering. When Al Smith's campaign for another term appeared to be in trouble, New York Democrats felt FDR was the only man who could beat the formidable Republic opponent, Albert Ottinger, who was not only of working-class Jewish origin but had a good record of fighting criminal stock manipulators. But their appeals fell on deaf ears.

'As I am only forty-six, I owe it to my family and myself to give the present constant improvement a chance to continue,' said FDR.

Roosevelt was still hoping against hope that one day he could walk again. So he stayed at Warm Springs and refused to take phone calls. He refused Smith when he called, and although she didn't want him to run, it was only when Eleanor was persuaded to telephone her husband and then hand the phone to Smith that Al got to talk to him.

According to Jean Edward Smith, Smith bore down on the man he was beseeching to succeed him in Albany. 'Take the nomination, Frank. You can make a couple of radio speeches, and you'll get elected. Then you can go back to Warm Springs. And after you have made your inaugural speech and sent your message to the legislature you can go back there for a couple of months.'

'Don't give me that baloney,' was FDR's reply.

But his colleagues were nothing if not persistent. Grabbing the phone from Smith, Herbert Lehman, a senior partner of the investment firm that bore his name who was one of the most respected figures in the party, told the reluctant candidate that he would he accept the nomination for Lieutenant Governor and deputize whenever necessary if FDR would run.

Silence from Warm Springs. Smith took back the phone. 'Frank, I told you I wasn't going to put this on a personal basis but I've go to. As a personal favor, can I put your name before the convention?'

Again the answer was no. Roosevelt repeated all his reasons for not accepting but could not get Smith off the phone.

'Frank, just one more question. If those fellows nominate you tomorrow and adjourn, will you refuse to run?'

This time there was hesitation. A couple of seconds passed and Smith seized his chance. 'Thanks, Frank. I won't ask you any more questions.'

When Egbert Curtis, manager of the Merriweather Inn at Warm Springs, asked FDR if he was going to run as he drove him back to his cottage, the answer sounded very much like Franklin D. Roosevelt.

'Curtis, when you're in politics, you've got to play the game.'

New York Major Jimmy Walker placed Roosevelt's name on the nomination the next day, and there was no opposition. FDR was chosen by acclamation. Eleanor cabled her regrets but said she understood. Louis Howe was less understanding. 'Mess is no name for it,' he wired. 'For once I have no advice to give.'

But of course the diminutive hustler had plenty to offer and set about ensuring that FDR became Governor of New York. It was a task beyond daunting. After starting on the campaign trail by train, FDR decided it would be easier to proceed by car, stopping at towns and villages across the state. Two large buses followed the candidate's car, carrying news media and staffers. Apart from Howe, Missy LeHand, and Frances Perkins, there was another staffer who became a long term and indispensable member of FDR's inner circle.

Sam Rosenman, a young member of the New York legislature, had been attached to the campaign to keep Roosevelt up to date with state issues. FDR, who made quick decisions about people, soon found Rosenman's detailed knowledge invaluable. It was a mutual appreciation. 'I have never seen anyone who could grasp the facts of a complicated problem as quickly and as thoroughly as Roosevelt,' Rosenman confided to friends.

And that was not all. Having survived the ordeal of typing out speeches on a swaying bus and helping to carry the candidate up and down the back stairs at stop after stop along the way, Rosenman recorded in his book *Working with Roosevelt*, 'It was not easy for a crippled man to carry on this kind of campaign . . . He always went through this harrowing experience smiling. He never got ruffled. Having been set down, he would adjust his coat, smile, and proceed calmly to the platform for his speech.'

Republican criticism that Roosevelt was not physically fit to run – 'There is something both pathetic and pitiless in the "drafting" of Franklin D Roosevelt' wrote the *New York Post* – was dealt with head on by the man himself. Referring to the 'sob stuff' in in the editorial columns, FDR told cheering crowds along the way, 'Too bad about the unfortunate sick man, isn't it?' And they cheered some more.

On election night, early returns, in both the presidential and state races, were tipped heavily against the Democrats. By midnight, the papers were headlining a Republican sweep in their early editions. Roosevelt, resigned to the worst, left the Democrats' ballroom with its popped balloons and went home to East 65th Street to get some sleep.

Only in one hotel room did the lights stay on. Louis Howe, Frances Perkins and Edward J. Flynn, Democratic boss of the Bronx, were not ready to give up, even though most of the remaining votes would be coming in from upstate New York, traditionally a Republican stronghold. But by 1:00 a.m. Ed Flynn noticed that this trend was not being followed. Something strange was happening. Had the crippled candidate in his open campaign car made an impression on all those little rural towns? Could it be so? Flynn got so excited he called Roosevelt, who was not pleased at being woken, calling him 'crazy'.

However, Flynn was a seasoned campaigner, and he recognized a trend when he saw one. Still, he was worried at the slow trickle of votes coming in, and, knowing how the GOP was inclined to hold back votes until they saw which way the wind was blowing, sent messages to polling centres, vowing to send a team of lawyers up state to prevent any election stealing. Whether that was necessary or was unclear, but the results speeded up, and with every return FDR's chances brightened. The gap narrowed, and by 4:00 a.m. Roosevelt pulled ahead and never lost his narrow lead, beating Ottinger by a majority of 25,608 out of four million votes cast.

It was only 10 months after he had settled into the Governor's Mansion in Albany that fate guided Franklin Roosevelt towards his destiny in the most appalling way. In October 1929 the Stock Market crashed and, overnight, millions were thrown out of work and left destitute. Unlike the newly-elected President, Herbert Hoover, and many other Republicans, who refrained from any bold government programmes which might have provided relief and assistance to those most heavily impacted by the financial crisis, Roosevelt proposed and implemented several state-wide programmes, including the Temporary Emergency Relief Administration which would provide assistance to more than one-third of New York's population until 1938.

FDR's swift action in New York did not go unnoticed nationwide, and, with the country reeling from the Great Depression, he made the leap from Albany to Washington DC To do so, he had to beat the persistent Al Smith to the Democratic nomination at the party's Chicago Convention in July 1932, which he did by the eventually decisive margin of 945 to 190. To everyone's surprise, FDR decided to make a late dash to Chicago in a Ford 5-AT Tri-Motor aircraft, which American Airlines pulled out of a hangar for his use. It was called The Tin Goose, but, flapping its wings through encroaching storms, it managed to get Roosevelt and his party to Chicago's Municipal Airport just about in one piece.

There were no storms in the Convention Hall. An organist led the delegates into a rousing rendition of 'Happy Days Are Here Again!' and soon the cultured tones that had become familiar to New York radio listeners but were unknown nationwide were gripping his audience. Striking at the heart of conservative opposition within his own party to progressive reform, Roosevelt said in his maiden speech as nominee, 'I warn those nominal Democrats who squint at the future with their faces turned to the past, and who feel no responsibility to the demands of a new time, that they are out of step with the Party. Ours is a party of liberal thought, of planned action, of enlightened international outlook, and the greatest good to the greatest number of our citizens.'

Then after listing an entire programme of reform, covering tariff reduction, securities regulation, public works and home mortgage guarantees, he finished in a rising voice with a phrase that would lodge itself in American history: 'I pledge you, I pledge myself, to a New Deal for the American people.'

Nationally, Roosevelt was a new voice, and, with Herbert Hoover having become a thoroughly unpopular President, the path to the White House was open. But the path FDR travelled was long. He consumed a total of 13,000 miles by car, train and plane, arriving in Baltimore on 25 October with a phrase that just about put the nail in the Republicans' coffin. There were, he said to wildly cheering crowds, just Four Horsemen of the Republican Apocalypse: Destruction, Delay, Deceit and Despair.

The final vote was not close. Out of 40 million votes cast, FDR received 22,825,016 to Hoover's 15,758,397. In his acceptance speech, the President-elect had singled out Louis Howe and James Farley as the two aides most responsible for his victory, but Howe was nowhere to be seen. Eleanor and Farley knew where to look. At his hideaway office on Madison Avenue, they found the tiny, slight figure pouring over the returns like, to quote Farley, 'a miser inspecting his gold'. Eventually, taking an ancient bottle of Madeira from a cupboard, a bottle he had vowed never to touch until victory had been achieved, Howe raised his glass 'To the next President of the United States'.

* * *

But for a wobbly chair, FDR might never have become the next President. Campaigning in Florida before his inauguration in March 1933, Roosevelt came within a couple of feet of being assassinated – an incident that seems to have drifted from people's memories some 80 years later. But not, probably, in Chicago because the mayor of that city, Anton Cermak, was the only one of five people hit who would ultimately succumb to his wounds. There were theories back in Chicago, a city never short on political intrigue, that Cermak was the target all along, but the assassin, an Italian immigrant of poor education called Giuseppe Zangara, insisted that the President-elect had been his target when FDR climbed onto a wobbly chair at Miami's Bay Front Park, where 20,000 people attending the encampment of the American Legion were gathered. Zangara, who had bought an $8 pistol (about $150 in today's money) from a nearby pawnshop, was only 5ft tall and needed height to get a view of his intended victim. Like a future President who would not be so lucky, Roosevelt was seated in the back of an open car. Zangara, his arm brushed by a woman who immediately realized what he was doing, fired off five shots. Having served in the Italian army in the First

World War, he would probably have been more accurate but for the chair wobbling beneath him.

By such weird circumstances is history shaped. The life of the 32-year-old Zangara, who was burdened by a hatred for the entire upper class, was shaped by the ineptitude of a local hospital whose care for the wounded Cermak did not extend to saving him from dying of peritonitis. Originally, the bricklayer had been sentenced to 80 years in jail, but when Cermak succumbed 19 days after the attack – just two days after FDR's inauguration – Zangara was given the death penalty and went to the electric chair.

The future President had cradled Cermak's head in his arms on the way to the hospital and waited until the Mayor came out of the emergency room. His composure throughout the ordeal was, according to observers, remarkable. Firstly, he had stopped the Secret Service from speeding his car away from the scene when Cermak was hit and insisted he be loaded onto his lap. At the hospital, he chatted with other patients as if nothing had happened. 'There was nothing,' wrote Raymond Moley, a Columbia University science professor who was helping FDR with some of his speeches, 'Not so much as a twitching of a muscle to indicate that this wasn't any other evening in any other place. Roosevelt was simply himself – easy, confident, poised . . .' And alive.

As President, he assumed control of America at the most daunting moment in its history. Many had lost faith in their country and were desperate. Millions were unemployed, homeless and hungry.

The pitfalls lying before a new, young President were huge, but Roosevelt did not panic. Outwardly he approached the situation with unflappable courage and optimism. His inauguration speech, only 15 minutes long, was seared into history with the famous line, 'We have nothing to fear except fear itself.'

One of FDR's first acts was to work with the outgoing Hoover cabinet officials to declare, in the most literal sense, a bank holiday. The purpose was to give the banks time to meet the liquidity needs of the American depositors who had lost confidence in the banking system. This would be just the first of a blizzard of new programmes and legislation proposed to Congress in what has since been referred to as 'The First One Hundred Days'.

Roosevelt was only a few days into his presidency, when, pressured by the immediacy of the financial crisis, he won the support of Congress to overhaul the United States banking system. To reopen after their enforced closure, each bank would need to get a licence from the US Treasury attesting to its financial soundness. Within 30 days of passing this bill, 80 per cent of all US banks had received their licence to reopen, suggesting much burning of the midnight oil.

Other legislation and programmes passed or adopted in FDR's first one hundred days included:

- An agricultural bill designed to raise the income of farmers by paying them to set aside land rather than farm it. The creation of a civilian conservation corps, which would offer employment to young workers who would help control floods and restore forested land.
- Authorization for $500 million dollars in relief for unemployed workers.
- Mortgage relief for homeowners.
- Regulation for investment firms.
- Issuance of public securities.
- A programme to re-habilitate the United States railroad system.

Extraordinary times call for extraordinary measures, and Franklin Roosevelt rose to the challenge, making the most of his powers to bring in numerous New Deal initiatives that constituted unprecedented actions by the Federal Government. Obviously, he benefited from Democratic majorities in both the US Senate and House of Representatives, but most of his legislation passed without significant or sustained debate. The severity of the crisis was partially responsible for this, but FDR himself had to take considerable credit for the manner in which he smoothed the passage of his ideas. Using a medium that was still less than a decade old as far as the mass of the populace was concerned, Roosevelt appealed directly to the people by radio. It was through the popularity of what became known as his 'fireside chats' that FDR established a rapport with the country and explained the reasons for such dramatic legislation.

Throughout the remainder of the 1930s a return to prosperity proved elusive for the American people. FDR's legislative success in the First Hundred Days was difficult to sustain, and critics were able to thwart many of the President's most cherished programmes. One of the most controversial of the New Deal programmes was the National Recovery Administration (NRA) – a set of initials with a very different connotation today.

The NRA was introduced in 1933 and was intended to help businesses by reducing what was viewed as counterproductive competition. For a nation born and built on the fundamental of belief of everyone's right to compete within the law, this was always going to be a hard sell. But FDR was stubborn, and he tried. Industries like coal would establish minimum pricing to help ensure profitability of the mines. Workers would also be paid a minimum wage and a range (limit?) of working hours was also established. Many business executives resisted the NRA because it eliminated their ability to succeed over competitors via lower-cost manufacturing or economy of scale. In 1935 the United States Supreme Court ruled that the NRA was unconstitutional, and the programme was dismantled.

This was just one of a series of rulings by the Supreme Court which struck down New Deal programmes on the grounds that they were unconstitutional due to the defined powers of the Executive Branch. FDR bristled. But he did not surrender easily and, in 1937, he suggested that the Supreme Court be expanded from nine to fifteen members. As the President has the power to appoint Supreme Court Justices, his motives were clear. Republicans threw around words like demagoguery, and even members of his own party were lukewarm. Changing tack, FDR tried taking his idea directly to the American people through his fireside chats, but his proposal didn't fare well in the court of public opinion either, and his attempt to 'pack' the Supreme Court was abandoned.

Despite these setbacks, Roosevelt's record of pushing through innovative and sometimes daring legislation is unparalleled in United States history. His audacity earned him many enemies, but the majority of the country stuck with him, and in 1936 he won re-election with 61 per cent of the vote, carrying forty-six states. Even so, the Depression proved to be a stubborn opponent and hung like a pall over his presidency throughout the latter half of the 1930s.

Although he came from a moneyed background and enjoyed most of the trappings of the Presidency, Roosevelt could never be accused of living lavishly. In the rooms he used at the White House, creature comforts were minimal. He turned the Oval Study on the second floor into his bedroom, and the bed itself appears to have been even narrower that Winston Churchill's at Chartwell. As described by Frances Perkins, who would become his Secretary of Labor throughout the Second World War, it was not the kind of bed one would have imagined the President of the United States using. 'Roosevelt used a small, narrow, white iron bedstead, the kind one sees in the boy's room of many an American house. It had a thin, hard-looking mattress, a couple of pillows and an ordinary, white seersucker spread. An old grey sweater, much the worse for wear, lay close at hand. He wore it over nightclothes to keep his shoulders warm.'

Eleanor, of course, had little to do with her husband's sleeping habits. The affair with Lucy Mercer had seen to that years before, and by the time they entered the White House, the President and First Lady were almost leading separate lives. Except for official functions, they did not even dine together, and, on the rare occasions Eleanor entered the Oval Office she was invariably carrying papers – the visit being entirely concerning business. There appeared to be no outward animosity; respect remained and, politically, the pair were still in tune, fully supporting each other's programmes. And Eleanor had plenty.

The First Lady worked tirelessly for women's rights, for the poor and for the working class. She gave her name and was involved in numerous liberal causes such as the Women's Trade Union League and League of Women's Voters and regularly received female friends, both personal and official, for afternoon tea in her sitting room on the second floor.

This took place at 5 o'clock, two hours before the President would have a routine of his own, named 'children's hour'. He would adjourn to the family room and begin mixing cocktails for members of his staff like Missy LeHand and Grace Tully as well as a variety of visitors. A tray was set up on the desk for him, and he went to work on his martini mix – usually two parts gin and one part vermouth. But as Samuel Rosenman, recounts, 'He never bothered to measure and seemed to experiment on each occasion.' Sometimes rum from the Virgin Islands got into the mix and, occasionally, to Rosenman's obvious concern, Benedictine. 'Not something to be tried at home.' In contrast to Churchill, who sipped watered-down whisky throughout the day, FDR rarely consumed more than two of his own concoctions.

Also unlike Churchill, who did not lack for lighter moments but could never totally switch off from the day's ordeals, FDR seemed able to close the door on the Oval Office. 'During cocktail hour no more was said of politics and war,' said the historian Doris Kearns Goodwin, 'the talk was all about gossip, funny stories and reminisces.'

Less amusing was the food. During FDR's long occupation of the White House, the cuisine was, according to innumerable sources, of a standard to make any self-respecting Frenchman faint. Ernest Hemingway, having spent so many youthful years in Paris, was particularly scathing. 'Rainwater soup followed by rubber squab; nice wilted salad and a cake some admirer sent in. An enthusiastic but unskilled admirer.'

Despite the fact that the running of the White House fell entirely under Eleanor's governance, the First Lady could not be accused, of course, of being a bad cook. She just didn't. But she bore full responsibility for the appointment of Henrietta Nesbitt, a 59-year-old Hyde Park matron who was active in the League of Women Voters and had no experience of running a household of any kind, let alone the White House. Appointing her to do just that Eleanor said, 'I don't want a professional housekeeper. I want someone I know. I want you, Mrs Nesbitt.'

The results were not happy for anyone of gastronomic tendencies. When Hemingway's future wife Martha Gellhorn was found consuming three sandwiches at Newark Airport on her way to Washington DC, she said, 'Eat before you go. Everyone knows the rules.'

Mrs Nesbitt, who did little actual cooking herself, believed in plain food, plainly prepared. To this end, she hovered around the chefs, 'making sure that each dish was overcooked or undercooked or ruined in one way or another,' as Jean Edward Smith relates. Even if she was not personally responsible for the fare that made its way to the White House table, James Roosevelt did not spare Mrs Nesbitt. 'She is the worst cook I have ever encountered,' he stated, a view he probably shared with his father.

The President went some way to improving the situation by bringing his mother's excellent cook, Mary Campbell, down from Hyde Park after Sara died in 1941, but Mrs Nesbitt stayed on. Confiding to his daughter Anna in 1944, FDR was probably speaking only marginally in jest when he said that the real reason he wanted to get elected to a fourth term was 'so I can fire Mrs Nesbitt'. In fact it fell to President Harry Truman to do the dirty deed. Acting decisively after Mrs Nesbitt had refused to bring a stick of butter to a lunch for the Senate wives' Bridge Club – 'because the White House is rationed' – he ended her reign of terror that afternoon.

Sara Roosevelt's death on 7 September 1941, two weeks before her 87th birthday, was greeted in the family by what the British would call a stiff upper lip. Eleanor, who had the most complicated relationship with the family matriarch, would write that little emotion was shown at the funeral, even by her husband. 'I kept being appalled because I couldn't feel any real grief or sense of loss and that seemed terrible after 36 years of fairly close association.'

As far as the reference to FDR's lack of emotion, his grandson Curtis was not having any of it. The son of Anna, FDR's oldest child, Curtis was obviously a highly sensitive boy, whose way of dealing with the lack of overt love he received from his mother in early age was to retreat into his own fantasy world. The love he received, during his days living in the White House, came mostly from the President and 'Granny'.

In *Too Close to the Sun*, Curtis wrote, 'The truth was that my grandfather had been deeply affected by his mother's death. Not revealing hurt or grief in public was simply his style.'

Curtis himself was certainly affected. Some of his fondest memories had been the morning ritual whereby he and his older sister would rush into Granny's room while she enjoyed her breakfast. 'Propped up in her bed, wearing something silk and lacy around her shoulders and smelling of lavender, as she always did, she'd be having her breakfast on a tray, just like Papa did. Our arrival was greeted warmly. Usually, she'd offer us a little titbit to taste, for which we competed with two yappy Pekinese dogs . . .'

Curtis had moved to Seattle with his mother and stepfather by 1941 and he recounted how difficult it was to deal with questions from friends at school when news of his great-grandmother's death became front page news. 'I even had to explain what a "great-grandmother" was to some classmates. The whole thing was surreal. It was impossible to convey how close I had felt to her, how much Sara Delano Roosevelt had meant to me.'

There had been times when this outwardly bossy woman had been heavily criticized in public and within her own family. But there was no criticism from her great grandson. Just love.

There is never a good time to lose one's mother, and this was certainly not a good time for Franklin Roosevelt. The pressure of the Presidency is always great, but few have had to deal with so many contrasting demands of such incredible import. A maniac was loose on the world scene with his Panzer divisions gouging their way across the civilization of Europe; in the Pacific, Japan's intentions were opaque, but no one felt confident they were pure, and then, digging in its heels, blocking its ears and shielding its eyes to reality was the powerful anti-war feeling at home, emanating, largely, from the Republicans.

They had hollered in indignation when the President and Prime Minister Churchill had met on warships off Newfoundland just a month before Sara Roosevelt's death, insisting that the meeting, held against such a military background, signified a prelude to war.

With every move he made, FDR had to take into consideration this vocal domestic opposition while dealing with Churchill's growl in the other ear. Churchill knew he could not win the war without America becoming totally involved. Roosevelt also knew it and, increasingly, his generals and closest advisers became resigned to it. No one will ever know how long the President would have held out in the face of Britain's increasingly desperate demands had it not been for the Japanese attack on Pearl Harbor in December 1941. It is inconceivable that he would have continued to stay away from the conflict had Britain been invaded because that would have meant Hitler not only conquering

Europe in its entirety, but also the whole of North Africa, the Middle East and possibly even India. America would have become the world's last bastion of democracy and the United States, especially with a man of Roosevelt's inclinations and courage in the White House, would have fought to preserve it.

The Atlantic Charter, after all, had just been written. Peace, tolerance and honour between nations. It was not something Hitler understood but both Roosevelt and Churchill, imperfect men with a perfect vision of what was tolerable and what was not, understood it very well.

Chapter 7

Churchill – A Lust for Danger

'If you can fill the unforgiving minute with sixty seconds worth of distance run...' Rudyard Kipling's poem was not published until 1910, but Winston Spencer Churchill had already got the message.

The son of an unkind and demanding father and a flighty American mother was already well on his way in the first decade of the twentieth century to making a better stab than most of his contemporaries at fulfilling the poet's promise that the earth and 'everything that's in it' would be his. But it took time. And only by filling every second with tireless, monumental endeavour was Churchill able to seize his moment in history and emerge as arguably the most dominant and extraordinary personality the world has seen in the past century.

For all his foibles, failures and freakish character traits, Churchill was a colossus, and a contradictory one at that. The pugnacity of his temperament took him to the very limits of acceptable behaviour, right up to having to accept charges of being a dogmatic bully. But there were lines he never crossed. If you cut through the cigar smoke and the smell of whisky on his breath in search of all the tell-tale signs of a dictator, you would have found instead a democrat, a man who derided yes-men, who invited constructive argument and, as he announced to his audience at Fulton, Missouri, one who owed all his success to the House of Commons 'whose servant I am'.

Dictators do not describe themselves as servants to anyone nor do they refuse the self-aggrandizement that comes with peerages and titles. Churchill did both. He flatly refused to go to the House of Lords, preferring to remain in the House of Commons where he could accept a knighthood and, therefore, after some persuasion, become Sir Winston. Yet the name that adorns his statue in Parliament Square, facing his beloved House of Commons, would have been most to his liking. It carries just one word: Churchill.

So how did a boy who was a backward student at school and derided by his father as good for nothing but the army because all he could do was play with toy soldiers grow so swiftly into the daring, ambitious young man he became? How did the wimpish teenager who wrote his mother imploring letters from Harrow, detailing how miserable he was, turn within the space of six or seven years into a cavalry officer at the forefront of the charge at Omdurman?

At Chartwell, the much-loved and beautifully-preserved Churchill family home in the depths of the Kent countryside, there is a portrait which hangs above the single bed in Winston's own small bedroom. It is of Lord Randolph Churchill – his father. The man he adored. Yes, the man he adored throughout his life, despite the near indifference and casual cruelty with which he had been treated. And it was his father's death at the age of 45 in January 1895, when Winston was still only 20, that may offer the clue to the startling transformation which overcame his son.

From the mewling, pathetic schoolboy, there emerged this extra-ordinary force of nature whose talents were so varied and abundant that one wondered how they could all be compressed into one life. He became a soldier, a politician, a statesman, a writer, a historian, an orator, a painter, a polo player and a bricklayer. Any visitor to Chartwell will see evidence of the latter talent. The gardens are enclosed by 10-foot walls. He built some of them. He was always, always filling the unforgiving minute, and he never, never gave up.

During his childhood years, it would have beggared the imagination to believe this would be so. It was not just his father who despaired of him. Before going on to Harrow in north London, young Winston was sent to St George's School at Ascot where his reports read 'History and geography, very good, especially history. General conduct – very bad. He is a constant trouble to everybody.'

According to author Max Arthur, this report proved too much even for Winston's doting mother, who told him, 'Your work is an insult to your intelligence. If you would trace out a plan of action for yourself and carry it out, and be determined to do so, I am sure you could accomplish anything you wished.'

Lady Randolph, who, as Jenny Jerome, had met her future husband at a ball given aboard HMS *Ariadne* on 15 April 1874 during the Cowes Regatta, was generally, more of a supporter than a critic, but it was to 'Woomany' – his nurse Mrs Everest – to whom the boy turned for comfort and understanding. 'I poured my heart out to her,' he wrote later.

There is no question that much of his childhood was unhappy. Some of his letters to his mother tug at the heartstrings.

'Let me at least think that you love me,' he wrote from Harrow in December 1891. 'Darling Mummy, I despair. I am so wretched. I don't know what to do. Don't be angry – I am so miserable.'

Let us fast forward and contrast this letter to the young man who somehow transformed himself – not without difficulty – into a subaltern with the 4th Hussars and who, after much arm-twisting, had got himself seconded to the Spanish forces fighting insurgents in Cuba. It was there, on his 21st birthday, that he saw action for the first time. The story might have ended right then. A bullet, fired from the undergrowth at their bivouac, missed his head by a couple of feet and killed a horse behind him. It was by no means the last time he came within inches of death, often because he continually thrust himself in the path of danger. He sought it, chased it and gleefully confronted it. What happened to 'Mummy, I despair; I am so wretched?'

By 1898, the desperate schoolboy was rapidly establishing himself as a man of action on the world stage, enhancing his reputation through his journalistic writings for such newspapers as *The Sunday Graphic* and *The Morning Post*. It was on 2 September of that year that he was to be found in the Sudan, taking part in the very last British regimental cavalry charge against the Dervishes at Omdurman. It achieved little other than death. Of the 300-strong contingent of Lord Kitchener's 21st Lancers, a quarter were killed or wounded within a matter of minutes but luck rode with young Churchill.

His mother soon received a very different letter from the one she had read with such despair less than a decade before. This was one of boastful triumph.

'I was under fire all day and rode through the charge,' Winston wrote on his way home.

> You know my luck in these things. I was about the only officer whose clothes, saddlery or horse were uninjured. I fired ten shots with my pistol . . . I never felt the slightest nervousness and felt as cool as I do now. I am sorry to say I shot five men for certain and two doubtful. I destroyed those who molested me and so passed without any disturbance of body or mind.

One of his victims was so close that Churchill's pistol touched him as he fell. Was there exaggeration in this account? Possibly. But only to a small degree. Less easy to accept is the transformation that had come over this man. One could put it down the natural growing-up process, but few people find their feet and grow in confidence to such an extraordinary degree in so short a space of time.

So what was at the root of this transformation? Historians do not seem to have come up with a clear answer but, in an irony that would fit their relationship, it would seem that the death of Lord Randolph in January 1895 – just a few months before his son was commissioned into the 4th Hussars – was a determining factor. Winston had joined the army because his father considered him 'not clever enough to do anything else'. Such dismissive paternal evaluation would have crushed many sons and has done so a million times over. But young Winston used it as a launchpad for greatness. When Lord Randolph died at such an early age, his son, at a later date, wrote: 'All my dreams of comradeship with him, of entering Parliament at his side and in his support, were ended. There remained for me only to pursue his aims and vindicate his memory.' He did that in some abundance.

Keen to keep the memory of his father alive, these thoughts and it seems incentives were laid out in a much-acclaimed biography of Lord Randolph that he wrote ten years later. But his father's career, which *The Spectator* described as being marked by 'instinctive rowdyism' would not have been quickly forgotten in any case. At once charming, rude and erratic, Lord Randolph rose to become Chancellor of the Exchequer in Lord Salisbury's government in 1886 and was never less than a star of the chamber, for better or worse.

But the fact that Churchill biographer Roy Jenkins calls Lord Randolph a preoccupied, ill-tempered and discouraging parent suggests that Randolph must have had some impact on his son's early struggles at school. Few of Winston's teachers missed the fact that he was different, but those who latched on to the talents that lurked beneath a confused and disruptive personality were rare. One such was Robert Somervell, his lower-school English master at Harrow, 'a delightful man, to whom my debt is great'.

Of that there is no question. Had Somervell not recognized and nurtured Churchill's literary abilities, the English language, indeed history itself, might have been less well served. Of his perceptive and persevering English teacher, Churchill wrote:

He was charged with the duty of teaching the stupidest boys the most disregarded thing – namely to write mere English. He knew how to do it. He taught it as no one else has ever taught it. As I remained in the Third Fourth (a very disregarded form) three times as long as anyone else, I had three times as much of it. I learned it thoroughly. Thus I got into my bones the essential structure of the ordinary British sentence – which is a noble thing.'

The man who went on to write *The History of the English Speaking Peoples* and hold a nation in thrall with his oratory put the ordinary British sentence to very noble use indeed. One shudders to think what might have happened if Churchill's prose had not been polished so painstakingly. Had he been a better student and escaped Somervell's lowly class sooner, that ability to enthral might have been less acute.

Another talent began emerging at school. The young man was developing a prodigious memory, an asset that served him well throughout his life. But he could forget, too. Needing to visit a tutor in the Earl's Court Road as he pursued admittance to the Military Academy at Sandhurst, Churchill was required to cram for French, Latin and mathematics. The latter, in particular, was not his favourite subject, and, like many of us who have had to take too much information on board in too short a space of time, Churchill found that 'this alien knowledge passed away like the phantasmagoria of a fevered dream'. Many will relate – if not with such elegance. Mr Somervell's tutoring was already on the wing.

From Churchill's point of view, his facility with a pen was a lifesaver. Despite being born at Blenheim Palace with an aristocratic father, the family was not moneyed in the traditional sense and, despite a tendency to live like a lord no matter the cost, Lord Randolph was not rich and never became so. The House of Commons is not the place to make one's fortune, unless you can augment the recognition it brings with outside talents, and Winston was not short of those. Writing came naturally to him, more so, initially, than public speaking and, having returned for a last polo-playing stint in India with the 4th Hussars, he resigned his commission. Initially, the idea was to follow his first love, politics. But in July 1899, he failed in his initial attempt to enter Parliament, losing narrowly at Oldham. So he had to look elsewhere, and a new adventure beckoned. With a reputation already established after Cuba and Omdurman, he was not short of journalistic offers and quickly accepted the best of them – £250 a month, all expenses paid, from *The Morning Post*, now known as *The Daily Telegraph*, to cover the Boer War in South Africa.

As we have noted, Churchill was living on limited funds, but that did not prevent him sailing on the *Dunottar Castle* accompanied by a valet, Thomas Walden, who had worked for his father, and a serious consignment of whisky, wine, port, vermouth and lime juice. The bill, it has been noted, was not settled for over a year and probably would never have been had Churchill's luck not held once again.

Soon after his arrival, the eager young correspondent ran into Captain Aylmer Haldane, an old friend from his time with the 4th Hussars on the North West Frontier in India. They met at a town called Estcourt, which was on the way to Ladysmith where Haldane's battalion, the Dublin Fusiliers, was under virtual siege. Captain Haldane had been unable to reach Ladysmith for reasons that would soon become clear. To make use of his time, Haldane had been ordered by the colonel in charge of the Estcourt garrison to take an armoured train on a reconnaissance mission up the track. Churchill, who had been heading for Ladysmith himself, was invited to go along.

Haldane was supposed to check for telephone messages along the route to receive orders on how far he should go. But on reaching the ravine of the Blaaw Kranz river, he failed to do so. 'Had I not had my impetuous young friend Churchill with me, I might have thought twice before throwing myself into the lion's jaws.' But he didn't, and, within minutes of crossing the ravine, Haldane, Churchill and the train driver, Charles Wagner, found themselves dodging bullets that pinged off the armour plating. Worse, they ploughed straight into the boulders thrown across the tracks on the instructions of the Boer commando, Louis Botha, the future Prime Minister of South Africa. Confusion followed; firing erupted all around; Churchill, reverting to army officer rather than war correspondent, began issuing orders, telling Wagner to get back in the cabin and reverse the train out of danger. Winston could have gone with him but opted not to. 'I can't leave those poor buggers to their fate,' he told Wagner, referring to some British soldiers he thought to be under fire in the shallow cutting. In fact, they were in the act of being taken prisoner – not a fate Churchill intended for himself when confronted by what he described as 'two Boers, tall figures, full of energy, clad in dark, flapping clothes, with slough, storm driven hats, poising on their levelled rifles'.

It was another moment that should have spelled the end for the impulsive young adventurer. Rather than raising his arms, he reached for his pistol – an invitation for the Boers to shoot him down. But he had left it on the train. There was nothing to do but surrender. And so his famous imprisonment began. Celia Sandys, Churchill's granddaughter, recalls it in detail in *Chasing Churchill*, recounting how she and her 13-year-old son Alexander visited Estcourt to take part in a ceremony to mark the centenary of the ambush. Amazingly, Sandys found, among those welcoming her, Charles Wagner, who carried the same name as *his* grandfather, the driver of the ill-fated train. Not one to forget those who had stood by him, Churchill had seen to it that Wagner's grandfather be awarded the Albert Medal, now displayed in a Durban museum, when he became Home Secretary ten years after the event.

After a two-day march and twenty-four hours on a train, Churchill was incarcerated at the States Model School in Pretoria. Sandys discovered that it still stands, a large single-storied brick building with a steep corrugated iron roof and wide veranda. It was declared a national monument in 1963 with a new road diverted around it.

Along with Captain Haldane, who had also been captured, Churchill suffered a few weeks of boring but comfortable detention. He was already something of a celebrity, and Louis de Souza, the Transvaal Secretary for War, interrupted the monotony by bringing important people round to meet Churchill, who responded by handing round cigars and promptly chairing political discussions! There certainly seemed to be a lack of animosity between captors and prisoner. Sandys discovered that de Souza's wife, Mary, had kept a diary of those weeks, in which she relates the occasion when her husband arrived with a basket of fruit. The three exclamation marks on the accompanying note apparently denoted the fact that, beneath the fruit, lay hidden a bottle of whisky, a beverage forbidden to the prisoners.

Despite the thoughtful hospitality, Churchill had words to write and places to go and had no intention of hanging around longer than absolutely necessary. So he planned an escape over the wall with Haldane and a Sergeant Brockie. It was all about timing. There were split seconds when the sentries were preoccupied or looking the other way and, being the impulsive one, Churchill seized his chance first. The other two, either through fear or hunger, didn't. They decided to break for supper. Later, when his escape made headlines around the world, Churchill was criticized for leaving his comrades behind. In fact, he waited for an hour in the garden adjacent to the wall before giving up. Putting on a slouch hat adorned with the colours of the Transvaal, the escapee mingled with evening crowds along Skinner Street before making his way to a small station called Koodoesport and leaping onto a freight train as it chuntered through.

After sleeping among coal sacks, he jumped off at dawn, hoping to find some nourishment with the intention of catching another train that evening. But none could be found. After scrambling through undergrowth and fording streams, he thought he saw the fires of a Bantu kraal, but it turned out to be the furnace of a coalmine at Witbank. Chancing his arm yet again, Winston knocked on the door of the first house he came to and, yet again, his luck held. The house belonged to the mine manager, and he turned out to be an Englishman, John Howard, who offered him food and whisky and hid him down a mineshaft the next morning. Even in those days of limited travel one could find some very odd coincidences among the people one met, especially when hurtling into the bowels of the earth. The man escorting Churchill to his new hiding place was Daniel Dewsnap, the mine's engineer, who happened to come from Oldham – where the aspiring politician had failed to win the seat.

On her journey re-tracing her grandfather's footsteps, Sandys found yet another grandson, Errol Dewsnap, who confirmed that the next two or three days had been less than salubrious for the family's unexpected visitor. 'His companions at the bottom of that shaft were rats as big as cats,' he said.

From then on, Churchill's rise from those depths quickened pace in every sense. Hidden in bales of wool, he was put on another train and, after a journey of forty-eight hours, was to be found in a somewhat dishevelled state knocking on the door of the British Consulate in Lourenço Marques (today Maputo) in Mozambique. A boat took him to Durban and he eventually made it back to where he had been captured six weeks before.

On being asked by General Sir Redvers Buller, head of the British army in South Africa, if there was anything he could do for him, Churchill asked for, and was given, a commission in the South African Light Horse so that he might take a more legitimate part in the battles that loomed. In order to circumvent the War Office edict that officers were not to write for the press, he took no pay. As a result he was able to chronicle, for his real employer, *The Morning Post*, the active parts he played at Spion Kop, Potgeiter's Ferry and Diamond Hill before being among the first to enter Ladysmith as his unit helped relieve the British garrison. If there was a battle, he was always thrusting himself forward into the thick of it and could have been killed or recaptured on numerous occasions.

However, when Pretoria fell, he knew the major part of the Boer War was over, and he found himself aboard the same ship, the *Dunottar Castle*, on which he had sailed nine months before, carrying him home to a very different, if no less dramatic, future.

Churchill docked at Southampton on 20 July 1900. The twentieth century and all that it would bring for the world and the man himself was barely born. But Churchill wasted no time in grabbing it from its cradle and nurturing the possibilities it held for his future. Within a

USS *McDougal*, with President Franklin D. Roosevelt on board, comes alongside HMS *Prince of Wales* in Placentia Bay, Newfoundland, 10 August 1941. (USNHHC)

USS *McDougal* alongside HMS *Prince of Wales* in Placentia Bay during August 1941. (USNHHC)

Winston Churchill is pictured coming aboard USS *Augusta* to confer with President Roosevelt in Placentia Bay, Newfoundland. The Prime Minister was welcomed aboard by Admiral Ernst J. King. (National Museum of the US Navy)

Aboard USS *Augusta*, Churchill is pictured having handed a letter from King George VI to President Roosevelt. Among those present are, left to right: Averell Harriman (right hand in pocket, smiling); Admiral Ernst J. King (right hand in pocket, head turned); Churchill, Ensign F.D. Roosevelt Jr.; Sumner Welles; Captain John R. Beardall; President Roosevelt; and Captain Elliot Roosevelt. (USNHHR)

Attendees of the Atlantic Conference pictured aboard USS *Augusta* having gathered for a dinner party. Seated, left to right, are: Sir Alexander Cadogan, Permanent Under-Secretary of State for Foreign Affairs; Air Chief Marshal Wilfred Freeman; Prime Minister Winston Churchill; President F.D. Roosevelt; Admiral Sir Dudley Pound; Field Marshal Sir John Dill; and Lord Cherwell. In the back row, standing, left to right are: Averell Harriman; Harry Hopkins; Admiral Ernest J. King; Admiral Ross T. McIntire; Sumner Wells; Major General Watson; Captain John Roosevelt; Admiral Harold R. Stark; Captain John R. Beardall; General George C. Marshall; and Ensign F.D. Roosevelt, Jr. Note FDR's dog, Fala, at his feet. (USNHHC)

President Franklin D. Roosevelt and members of his entourage coming on board HMS *Prince of Wales*, from USS *Augusta*, during the Atlantic Charter meetings. (National Museum of the US Navy)

A church service underway on the after deck of HMS *Prince of Wales*, in Placentia Bay, Newfoundland, during the conference. President Franklin D. Roosevelt and Prime Minister Winston Churchill can be seen seated in the centre of the image. (USNHHC)

President Franklin D. Roosevelt and Prime Minister Winston S. Churchill on the deck of HMS *Prince of Wales* following the church service held during the Atlantic Charter conference. (National Museum of the US Navy)

Winston Churchill shown during ceremonies on board HMS *Prince of Wales* during the Atlantic Charter conference. (National Museum of the US Navy)

Winston Churchill pictured walking the deck of HMS *Prince of Wales* during the Atlantic Conference, 1941. (Historic Military Press)

A portrait of Sumner Welles, circa 1940. (Library of Congress)

A portrait of Harry Hopkins, circa 1940. (Library of Congress)

MOST SECRET

NOTE: This document should not be left lying about and, if it is unnecessary to retain, should be returned to the Private Office.

PROPOSED DECLARATION

ALTERNATIVE VERSION — VERSION "A"
INCORPORATING NEW PARAGRAPH PROPOSED BY
CABINET IN ABBEY TELEGRAM NUMBER: 31.

The President of the United States of America and the Prime Minister, Mr. Churchill, representing His Majesty's Government in the United Kingdom, being met together, deem it right to make known certain common principles in the national policies of their respective countries on which they base their hopes for a better future for the world.

First, their countries seek no aggrandisement, territorial or other;

Second, they desire to see no territorial changes that do not accord with the freely expressed wishes of the peoples concerned.

Third, they respect the right of all peoples to choose the form of government under which they will live; and they wish to see self-government restored to those from whom it has been forcibly removed.

Fourth, they will endeavour, with due respect to their existing obligations, to further the enjoyment by all peoples of access, on equal terms, to the trade and to the raw materials of the world which are needed for their economic prosperity.

Fifth, they support fullest collaboration between Nations in economic field with object of securing for all peoples freedom from want, improved labour standards, economic advancement and social security.

Sixth, they hope to see established a peace, after the final destruction of the Nazi tyranny, which will afford to all nations the means of dwelling in security within their own boundaries, and which will afford assurance to all peoples that they may live out their lives in freedom from fear.

Seventh, they desire such a peace to establish for all nations safety on the high seas and oceans.

Eighth, they believe that all of the nations of the world must be guided in spirit to the abandonment of the use of force. Because no future peace can be maintained if land, sea or air armaments continue to be employed by nations which threaten, or may threaten, aggression outside of their frontiers, they believe that the disarmament of such nations is essential pending the establishment of a wider and more permanent system of general security. They will further the adoption of all other practicable measures which will lighten for peace-loving peoples the crushing burden of armaments.

Private Office.
August 12, 1941

The original draft of the eight-point Atlantic Charter showing Winston Churchill's handwritten changes. (Randolph Churchill)

Edwina Sandys called this painting of her grandfather painting 'Brush with History'. It includes many of his favourite things - books by him and about him; bottles of his favourite drinks and the flowers from the garden that he was painting. 'Some people think painting is a form of relaxation,' says Edwina. 'In fact it takes great concentration and uses a different part of the brain. And that was exactly what Grandpapa needed - something to take his mind completely away from the affairs of State.' (Copyright: Edwina Sandys 2016)

matter of ten weeks after stepping ashore, he had rejected an offer to run as an MP for Southport and got himself elected at Oldham. He had not forgotten the encouragement offered by Dan Dewsnap in that South African mineshaft. 'They'll all vote for you next time,' he had said. As it turned out just about enough did so, giving him a swing of only 6 per cent from the previous election.

He was elated but not carried away. The problem of earning a living remained. Members of Parliament at the turn of the century were rich. He was not. Although accumulating a fortune was never a specific goal, he was realistic enough to realize that he could not enjoy his lifestyle without earning the means to support it. So, almost immediately after being elected, he sailed for America. He had enjoyed a lucrative speaking tour of Britain on his return from the Boer War – he was, after all, not short of material – and grabbed the opportunity to capitalize across the Atlantic. As it turned out, a booking agent who did not live up to the industry of his British counterpart left Churchill disappointed with the financial return, especially in the United States. Not surprisingly Canada, being more closely aware of the Boer War, proved more successful and he returned home with a reasonable sum of money – £80,000 at today's rates.

Britain had changed, symbolically, in one important aspect while Churchill had been away: on 22 January 1901, Queen Victoria had died. The country had entered the Edwardian age with all its grandeur, extravagance and elegance, taking its cue from a king, Edward VII, who became one of Britain's most popular monarchs.

Needless to say, Winston Churchill did not enter the House of Commons as your average new boy. He was the son of a famous father, and he had created his own mantle of fame, not to say of notoriety, as a result of his daring exploits abroad. Always forward thinking, he was ready to embrace the new era, and, of course, he did not tip toe quietly to his seat on the backbenches. It soon became evident that he opposed many of the policies of Arthur Balfour's Conservative government.

As his career unfolded, it was never easy to follow the pattern of Churchill's politics. Although a man of firm convictions, he never allowed himself to be bound by party dogma and proved it very early on by railing against Balfour's large defence budget and tariffs. To his core, Churchill was a Free Trader and, in so being, was quite prepared go against the best interests of the Empire, to which he was devoted.

Waving contradictions aside, he expressed his feelings as only he could: 'Why should the world's shipping labour in the chops of the Bristol Channel, or crowd up the dreary reaches of the Mersey? It is because our harbours are more nearly as nature made them; because the perverted ingenuity of man has not been occupied in obstructing them with fiscal stake nets and tariff mud bars. That is why they come.'

History tells us that although the budding statesman began and ended his long career as a true Conservative, the conditions he discovered while touring his own country were more than his innately decent nature could abide. When he read Seebohm Rowntree's book on conditions in York, he said, 'The book has fairly made my hair stand on end. Poverty in York extends to 1/5th of the population . . . That I call a terrible and shocking thing. People have only the workhouse or prison as avenues to change their present situation.'

The Conservative drift towards protectionism enraged him, for it was his profound belief that tariffs meant handing over fiscal politics to the competing pulls of different industrial interests and that those with the longest purses and least scruples would get the largest benefits. These were hardly right wing thoughts and, in the absence of the yet unformed Labour Party, he found his thinking, aided and abetted by his new friend David Lloyd George, becoming more and more aligned with Liberal philosophy.

Soon, in May 1903, he took the plunge and wrote to Prime Minister Balfour: 'I am utterly opposed to anything that will alter the free trading policy of this country. Preferential tariffs are dangerous and objectionable. If your mind is made up and there is no going back, I must re-consider my position in politics.'

For a 28-year-old who had yet to complete three years in the House, it was a bold and brash stance to take, but, although many Conservatives hated him for it, none could doubt his conviction. So it did not come as a complete surprise when on 31 May 1904, Churchill entered the chamber, hesitated at the bar for a second, and then turned right towards the Opposition benches, finding a seat, not, perhaps by chance, next to David Lloyd George, the future Liberal Prime Minister. Literally and politically, he had crossed the floor.

Despite being urged by friends not to cloud his convictions with too great a show of overt ambition in seeking a government position when the Liberals gained power in the General Election of 1906, the lucidity and vehemence of the young man's speeches had already made it inevitable that he was destined for high office.

Speaking before the election in Manchester, Churchill, referring to the Prime Minister under whom he had served only months before, said this:

The great leader of the Protectionist party, whatever else you may or may not think about him, has at any rate left me in no doubt as to what use he will make of his victory should he win it. We know perfectly well what to expect – a party of great vested interests, banded together in a formidable confederation, corruption at home, aggression to cover it up abroad, the trickery of tariff juggles, the tyranny of a party machine, sentiment by the bucketful, patriotism by the imperial pint, the open hand at the public exchequer, the open door at the public house, dear food for the million, cheap labour for the millionaire.

It was a withering assessment, and no doubt his working-class Mancunian audience lapped it up. He was elected for Manchester North West not long after. The world has long become acquainted with quotes from Churchill's great speeches in later years, but few would associate him with attacking patriotism by the imperial pint or cheap labour for millionaires. Even for a new and enthusiastic Liberal these were the views of a man veering left of centre – an aspect of Churchill's political career that has been mostly lost in the mists of time.

Given his prominence, it was inevitable that the new Prime Minister, Sir Henry Campbell-Bannerman, would waste no time in offering Churchill a position in his Liberal administration. Having been summoned to the new leader's house in Belgrave Square, the young man who was supposedly too ambitious for his own good, promptly turned down the position first offered to him – that of Financial Secretary to the Treasury, the most highly regarded of all junior posts because it had almost always led to the Cabinet.

However, Churchill realized immediately that he would be placed in a very secondary position under Herbert Asquith, the new Chancellor of the Exchequer, who was being widely, and correctly, touted as the future Prime Minister. In avoiding the shadows of a greater figure, Winston cleverly suggested the Colonial Office where, given his history, he would be able to speak with great authority. And that was not all. He knew that the Earl of Elgin (grandson of the earl of Elgin Marbles fame) had been appointed Secretary of State for the Colonies and would be leaving much of the public work in the Commons to his deputy as he would be in the House of Lords. In fact, the white-haired Earl with his fuzzy whiskers would prefer to spend even more time on his estate in Scotland.

So, on being given the role of Under-Secretary for the Colonies, Churchill seized as much work as he could, much to the displeasure of department's permanent civil servant, Sir Francis Hopwood, who wrote to Elgin: 'He is most tiresome to deal with . . . The restless energy, uncontrollable desire for notoriety and the lack of moral perception make him an anxiety indeed.'

In his biography *Churchill*, Roy Jenkins, a future Chancellor of the Exchequer, amusingly revealed the extent to which Elgin kept his interactions with his rambunctious deputy brief. On receiving a long and grandiloquently expressed dissertation on all matters Colonial from Winston, which ended, 'These are my views. W.S.C.' his boss responded, 'But not mine. E.'

Perhaps it was no surprise that, having worked furiously to finish his huge book on his father, Lord Randolph, which had been completed just before the election, and having dealt with the stress and strain of switching parties and entering government, Churchill, by the end of 1905, fell seriously ill. The problem affected his tongue, throat and heart and confounded the medical profession. Rest was obviously of the essence, and Churchill retired to the country seat of his good friend Lord Wimborne at Canford Manor (which was turned into Canford School in 1923) to recuperate. Apparently heavy massage, delivered by a fearsome and elderly American woman, was on offer as treatment.

Writing to his mother from Canford on 4 December 1905, he explained that part of the problem was caused by ligament damage to his tongue. This raises some interesting questions. Was this the cause of the lisp that became part of his speech from then on? Or had it been there since childhood? And how serious was this affliction? Serious enough, apparently, for the budding politician to joke in another letter to 'Mama' that his doctor, Sir Felix Semon, 'has refused to cut off my tongue'. Without exaggeration, it could be said that any kind of incision on the Churchill tongue could have changed the history of the world.

It is unquestionable that Churchill's oratory defined him and became his greatest political tool, despite being affected by a lisp. Although Franklin Roosevelt's affliction was far more debilitating, it is worth noting, as we have in the previous chapters, he also used his handicap to his advantage in requiring that all visitors came to him. As it was, Churchill seemed cured by the New Year and quickly threw himself back into the political fray. However, while discussing the way he spoke, the question of Winston's accent might also be raised. As one can hear from listening to MovieTone newsreels, prior to the Second World War, upper-class accents in Britain were far more exaggerated than they are today. The speeches of Neville Chamberlain offer another example. Strangely, considering the milieu in which he moved, Churchill did not talk like that. His vowels were flatter, possibly, as his granddaughter Celia Sandys suggests, because of his having grown up listening to his

American mother. Considering what he was called upon to do later in life, this was, to say the least, fortuitous. The speeches he delivered in his early days as Prime Minister were, as a result, delivered in tones which would have been much more accessible to the mass of the British public, especially the working class, than his Conservative colleagues would have been able to. There is no doubt that Churchill's speeches were of huge import at that moment in history, and it is reasonable to assume that it was his accent, as well as his words, that helped rally the morale of the nation.

Even during his time at the Colonial Office, the social situation of Britain's working class was never far from his mind, and, when Churchill did achieve Cabinet rank at the Board of Trade under Asquith in 1908, he was able to do something about it. Again the opening of Labour Exchanges or, in effect, Job Centres, was central to Churchill's attempts to alleviate suffering and is not something that comes readily to mind while assessing his achievements today. Yet he worked assiduously on the project, linking it to a scheme of unemployment insurance and, physically, making his presence felt. On 1 February 1909, Churchill, accompanied by his wife Clementine, visited no less than seventeen Labour Exchanges that were opening that day in London.

As British historian Max Arthur relates, Churchill's two years at the Board of Trade saw him become a strong advocate of state aid for the sick and the unemployed. Just prior to the opening of the Labour Exchanges, Churchill had spoken on behalf of Asquith at East Fife in Scotland:

> Dimly across the gulfs of ignorance I see the outline of a policy that I call the Minimum Standard. In the centre of this scheme stands the great principle of national insurance against unemployment, sickness, infirmity and the death of the breadwinner. This is linked with the system of labour exchanges now being established, with large projects for reforming the Poor Law, for rescuing children from the work house; for providing for proper treatment for the feeble-minded, for inebriates . . . and for discounting between the honest worker in search of a job and for the idle loafer in search of a tip.

The latter phrase, if little else, would resonate with those right-wingers who like to align themselves with the great man today.

As we mentioned, Churchill was accompanied on his tour of the Labour Exchanges by his wife, Clementine, whom he had married in September 1908 at St Margaret's, Westminster, having proposed at

Blenheim Palace where he had been born. The couple had met over four years before at a ball, and first impressions, at least from Miss Clementine Hozier's side, had not been promising. She described the young man as being untypically monosyllabic, gauche and too timid to ask her for a dance. However, the relationship developed as the pair met casually during Winston's early years in Parliament and Clementine showed sufficient interest to buy Winston's biography of Lord Randolph. Soon, there began an initially stiff, but later more fluent, correspondence – the first of more than 1,700 letters or notes they would send each other during the course of an oft-disrupted but never questioned love affair.

The first signal of a desire for a more intimate relationship came from Winston soon after he had suffered an agonizingly narrow loss by just 429 votes at Manchester North West. 'I was under the dull clouds of reaction on Saturday after all the effort and excitement of that tiresome election,' he wrote to Clementine. 'How I should have liked you to be there. Write to me again. I am a solitary figure in the midst of crowds. Be kind to me.' It was a plea that Clementine strove to answer for the rest of her life.

Prior to his marriage, Winston had never been a ladies man, certainly not when compared to some of the young swells making the most of the more a more openly social Edwardian age. Inevitably, however, there were moments when a lady caught his eye. There had been a flirtation with Pamela Plowden, later Pamela Lytton, with whom he remained friends through the following decades. There had been the well-chaperoned motor tour of central Italy in 1906 with Muriel Wilson, the daughter of a rich shipowner from Hull who teased him when, a little later, there were rumours of an engagement with the daughter of Louis Botha, the future South African Prime Minister who had captured him during the Boer War. Roy Jenkins quotes her as writing about looking forward to welcoming him and his wife 'with all their little Bothas' to her place in the South of France. But it was little more than gossip.

That might also have been true of a supposed relationship with Ethel Barrymore, a famous American actress of the period, who spent much time in London at the turn of the century. Many thought it little more than stage-door gossip, although it could well have been through Barrymore that Churchill met Maxine Elliott, another American actress of great beauty, who was a star of the West End stage during the immediate pre-war years. Maxine became a lifelong friend until her death in 1941, frequently inviting Winston to stay, often without Clementine, at her villa near Cannes. But there was never any hint of romance. In the early years of their friendship, Maxine was, in any case, far too involved with the dashing Wimbledon champion Anthony Wilding, a New Zealander who was killed in Flanders in 1915.

It fell to another dinner companion to offer a rare insight into exactly what Churchill was like socially at the start of his political career. Violet Asquith, whose father would shortly become Prime Minister, was nineteen when she found herself seated next to him at a dinner in London in 1906. Arthur Balfour and Hilaire Belloc were among the guests. But, afterwards, Miss Asquith, later to become Lady Violet Bonham Carter, could not even remember who was sitting on her left. She had, by her own admission, become totally star struck.

'He seemed to me to be quite different from any young man I had ever met,' she wrote in *Winston Churchill As I Knew Him*, published in 1965.

> For a long time he remained sunk in abstraction. Then he appeared to become suddenly aware of my existence and asked me abruptly how old I was. I replied that I was nineteen. 'And I,' he said almost despairingly, 'am thirty two already. Younger than anyone else who COUNTS, though,' he added as if to comfort himself. Then, savagely, 'Curse ruthless time, curse our mortality!' . . . and he burst forth into an eloquent diatribe into the shortness of human life, the immensity of possible human accomplishments – a theme so well exploited by poets, prophets and philosophers that it might seem difficult to invest with it with a new and startling significance. Yet for me he did so in a torrent of magnificent language which appeared to be both effortless and inexhaustible and ended up with the words I shall always remember: 'We are all worms. But I do believe I am a glow-worm.' Until the end of dinner I listened to him spell bound . . . I was transfixed, transported into a new element . . . His ear for the beauty of language needed no tuning fork.

Her friends were far from unanimous in this appraisal of her new acquaintance, but she was not surprised. Violet's father had forewarned her when, as was her habit, she went into his bedroom that night to recount the doings of her day. Herbert Asquith, customarily known as H.H, responded to her exhilarated assertion that she had encountered genius with a knowing smile. 'Well, Winston would certainly agree with you there – but I am not sure you will find many others of the same mind. Still, I know exactly what you mean. He is not only remarkable but unique. He will now have every chance to extend himself and show his paces.' Asquith ensured that he was given the chance. By 1911, after two other Cabinet posts, the Prime Minister made him First Lord of the Admiralty.

Clementine Hozier was already a friend of Lady Violet's by the time her engagement to Winston was announced and it is impossible to imagine there was not an element of jealousy. But none of it emerged in her writing and, having admitted to being awestruck by Clementine's 'flawless beauty and wide experience of the world' Violet spoke of a 'long friendship which no vicissitude has ever shaken'.

It helped that Clementine turned out to be even more of a Liberal in the political sense than her husband, and although at the outset, she was thought to be by far his inferior intellectually, she became his moral anchor, totally devoted in public but far from afraid to rail against his excesses in private – even if the staff were in earshot. They spent a great deal of time apart but remained devoted to his each other, and he was always contrite after an argument, never doubting that he needed that anchor as well as the love she offered.

Edwina Sandys, the couple's granddaughter and celebrated artist, has no doubt as to the importance of the relationship. 'If he had married the wrong woman,' she told us recently, 'the world would be a very different place. She was very strong, very beautiful and very wise.'

Despite his meteoric rise, which saw the young minister in charge of Britain's navy at the Admiralty during the crucial months leading up to the First World War, his fall, when it came a few years later, was heavy. From one of three ministers Asquith relied on more than any others at the start of the war (Lloyd George and Foreign Secretary Edward Grey were the others) Churchill found himself relegated to the role of an Army major in the trenches of the Somme. This drastic demotion had everything to do with one of greatest military disasters in British history: Gallipoli. It also brought about the disruption of the Liberals needing to form a coalition government and the eventual resignation of Prime Minister Asquith – but not before Churchill had been shunted off to the lowly post of Duchy of Lancaster. The only crumb he was thrown was a seat on the War Council.

The disaster at Gallipoli, which ultimately cost 46,000 Allied lives, was as complicated a catastrophe as Britain has ever suffered and, although there were many faults and errors of judgement made lower down the lines of command, it was, inevitably, considering his position and personality, Churchill who bore the brunt of it. As the war became ever more bogged down in the mud of Flanders, it was the First Lord of the Admiralty who had argued strongly for diversionary tactics. He felt it imperative to open up a sea link with Russia through the Dardanelles, the narrow straits which led into the Sea of Marmara, between the Aegean and the Black Sea, and was heavily guarded by Turkish troops fighting on Germany's side. This was attempted, with the immediate loss of three Royal Navy ships in February, and, in the summer, landings on the shores of Gallipoli in which Allied troops, largely drawn from Australian and New Zealand regiments, suffered appalling losses. All manner of contradictory orders were issued and, at one point, the Secretary of State for War Lord Kitchener refused to deploy the additional forces his generals were calling for. The object was to threaten Constantinople with bombardment and in so doing force Turkey out of the war. It was never achieved.

With historical perspective, Churchill's entire time at the Admiralty proved of immense use to him when he became Prime Minister. For a start, his own personality would ensure that lines of command would be cleaner and more effective and eliminate much of the bickering that had taken place between him, Lord Kitchener and Lord Fisher who he had brought back to the Admiralty as First Sea Lord. In retrospect, this was not a great idea as Fisher, regarded by many as Britain's greatest sailor after Lord Nelson, was 73 years old but still convinced he knew more about the Navy than any living soul. The feisty old man resigned six times before finally walking away during Churchill's last days at the Admiralty.

The endless disagreements only helped sow the seeds of defeat at Gallipoli. It is hard to believe Churchill was not remembering that time when, on being appointed Prime Minister all those years later, he made his famous remark about feeling 'that my past life had been a but a preparation for this hour and this trial'. The preparation had been brutal but had not been forgotten.

Commenting years later to biographer Martin Gilbert, Clementine said of her husband's mood at the time, 'I thought he would die of grief'. His indomitable spirit would never allow that, of course, but the method he chose to raise his spirits was an unusually placid one. He began to paint. In future years, he would use painting to soothe his soul and, eventually, he not only improved but became prolific. In 1915, he had not yet acquired Chartwell and its lovely views over the Kent countryside, but the vast estate of Knole, once owned by King Henry VIII, was but a few miles away and when he received an invitation from the family of Vita Sackville-West, who grew up there, he planted his easel and set about producing some of his earliest canvasses amidst the parkland setting where, to this day, deer still roam.

By then he had progressed to oils, but early watercolours were painted at a small manor house, Hoe Farm, near Godalming in Surrey which he and Clementine were renting. As usual, he was short of money, a fact that was implied in a letter to his brother Jack. 'We live very simply here,' he wrote. 'But with all the essentials of life well provided for – hot baths, cold champagne, new peas and old brandy.' As a map to Winston's heart, these 'essentials' provide a good guide.

Churchill, of course, could not sit still for too long and, having been demoted to the position of Chancellor of the Duchy of Lancaster, with its dingy offices near Waterloo Bridge, he headed up north for a very rare visit to his Scottish constituency in Dundee. Here again the Bulldog was to the fore, offering a brief glimpse of the eloquence which he would display when lifting British spirits during the darkest hours of 1940. Casting aside the personal humiliation he had suffered in Westminster, he received rousing cheers from his audience as he told them:

> Then turn again to your task. Look forward, do not look backward. Gather afresh in heart and spirit all the energies of your being, bend again together for a supreme effort. The times are harsh and the need is dire, the agony of Europe is infinite, but the might of Britain hurled united into the conflict will be irresistible. We are the grand reserve of the Allied cause and that grand reserve must now march forward as one man.

He was not, of course, asking them to do something he was not prepared to do himself. After a few frustrating months of trying to clean up the mess of Gallipoli without the tools to do it as just one voice on an increasingly large War Council – now infiltrated by Bonar Law's Conservatives – he wrote Asquith a letter of resignation on 11 November 1915. Having pointed out his inability to make major decisions and abhorring 'well paid inactivity', Churchill wrote in his closing paragraphs:

> I therefore ask you to submit my resignation to the King. I am an officer, and I place myself unreservedly at the disposal of the military authorities, observing that my regiment is in France.
>
> I have a clear conscience which enables me to bear my responsibility for past events with composure.
>
> Time will vindicate my administration of the Admiralty and assign me my due share in the vast series of preparations and operations which have secured us the complete command of the seas.
>
> With much respect, an unaltered personal friendship, I bid you good bye.

Within a matter of days, a man who had been in charge of the Admiralty just a few weeks before arrived in Boulogne as an Army major, soon to be assigned to the 2nd Battalion of the Grenadier Guards. But rank only counted for so much. He was still Winston Churchill of course and, as such, found himself met by a staff car sent by Field Marshal Sir John French, the commander of the British Expeditionary Force, which promptly whisked him off to General Headquarters at St Omer, where he was able to spend his first night dining at the Commander-in-Chief's table and sleeping in a beautiful chateau. A few nights later, reality set in. He was in the trenches. It was the end of November and the mud and the cold and the rats engulfed all who fought there. The reception Churchill had received from the Grenadiers' hierarchy had been chilly, too, but suspicion soon evaporated as it became clear that the former Cabinet Minister was there to fight, to endure and to do his duty. In turn, Churchill quickly developed much admiration for the Grenadiers. 'The discipline of this battalion is very strict,' he wrote on 27 November. 'But the results are good. The spirit is admirable . . . A total indifference to death or casualties prevails. What has to be done is done and the losses accepted without fuss or comment.'

Churchill's main complaint in his early days with the Grenadiers was the fact that strong tea with condensed milk, which he described as a 'very unpleasant beverage', was the only drink on offer at Battalion headquarters. But he soldiered on and soon enjoyed another visit from Lady Luck. Reluctantly obeying an order from the corps commander to visit him, Churchill set off with his batman across three miles of muddy fields to the appointed rendezvous. They had not gone 200 yards when the crack of shells split the air and, turning, they saw sheets of flame light up the trenches they had just left. On returning later, Churchill was told by his sergeant that his kit had been moved from his shelter but that he should not go in. 'Sir, it's an awful mess.' The shell had hit five minutes after Churchill had left, killing the remaining occupant.

Always assured of his own abilities, Churchill had set his heart on being given a brigade and paid little heed to cries of outrage from opposition benches in the House of Commons when rumours to that effect began circulating. It was pointed out that, in the entire history of the British Army, no major had been elevated to brigadier at such short notice and with so little experience. Asquith, who had intimated to Winston that he would get his brigade, had a change of heart and, when Sir Douglas Haig took over from French, the offer was downgraded to a battalion.

So it was as a colonel that Churchill was assigned command of the 6th Royal Scots Fusiliers on New Year's Day, 1916, and set off to find his command post, which turned out to be a dilapidated farm house situated just behind the front-line trenches which, themselves, were no more than 300 yards from the German lines. A Royal Fusilier Captain, A.D. Gibb, who went on to become Regius Professor of Law at the University of Glasgow, wrote in *With Winston Churchill at the Front* that the newcomer's arrival was met with foreboding as his predecessor had been very popular.

It did not take Lieutenant Colonel Churchill long to assuage their fears. Addressing his stony-faced officers for the first time, he declared an outright war . . . on lice. There followed a historical dissertation on the dastardly part played by the louse in previous wars and orders were issued for much work with hot irons and other methods of how to eradicate the menace. Apparently it was successful, leaving the 6th Battalion as the only lice-free unit at the front. If that was a morale booster, so were the games of football, the singsongs, lessons in building sandbags and bricks, parapets, half moons and ravelins (much of it out of his own imagination) and his tendency to be less strict with punishments.

After a few of months, Captain Gibb, a man of good-tempered cynicism who thought the army mostly stumbled along, had revised his earlier opinion of his celebrated colonel and wrote: 'I am fairly convinced that no more popular officer ever commanded troops . . . He was always the first on the scene of misfortune and did all he could to help and comfort and cheer.'

Churchill loved being a soldier, loved the excitement and danger of it to an extent that most people would find incomprehensible. But the trumpet of ambition was always sounding in his ears, and he knew his destiny lay closer to the dispatch boxes of the House of Commons than the trenches of Flanders. So when he asked to be relieved of his command after little more than six months in France, he was not fleeing the war but rather seeking to have a greater influence upon it. This, he knew, could only be done from Westminster.

However, it may come as no surprise to learn that his reappearance in Parliament did not go smoothly. In fact, all hell broke loose when Churchill gave a speech assessing the state of his former stamping ground at the Admiralty and, after some measured criticism, stunned his colleagues on both sides of the House by calling for the return of the ageing Lord Fisher as First Sea Lord. Such a suggestion seemed unfathomable to almost everyone. This was the man who had been the cause of Churchill's downfall eleven months before and who, by now was a seen as an old admiral wobbling on a shifting deck. But as Roy Jenkins points out, 'They had an amazing and almost indestructible fascination for one another.' Even pleas from Clementine, who was not shy of pointing out that Fisher had ruined him once and was capable of doing so again, fell on deaf ears. 'Leave him alone!' she was reported to have said with some vehemence when Fisher was invited to dinner at their Cromwell Road residence on the eve of Churchill's disastrous speech on 7 March 1916. But to no effect.

So bereft of friends and supporters was Churchill afterwards that Asquith was one of many who urged him to return to his regiment in France. This he did in a state of almost complete disorientation. On his way he changed his mind at least four times, sending and cancelling missives to Asquith before eventually returning to his command of the Royal Fusiliers. Amazingly, as Churchill grappled with his angst, neither Captain Gibb nor any of his brother officers noticed any lessening of his authority nor any hint of outward distress. How long he could have continued is open to doubt, but Fate galloped to his rescue. It was decided that the 6th and 7th battalions of the Royal Scots Fusiliers, both reduced in strength by casualties, were to be amalgamated. The colonel of the 7th was senior to Churchill, so the job fell to him, which offered Winston a lucky escape route back to London. At the beginning of May, he left the war zone for the last time as a soldier.

Churchill returned to Parliament with his enthusiasm for long speeches undiminished, although many were not well received by a House that had not forgotten his blunder over Lord Fisher. However, his unrivalled knowledge of all things naval and his first-hand experience of the front, presented with such seductive use of the English language, slowly brought people round. He spoke powerfully within weeks of his return about what he described as the 'trench population' and the 'non-trench population' of the army – the first living in constant danger and conditions that were often knee deep in mud, while the second lived in comfort away from danger, and with better pay. It was more than his sense of fairness could countenance, and he railed against it. But his rehabilitation was as yet incomplete, and little was achieved.

The year of 1916 saw little more than stagnation in Flanders, punctuated by futile attempts to break through German lines, which resulted in yet more deaths on a scale that, from a distance in time, is almost impossible to reconcile. Shipping losses were appalling, too, and it was inevitable that change in leadership would come. Eventually, on 5 December, Asquith lost the Premiership, and Lloyd George took over. This change did not bring any immediate change in fortunes for Churchill, despite his friendship with the fiery Welshman, and it took a year for this unceasingly controversial figure to regain some influence.

Soon after President Wilson brought the United States into the war on 6 April 1917, Churchill managed to persuade David Lloyd George to agree to a secret session of the House of Commons so as to examine war strategies and possible solutions away from the glare of the public gaze. So on 10 May, the exact date that, 23 years later, would see him become Prime Minister, Churchill opened the debate. His speech lasted an hour and fifteen minutes and it proved a turning point for him.

He made much of the fact the front lines in France were congealed in every sense while British shipping was being destroyed at an alarming rate by a renewed German submarine campaign. He called for 'every resource and invention' to be applied and 'let the anti-submarine war claim priority over every other form of British effort'.

Churchill had seized the attention of his audience and finished in full stride:

> Let the House implore the Prime Minister to use the authority which he wields to prevent the French and British High Commands from dragging each other into fresh bloody and disastrous adventures. Master the U-Boat attack. Bring over the American millions. And meanwhile maintain an active defence on the Western Front, so as to economize French and British lives, and so as to train, increase and perfect our armies and our methods for a decisive effort in a later year.

It all made sense. Churchill had re-found his compass and was a force again. The House sensed it and, more importantly, so did Lloyd George who, facing down opposition from the Conservative benches, promptly offered him the important, if not very prestigious, post of Minister of Munitions. Being so closely linked to the war effort, it enabled Winston to make use of his detailed knowledge of all things military. What had changed the Prime Minister's mind? The speech in close session, the reinforced realization that Churchill was far more use at his side than grumbling from afar and, interestingly, perhaps a more personal reason. Maybe he remembered with fondness the days when he and Churchill were the bright sparks of the Asquith government and just needed a friend. Lloyd George's wife, Frances Stevenson wrote in her diary on 19 May that year: 'He says he wants someone who will cheer him up and help and encourage him and who will not be continually coming to him with a long face . . .'

Presumably, Churchill performed this duty well, for he remained at the Ministry of Munitions for the remaining sixteen months of the war, headquartered at a hotel on Northumberland Avenue, where he often slept, and making numerous visits to France. His love of being where the action was his primary motivation, but, throughout his life, he always loved France. Once, on taking a break from touring the Front, he wrote Clementine from his rooms at the Ritz in Paris: 'Next time you should really try to accompany me and spend a few days in this menaced but always delightful city.'

But his mind was more concentrated on war than romance and, with his first-hand accounts of his conversations with Georges Clemenceau, the aging but still energetic Prime Minister, and his French generals, Churchill was able to have a greater influence in the decision making once he returned home than his lowly ministerial post would have suggested.

A full week visiting forward positions and interacting with Field Marshal Haig and General Rawlinson, as well as General Foch in March 1918, enabled Churchill to understand the urgency of getting American troops into battle. Rawlinson's Fifth Army had suffered horrendously from a recent German onslaught and the need for replacements was paramount. To that end, Churchill managed to persuade Clemenceau and Lloyd George to go straight to President Wilson with a request for 480,000 US troops to cross the Atlantic as fast as possible rather than wait for General Pershing to gather and train his entire army before embarking for France. A first contingent of 14,000 soon arrived and, by the end of hostilities, more than a million Americans in various capacities had come to the rescue of Britain, France and its allies.

By staying close to Lloyd George during the inevitable jockeying for position at Westminster once the war came to an end on 11 November 1918, Churchill ensured that he would remain in the Cabinet and, indeed, there was even talk of a return to the Admiralty. In the end he gladly accepted the War Office, with its wider scope (including the nascent Royal Air Force) and set about trying to help solve all the problems four years of devastating destruction and loss of human life had brought.

As Secretary of State for War, Churchill marauded on the fringes of those momentous early months of 1919 in Paris when the victorious nations laboured over the details of re-inventing large swathes of Europe at the Peace Conference. Beginning in January 1919, it followed close on the heels of the Treaty of Versailles, a flawed document that, in its imbalance towards Germany, would play an unhappy part in re-igniting Germany's nationalism, with Hitler fanning the flames.

The extent of problems facing the four men who took on the brunt of the task – US President Woodrow Wilson, British Prime Minister David

Lloyd George, French Prime Minister Georges Clemenceau and Italian Prime Minister Vittorio Orlando – became clear as they tried to redraw the map of Europe. By the time they had finished, the Austro-Hungarian Empire, which had encompassed such cities as Krakow, Prague, Vienna, Budapest, Trieste and as far south as Split and Sarajevo, vanished. New states, primarily Czechoslovakia, Yugoslavia and the newly-separated Austria and Hungary emerged. Further east, the Russian Empire was cut back to allow Poland and the smaller Baltic states of Estonia, Latvia and Lithuania to govern themselves.

All this was accomplished against the background of the Russian Revolution in 1917 and the arrival on the political scene of Lenin and the Bolsheviks. For a while, it created chaos. No one in Paris had a clue what was happening in Russia. Only the American journalist Lincoln Steffens seems to have made it to Moscow and, on leaving, he famously remarked, 'I have seen the future and it works'. His word was not to be trusted, and Churchill was one of those who didn't. In an assessment that must have made his pragmatic relationship with Stalin during the Second World War all the more indigestible, he stated, 'The essence of Bolshevism as opposed to many other forms of visionary political thought is that it can only be propagated and maintained by violence.'

Despite an attempt, early on in January, by Lloyd George to bring some cohesion to the proceedings by forcing the Supreme Council, which included the Big Four and Japan, to choose three options, the infighting created little but incoherence. Lloyd George had suggested three options on how to deal with Russia: 1. Destroy Russian Bolshevism. 2. To insulate the outside world from it. 3. To invite the Russians, including the Bolsheviks, to the peace table. The British Prime Minister, renowned for his charm and persuasive abilities, chose the third despite being urged by Churchill to choose the first. But he could not get his fellow negotiators to agree. As Margaret Macmillan relates in her masterly book *1919*, Allied policy towards Russia throughout the Peace Conference was hopelessly inconsistent – never firm enough to overthrow the Bolsheviks but hostile enough to convince them that the Western Powers were their implacable enemies. The consequences were dire, and to Churchill they came as no surprise. Even at the time, over the course of his visits to Paris during the Conference, Churchill felt that the 'frightful rancour and fear and hatred', as he put it later, which pervaded the proceedings would lead to disaster.

He stated his fears clearly in a speech at the Imperial Conference in London two years later, saying that he had wanted Britain to be both an ally of France and a friend of Germany. Speaking of that rancour and hatred Churchill prophesized with deadly accuracy that, 'if left unchecked will almost certainly, in a generation or so, bring about a renewal of the struggle of which we have just witnessed the conclusion'.

Decades later, in an address televised on NBC News, Churchill revisited the point: 'The idea that the vanquished could pay the expenses of the victors was a crazy and destructive delusion. The failure to strangle Bolshevism at its birth and to bring Russia, then prostrate, by one means or another, into the general democratic system lies heavy on us today.'

No matter what warnings Churchill might have been murmuring in the ear of his friend Lloyd George, President Wilson, with his vision of a League of Nations offering scant ideas of how it would encompass a bankrupt Germany, led the way to the signing of the treaty in the Hall of Mirrors at Versailles, an opulent and historic setting that did not, from any angle, reflect the dangers that lay ahead. For Churchill, there was nothing but frustration. Not for the last time, he had a vision that few shared and when his prophecies concerning the way in which a humiliated Germany would react came true, he would find himself a lone voice once again as he tried, tirelessly, to warn Parliament of the dangers he had foreseen.

Chapter 8

Ignored, Humiliated, and Finally Acclaimed

The date of 19 October 1922 was not one that Churchill remembered with fondness. It was the day Lloyd George was forced out of the Premiership and one that saw Churchill undergoing an emergency appendix operation at a private hospital in Dorset Square. Recovery from appendicitis was not as quick or routine as it is today, and the patient took a long time to recover. Worst of all, from Winston's point of view, was his inability to take part in the election campaign necessitated by the Prime Minister's resignation. His presence was badly needed in Dundee, and he sent Clementine up to Scotland to make some speeches for him. But the mood had changed, and Mrs Churchill was not spared the wrath of some of her husband's former working-class supporters who cared not one jot that the poor woman was travelling with a two-month-old baby.

The result was a disaster for Churchill, who lost heavily to the persistent Labour Party candidate, Edwin Scrymgeour, whose 32,000 votes tripled his total from the 1918 General Election. Churchill had managed to get himself to Dundee just a few days before, but it was all too late. Catching the sleeper back to London with his wife and baby, he wrote: 'I return without an office, without a seat, without a party and without an appendix.'

The fact that he felt himself without a party was prophetic because, although the Liberals still wanted him, the number of available seats they had to offer had diminished, and, at the start of 1924, Churchill found himself cast out of Parliament. His response, hiding periods of intense depression, was to take Clementine to the South of France, where she could play in all the spring Riviera tennis tournaments while he worked on his latest book, *The World Crisis*.

On his return, Churchill considered another run in a Manchester constituency, but for reasons that were never fully explained, opted for a seat in Leicester. Again he lost to the Labour candidate and that experience, following so soon on Dundee, started to edge him away from his previous position as left of centre in British politics. Although still a Free Trader and wholly sympathetic to the plight of the poor, he could not abide the thought of a Liberal alliance with the burgeoning Labour Party. But that soon came to pass when Stanley Baldwin's Conservatives lost 86 seats in the 1923 election – a depletion that prevented them from forming a majority government.

The Conservative total was 286, but Labour won 191 and the Liberals 158. So when the Liberals threw their support behind a party now clearly defined as 'socialist', it was the Labour Party leader Ramsay MacDonald, who became Prime Minister. The election result had done little to clarify the political landscape, but for Churchill, there was a tide pulling him back to his original shore. It began, as so many things do, with the chance occurrence of the death of the sitting member for Westminster, J.S. Nicholson. After tedious travels to Dundee, a by-election on the very doorstep of the Houses of Parliament was irresistible to Winston. He would challenge for the seat. But as what? Two press lords, Rothermere and Beaverbrook, were urging him on, presumably to stand as a Conservative. But the party he had joined as a young man was not quite ready to welcome him back. He had, inevitably, by style and substance, angered them continually over the years, and the wounds were still open. So he had to think of something else and came up with the uncompromising title of 'Independent Anti-Socialist'.

If that was not enough to gain attention, a new acolyte, the 23-year-old Brendan Bracken, who would remain at Churchill's side for the rest of his life, made sure that no one could miss the campaign of this peculiar political specimen. Bracken had Churchill driven around Whitehall, Pall Mall, Victoria Station and part of Soho in a 'coach & four' with a trumpeter on the box and chorus girls from Daly's Theatre to cheer him on. After it was all over and he had recovered tearfully from an agonizingly close defeat by a mere forty-three votes, Churchill described it as 'the most exciting, stirring, sensational election I have ever fought'.

His performance did much to smooth his path back towards the Conservative Party, and it became inevitable that, the next time he fought an election, it would be in their colours. A speech he gave in Liverpool to the Conservative Working Man's Association – the first to a Tory group in over 20 years – was billed as 'Present Dangers of the Socialist Movement', and the die was cast.

A Labour defeat in the House of Commons in October 1924 meant a third General Election in three years, and Churchill made the most of it, winning a safe seat in Epping (now called Woodford) in Essex by a wide margin. He was back where he felt he belonged: in Parliament.

Under Stanley Baldwin's leadership, the Conservatives found themselves back in power with 419 MPs, enough to give them a solid majority. Churchill was expecting a Cabinet post but when it was offered, it was more than he could have counted on. Baldwin asked him to become Chancellor of the Exchequer, generally regarded as the No. 2 position in the Cabinet. He had been lucky in that Neville Chamberlain, the man he would replace as Prime Minister in 1940, had declined the Chancellorship in favour of the Ministry of Health, but that in no way diminished Churchill's delight.

Churchill's time in charge of Britain's money will forever be tainted by the fact that he tried to turn it into gold. In fact, in a less than literal sense, he did just that. He put Britain back on the Gold Standard. Hindsight will tell a different story but, at the time, it was universally considered the right thing to do. When sterling had been had been tied to gold before the war, it was at parity with the dollar. But imbalanced expenditure, inflation and a rapid rise in prices (double in the UK and triple in France) during the conflict had made that impossible to sustain.

However, when Australia, New Zealand and other Commonwealth countries reverted to gold, the pressure mounted on a Chancellor who was still harbouring doubts. Although surrounded by a pro-gold group of advisers and political colleagues, he searched, almost in desperation, for the opposite viewpoint. He did not have to look past the economic guru of the time, John Maynard Keynes, or Reginald McKenna, one of Churchill's predecessors as Chancellor in 1915–16. Keynes was rigidly against the idea of returning to the Gold Standard. McKenna was intuitively aligned against it while fearing that it might become inevitable. So, never wanting to waste the opportunity of hosting a good dinner where opinions might flow freely with the wine, he invited them both to his residence at No. 11 Downing Street along with Otto Niemeyer, Controller of Finance at the Treasury, Sir John Bradbury, who had been the Government's chief economic adviser during the war, and P.J. Grigg who had been principal private secretary to no less than five Chancellors, Churchill being the fifth. It might be an exaggeration to say that the future of Britain's economy, encompassing the General Strike and the world-wide Depression, hung on this dinner but it certainly had an effect. By cognac time, it was clear that a majority were in favour of gold.

Reports suggested that a Keynes-McKenna alliance stood wholly against reverting to the Gold Standard but, in a detailed review of what became described as 'the famous dinner' A.C Pigou, a leading welfare economist, quoted McKenna as saying, 'You have to go back [to gold]. But it will be hell.'

Churchill would have needed another gulp of brandy on hearing this because McKenna, an austere, unclubbable man from all accounts who was a member of the Cambridge crew that won the Varsity Boat Race in 1887, had scuppered his last hope of building a strong argument against gold.

The situation highlighted the frequently ignored necessity of appointing Ministers to departments at which they might know what they were talking about. There had been no problem for Churchill in this respect when he was in charge of the Colonial Office, the Home Office, the Admiralty, the War Office or the Ministry of Munitions. But he was no economist, a fact to which Clementine, infinitely better at balancing a family budget than he was, would attest.

So Winston found himself having to rely on the expertise of others, a position he found exceedingly uncomfortable. However, it did not stop him from taking the plunge. With the tacit agreement of his Prime Minister, he announced in his Budget speech on 28 April 1925 that he was putting Britain back on the Gold Standard, giving parity to the dollar and the pound at $4.86.

Keynes, in his anguish, did not spare him. 'Why did he do such a silly thing?' he declared. 'It is because he lacked instinctive judgment, was deafened by the clamorous voices of conventional finance and, most of all, because he was gravely mislead by his experts.'

Given the crumbling worldwide economy and the looming Depression, it was amazing that Churchill remained Chancellor for another four years, weathering the General Strike of 1926, which started on 3 May and lasted nine days. Despite the fact that the mine owners were demanding that the miners work longer hours for less pay, the mood of the country was not with them and it took an unusual interjection from King George V to offer a little balance when he stated, 'Try living on their wages before you judge them.'

Churchill, forgetting his old Liberal tendencies, was far less forgiving and started behaving, in the view of some critics, like Napoleon. Startlingly, he wanted to use the newly-created BBC as a propaganda mouthpiece, but when that idea was rejected, he seized on the fact that most newspapers were on strike to make use of *The Morning Post*'s plant and produce his own newspaper, *The British Gazette*, virtually overnight.

With little else to read at such a turbulent moment, the public seized on this anti-strike sheet which, in the space of the nine days, managed to produce a circulation figure of 2.2 million. For Churchill – the creator, promoter and self-styled editorial director whose nit-picking over sentence construction drove his editors mad – it was quite an achievement, yet another example of his boundless energy.

Once the strike ended, he calmed down and played a leading role in settling the dispute, albeit with strong leanings towards the owners rather than the workers. As ever, Churchill's ebullient personality played its part. A few weeks later, when there was serious potential for bad blood and recriminations to emerge at a House of Commons debate, Churchill swatted it away by mocking himself. 'Make your minds perfectly clear,' he began with a threatening edge in his voice, 'If you ever let loose upon us again a General Strike, we will let loose upon you . . .' And he paused as the Opposition benches tensed, 'another *British Gazette!*' Even Labour members burst out laughing, seduced, as so many had been before, by this brilliant manipulator of Parliamentary mood.

However, the Gold Standard decision, with all its repercussions, haunted Churchill, who would refer to it in later years 'as the greatest mistake of my life'. As far as the Stock Market crash was concerned, it was, personally, an expensive one. It cost him half a million pounds.

His term as Chancellor of the Exchequer came to an end with the General Election on 30 May 1929, when, for the first time in their history, the Labour Party won more seats than the Conservatives. The tally was 289–260, with 58 seats going to the fading Liberals. Stanley Baldwin resigned immediately, and Ramsey MacDonald returned to No. 10 Downing Street. Churchill's Epping seat was safe, but he was out of government and would remain so for ten frustrating years.

If Churchill's so-called 'Wilderness Years' give rise to a picture of a miserable old man huddled in the Kent countryside suffering from bouts of what he termed his 'black dog of depression' it was rather wide of the mark. Only if wilderness can be described as a verdant, productive and many-coloured thing would the description fit.

From 1931 to 1939, right up to the moment his country called him, his output was beyond prodigious. Eleven volumes of history, over 400 articles, 386 speeches, which including another speaking tour of the United States; frequent – his critics would say too frequent – visits to the House of Commons to rail against independence for India, which put him on the wrong side of history, and on the right side of it as he warned, time and again, of the ever-growing threat from Nazi Germany.

If he had given up polo, the only sport he ever played with any enthusiasm apart from fencing at school, he did not shy away from physical work. At Chartwell, he not only built some of the walls but a swimming pool 'filtered to limpidity' – his descriptive phraseology as luminous as ever – and he also helped with the construction of a cottage where, today, one can view the results of his work with the paintbrush. Writer, speaker, artisan, artist, labourer: all this from a man moving in his sixties.

He achieved it all by the eccentric but detailed organization of his thrusting life, never letting that unforgiving minute fall into lassitude and by using his prodigious memory to sweep up and store pieces of information, often mere throwaways at a dinner table, to furnish later writings.

As his biographer William Manchester relates, Bill Deakin, hired as a literary assistant in 1936, was often astonished by the way Churchill would pick up on a memorandum given him before dinner and weave it into dictation after midnight. 'He would walk up and down dictating,' Deakin, soon to be a war hero in Yugoslavia and later Warden of St Anthony's College at Oxford, recalled. 'My facts were there, but he had seen it in deeper perspective. My memorandum was only a frame. It ignited his imagination.'

And the frame was always full of colours, whether they sprung from his brush and palette or from the careful construction of yet another 'noble' British sentence. The desire for colour in the literal sense sent him off in search of it, mostly to the South of France. where he enjoyed the light of the Mediterranean as he sat at his easel as much as Clementine enjoyed the red clay courts at Monte Carlo, Beaulieu and Cannes.

These were not unpleasant times, but, as the world lurched through the uncertain 1930s, Churchill's frustration was palpable. He had tasted power too often not to crave it in such a tenuous and forbidding moment of history. But for years he had no way back in. His defiant stand on India and memories of a 'less-than-successful Chancellorship as the Depression hit saw his support in the House dwindle, and hands were clasped against most ears when he began expounding on the need to match Hitler's rearmament programme.

It is important to understand both the extent and the tardiness of the pacifist mood that gripped Britain at the beginning of the 1930s. For the first ten or so years after the guns had fallen silent on the Western Front, the British people cared only that there was no more killing. The figures beggared rational understanding. The Commonwealth nations had lost 1,165,661 lives in France, 962,661 from Great Britain alone. Another million were injured, mostly scarred for life in an age when medical care was rudimentary by today's standards.

For the youth in the 1920s, who were just happy to be alive, there was jazz and flappers dancing the Charleston. Without television and only the most basic coverage of war images in the cinemas on *Movietone News*, reminders of the carnage in France were limited. Chroniclers of what had happened seemed stunned at first, unable to get sufficient hold on their emotions to put pen to paper. But when they did, all the pent-up feelings and desperate memories came bursting forth.

Robert Graves wrote *Goodbye to All That*, Siegfried Sassoon followed with *Memoirs of an Infantry Officer*, and Robert C. Sherriff's play *Journey's End* began a long run at the Savoy Theatre, a tale so vividly told that audiences were left in shock. And by the end of 1929, there were offerings from the other side, led by Erich Maria Remarque's *All Quiet on the Western Front*.

Even more stunning perhaps was the mood of the country's educated youth. On 9 February 1933, the Oxford Union approved a resolution stating that 'This House will, in no circumstances, fight for King and Country.'

It was the antithesis of everything Churchill felt in the fibre of his being, and he was furious. But, in the starkest fashion, it showed him what he was up against as he tried to warn the country of the very different mood that was blossoming under Hitler in a Germany where Jews were already starting to feel threatened.

In Britain, the situation was exacerbated by the seduction of many of the country's intellectuals by Soviet Communism. A clever Stalinist propaganda expert called Willi Murzenberg worked hard to make believers of such writers as Ezra Pound and P.G. Wodehouse as well as the journalist Lincoln Steffens, who returned from a carefully-guided tour of the Soviet Union to announce, 'I've seen the future, and it works.' Steffens, as most other visitors, had been shielded from the labour camps and the fact that Stalin had moved 25 million farmers into collectives, murdering in their thousands those who dared protest.

In much less overt fashion, two Cambridge University undergraduates, Donald Maclean and Guy Burgess, both of whom were to work in high positions in British intelligence and diplomacy, were recruited as Soviet agents. They were not outed till after the Second World War, and, even later, Kim Philby was uncovered as The Third Man of whom the British press had been writing for decades. Ironically Philby was a journalist himself, writing for the *Observer* in the Middle East, when he finally had to flee to Moscow. Philby's ability to keep his secrets in a watertight portion of his brain when the rest of it was flooded in alcohol almost every night stunned his foreign correspondent colleagues, some of whom had to help the legless spy to bed. Not once did he give himself away until MI6 tracked him down.

Stalin's foreign supporters with left-leaning inclinations saw him as a bulwark against the rise of fascism in Germany, while those on the right became equally bedazzled by Hitler. As with Stalin, a stream of intelligent, highly-educated and worldly-wise men returned from visits with stars in their eyes after meeting Hitler. Amazingly David Lloyd George, never a Conservative, was one of them. Espousing the 'personal admiration' he felt for the Nazi leader, Lloyd George added that he was sure Hitler 'would never invade any other land'.

What Churchill had to say to his long-time colleague-in-arms after this demented statement has not been recorded, but he must have been aghast. Had not Lloyd George taken any heed of what Churchill had written in the *Daily Mail* in 1932, even before Hitler been appointed Chancellor? 'Germany will do what she thinks fit in rearmament. Very grave dangers lie along these paths and if Great Britain encouraged Germany in such adventures, we might, in an incredibly short space of time, be plunged into a situation of violent peril.'

But no one was listening, and it was not only British statesmen who were duped. On 19 May 1933, Walter Lippman, the long-serving columnist for the *New York Herald Tribune*, reacted to a speech he heard Hitler make with these words: 'We have heard once more, through the fog and the din, the authentic voice of a genuinely civilized people. I am not only willing to believe that but all historical experience compels one to believe it.' But worse was to come. Later in the column, Lippman, who came from a family of German Jews, suggested that persecuting Jews served the purpose of satisfying the Germans' yearning to conquer somebody and that it was a lightning rod 'which protects Europe'.

Yet, incredibly for a journalist who went on to become one of the most renowned and respected in the world, Lippman wrote the following in *The Literary Digest* just seven days later about a Nazi book-burning festival in Berlin, where the works of authors such as Ernest Hemingway, Jack London and John Dos Passos went up in flames. 'What does it [the book burning] symbolize? Nothing less than the conviction of the present rulers of Germany that violence is the means by which human problems must be solved.' What happened to a 'genuinely civilized people'? Lippman never explained.

The election of 1935 saw the Conservatives return to power, with Stanley Baldwin replacing Ramsey MacDonald as Prime Minister. Just eleven days later, an Anglo-German Naval Agreement was signed. Churchill, naturally, thought it a huge mistake, not least because it infuriated the French who were not informed of its content. Three months earlier, Hitler had renounced the Treaty of Versailles, and now he had been given permission under the rules of the Agreement to build five battleships, twenty-one cruisers and sixty-four destroyers, not to mention a potentially unlimited number of submarines whose effectiveness in the Atlantic would become shockingly apparent at the outset of the war just four years later.

Churchill was more fired up than ever as he produced figures refuting Baldwin's claim that the RAF was keeping pace with the Luftwaffe's production of aircraft, and although it must have hurt him to admit it, he found he had more time to concentrate on the German threat when the Government of India Act was signed in August that year. Churchill had been fighting a losing battle over India, and the issue had done nothing to repel critics of his judgement. Now, with the Act acknowledging that India would join the Commonwealth as an independent nation, the fight was over, and Churchill reacted gracefully.

Having scorned Mahatma Gandhi some years earlier with his famous description of the peaceful independence advocate as a half-naked fakir, Churchill now invited one of Gandhi's chief aides, G.D. Birla, to lunch, an occasion which Birla later described as 'one of my most pleasant experiences in England'. According to Birla, Churchill had told him that Gandhi had gone 'very high in my esteem since he has stood up for the Untouchables [India's lowest caste]'. Churchill, in one of his more conciliatory moods, insisted he did not care whether Gandhi was more or less loyal to Great Britain but urged him 'to give the people more butter'.

Much later, Churchill met Jawaharlal Nehru, regarded as India's greatest leader, and quickly established a fine working relationship with India's first Prime Minister, even though they probably didn't dwell too heavily on their school days. Both had gone to Harrow.

For his own sake, Churchill was well rid of the India problem, but another strike against his reputation was in the offing. For twenty-five years he had been a good friend of the Prince of Wales, Edward, and when George V died in 1936, the natural succession was far from straightforward. In one of the most prominent scandals of the century, the man who would be king had fallen in love with an American divorcee, Mrs Wallis Simpson, a woman from Baltimore of no particular social pedigree. She was still married to her second husband when she met the future King, and although the affair was kept from the British public for months by an obedient press, when the story broke there were some serious constitutional questions to answer.

Firstly, Baldwin wanted to know if the King intended marrying Mrs Simpson when her divorce came through. The answer was a resounding 'Yes!' In that case, the Prime Minister replied, there was a major problem. The King was the Defender of the Faith of the Church of England, which did not recognize divorce. At the very least, Edward's wife could never become Queen.

Churchill's position was one of full support for King Edward VIII. For a start, he considered himself, above all personal ambition or political position, to be a loyal subject of the Crown. But on a personal note, he was overjoyed at the thought of his friend becoming King because, alone amongst all the sovereigns he would serve during his career, the stiff and distant George V was the only one with whom he did not have a strong rapport.

To keep him out of the limelight, Baldwin had suggested King Edward sequester himself at Fort Belvedere, a house in the grounds of Windsor Castle and see no one. However, as the crisis grew, Edward felt he desperately needed some friendly advice, and Churchill was summoned to dine with him the night after Winston had made a well-received speech at the Royal Albert Hall calling for stronger opposition to Nazi Germany on 4 December 1936.

Churchill was starting to walk on uncertain constitutional ground. He wanted Edward to be crowned King but Baldwin, reflecting the mood of the country who had no time for Mrs Simpson, was not prepared to make allowances. If Churchill moved against the government, forming in essence a King's Party, Edward would be hopelessly compromised. No British monarch is allowed to become embroiled in politics. So Churchill took the improbable view that, somehow things would die down if everything were allowed to run its course. When he stood up in the House of Commons on 8 December and started to suggest as much, all hell broke loose. He was literally shouted down from both sides of the House. All the steady work he had done in rehabilitating himself as voice worth listening to over Germany was torn to shreds.

The explosion of anger may have had deeper roots than just the question of the possible abdication of King Edward which, of course, came to pass just two days later. Churchill had been an uncomfortable fly in the ear of the House for the previous five years over Hitler (and a noisily buzzing one at that). Most members, gritting their teeth, knew that his arguments were based on sounder ground than theirs and that their counter-arguments were beginning to sound thin. But this was different.

Here was a chance to get at him and they seized it with gusto. *The Times* called it the most striking rebuff in modern Parliamentary history.

Churchill was forced to leave the chamber, and many believed it was the end of his political career. If so, it would have been a question of clutching defeat from the jaws of victory. Only a month before he had moved many towards his way of thinking over rearmament in the face of Hitler's threats when, seizing on a remark in the House by First Lord of the Admiralty Duff Cooper, soon to be a close ally, Churchill launched into another withering assessment of the government's inertia.

> Everything, the First Lord assured us, is entirely fluid. I am sure that is true. The government cannot make up its mind, or they cannot get the Prime Minister to make up his mind. So they go on in strange paradox, decided only to be undecided, resolved to be irresolute, adamant for drift, solid for fluidity, all powerful to be impotent. So we go on preparing for months and years – precious, perhaps vital to the greatness of Britain – for the locusts to eat.

After that salvo, one could not think that Baldwin was anything but munched up. In fact, lifted by the way he had handled the abdication crisis, he soldiered on until the Coronation of King George VI on 27 May 1937. Then, after being given a warm farewell, Baldwin handed over to Neville Chamberlain, a far more assertive and self-assured figure.

The year of 1937 was one of the most miserable and least productive, politically, of Churchill's life. He had lost his last remnants of support in the House and could only watch in horror as his Conservative colleagues did everything possible to avoid annoying Hitler. In this they were backed to the hilt by the editor of *The Times*, Geoffrey Dawson, whose paper turned into a virtual mouthpiece for Nazi Germany. *Times* correspondents based in Berlin filed factual reports of the anti-Jewish horrors that were unfolding but found them being cut to ribbons or even totally discarded by an editor who was abusing every tenet of honest journalism. Happily, Rothermere and Beaverbrook, despite keeping an open ear to the arguments for appeasement, encouraged their editors to make space for Churchill's articles in the *Daily Mail*, *Daily Express* and other publications, so the British public were not unaware of what was actually happening.

Churchill did, in fact, become the most informed man in Britain as far as armament build-up between Britain and Germany was concerned, and he achieved it through what can only be called a network of spies. Self-serving politicians in the House might have scorned him but he was far from friendless in other quarters. In particular, his long-standing connections with the military started to serve him well, as he turned Chartwell into what was described by Professor Herbert Nicholson at Oxford as 'a private information centre, the information of which was often far superior to that of the Government'.

All manner of people were received at Chartwell: foreign leaders, refugees and students from all over Europe, bringing him first-hand information. Then there was the neighbour with whom he could meet by walking across adjacent fields, Major Desmond Morton, who had been wounded in Flanders but went on to gain a most sensitive post at the Industrial Intelligence Centre. A firm opponent of appeasement, Morton was willing to pass on much of what he knew as they strolled in Chartwell's gardens.

Another willing informant was Sir Robert Vansittart, a Permanent Under-Secretary who had been warning of Hitler's intentions even before the Chancellor's rise to power, pleading with people to read *Mein Kampf*. Too few did. 'Van,' as he was known, had a mole in the office of the Luftwaffe commander Hermann Göring in Berlin, and so when Churchill quoted numbers regarding the build-up of the Luftwaffe, he knew exactly what he was talking about. Equally, Churchill had a precise idea of the RAF's weaknesses. Group Captain Lachlan MacLean, introduced by another RAF officer, Wing Commander Torr Anderson, made numerous visits to Churchill's flat at Morpeth Mansions, bringing charts and documents which revealed just how far behind the RAF had fallen compared to the Luftwaffe in the production of fighters and bombers. It was cloak-and-dagger stuff, and all Churchill's informants were putting their careers at risk. But, unlike the politicians, they recognized the danger and were prepared to act.

This was true even of some German army officers, one of whom, Major Ewald von Kleist-Schmenzin, was brave enough to travel to London and check into the Park Lane Hotel on Piccadilly. From there, he was driven by one of Churchill's local taxi drivers to Chartwell where he told Winston, while his son Randolph took notes, that 'nobody in Germany wants war except H. [Hitler]'.

That was palpably untrue, but Major von Kleist obviously came as the representative of a large number of German officers who were convinced that, if Hitler invaded Czechoslovakia, Germany would face war with Britain and France. He insisted his friends were willing to challenge Hitler but 'needed a little encouragement'. He received some from Churchill in the form of a signed letter, but it obviously meant little unless it was backed by the Prime Minister. When Chamberlain received the information Churchill forwarded to him, it was cast aside. 'I think we must discount much of what von Kleist says,' was Chamberlain's reaction.

To recap on the timeline of the events that Churchill had endured as almost a lone public voice against the rise of Nazi tyranny, the following had occurred:

- In 1935, Hitler had made his intentions clear by renouncing the Treaty of Versailles.
- In 1936, Hitler's forces had reoccupied the Rhineland, which had been designated as a demilitarized zone after the First World War. Also in July of that year, civil war broke out in Spain.
- In 1937 Hitler refrained from actually grabbing any more land but discussed with his generals plans for further expansion towards Eastern Europe and Russia.
- In 1938 the *Anschluss* took place on 14 March, as Hitler's forces marched into Austria. On 15 October, Hitler annexed the Sudetenland, the part of Czechoslovakia inhabited largely by German-speaking people.
- In 1939, Hitler invaded Czechoslovakia on 15 March, and in August the West was shocked as Hitler and Stalin suddenly become allies under the so-called Molotov-Ribbentrop Pact. This was followed by the invasion of Poland on 1 September, with the result that Chamberlain declared war on Germany two days later.

Missing from this list of events is the face-to-face interaction between Hitler and Neville Chamberlain. It resulted in one of the saddest and most humiliating pieces of diplomatic duplicity between two major leaders. Chamberlain had flown to Munich and then continued by train and car up to Hitler's Berghof retreat at Berchtesgaden on 14 September 1938. He was greeted by a truculent *Führer* who told him, in a lengthy diatribe, that the Sudetenland's three million Germans must become part of the Reich and that he was prepared to go to war if they did not.

Chamberlain replied plaintively: 'Then why did you let me come? I have wasted my time.'

Hitler's mood changed somewhat, and he laid his trap. Would Chamberlain agree to a peaceful solution if the Sudetenland were given 'liberation' through self-determination? With the proviso that he would have to talk with his Cabinet and get the agreement of the French, Chamberlain, so desperate to return home with something, said yes. He had just given away the Sudetenland.

Incredibly, Chamberlain left Germany believing, as he wrote to his sister Ida that, 'despite the hardness and ruthlessness I saw in his face, I got the impression that here was a man who could be relied upon when he had given his word'.

Self-deception can be an astonishing thing, but this was taking it to the limits of credibility. Hitler had already torn up agreements and murdered political enemies, but Chamberlain convinced himself he could be trusted. He did not, of course, convince Churchill, who continued to be outraged when the Prime Minister told the House that Hitler had assured him he did not want Czechs in the Reich and that in his view 'Herr Hitler is telling the truth'. Tragically for the future of Czechoslovakia, the French government had agreed to go along with this delusion.

In Washington, President Roosevelt summoned the British Ambassador and told him that the Anglo-French proposal was 'the most terrible remorseless sacrifice that has ever been demanded of a State'. FDR even went as far to suggest a mid-Atlantic conference of world leaders that he himself would attend. With a singular show of arrogance and disrespect, Chamberlain ignored the leader of the world's most powerful nation.

Churchill continued to denounce the decision. 'It is not just Czechoslovakia alone that is menaced,' he thundered, 'but also the freedom and democracy of all nations. The conviction that security could be bought by throwing a small State to the wolves is a fatal delusion.'

Meanwhile, Hitler had agreed to meet Chamberlain again and, on 22 September, the Prime Minister was off for a second meeting, this time at the small town of Godesberg on the Rhine. The delusion did not last long. Almost before Chamberlain had a chance to tell Hitler of the Anglo-French resolution, he was interrupted. 'I am very sorry . . . that is no long possible,' Hitler said.

Hiding behind demands from Poland and Hungary that they, too, had claims on parts of Czechoslovakia, Hitler stated that the Sudetenland must be occupied by 26 September, and consequently there would be no time for any kind of self-determination by the residents, many of whom were Czech miners and not German at all. Appalled, Chamberlain claimed that Hitler was giving him an ultimatum. Snidely, Hitler refuted that and, pushing a piece of paper under the nose of the Prime Minister, insisted that it wasn't a *diktat* at all but a *memorandum*' a word used in both languages.

Then, wishing to keep Chamberlain on the hook, Hitler said he would do something that he had never done before and offer a *konzession*. He would push the date for his troops to begin occupation of the Sudentenland on to 1 October. Chamberlain might well have said, 'Big deal!' Instead, he expressed appreciation and offered the Nazi leader a hearty farewell. It was, he told a reporter, 'now up to the Czechs'.

When Mussolini decided to inject himself into proceedings and suggest another meeting, Hitler agreed. Chamberlain was handed the note while he addressing the House, and when he interrupted himself to announce that Hitler had invited him to Munich, cheers broke out. Despite the warnings from the man who sat slumped and grim-faced in the corner, the mood was still one of wanting peace, of appeasement at almost any cost.

Chamberlain flew out once again, this time to meet with Hitler, Mussolini and the French Prime Minister Edouard Daladier. Two of them were eager to negotiate. Hitler and his Italian cohort were not. A new *memorandum* was produced. Chamberlain and Daladier stared at it in disbelief and then tried to work their way through, trying to alter this, reword that, but by 1:00 a.m. they gave up.

And gave in. They had capitulated. The Sudetenland was to be occupied immediately, and Hitler had gotten practically everything he asked for.

What Chamberlain got was the Nazi's signature on a piece of paper that he had brought with him. It was billed as a joint Anglo-German declaration but, in effect, said little other than the two nations would try to work together for peace. The irony was not lost on the members of the Czech delegation, who had been held as virtual prisoners of the Gestapo at the nearby Regina Hotel. When they were handed the result of the Sudetenland Declaration it was 2:30 in the morning. They look stunned. The French appeared to be embarrassed. Chamberlain yawned.

Back in London, Chamberlain was greeted by cheering crowds at Heston Airport (adjacent to what is now Heathrow) and was immediately summoned to Buckingham Palace to receive the congratulations of King George VI. But it was his gesture at the window of 10 Downing St that history will remember. At the urging of his wife, he waved that meaningless piece of paper and told the crowds below, 'I believe it is peace with honour.' It was an unfortunate phrase. He had not secured peace, and honour played no part in it.

No one needed to tell Churchill. Dining at the Savoy, he was incandescent. According to Colin Coote, then at *The Times*, Churchill berated the two ministers present, First Lord Duff Cooper and Secretary for Scotland Walter Elliott, his voice sounding to Coote like a sonic boom. 'How can men with wide experience and fine records in the Great War condone a policy so cowardly? It was sordid, squalid, subhuman . . . and suicidal.'

Suicidal or not, it ended Duff Cooper's time at the Admiralty. Just before the House of Commons debated the Munich Agreement, Cooper resigned. The debate continued for three days while Churchill sat in silence. Then at 5:10 p.m. on the third day he rose. Inevitably, it was a long speech, but it was measured and only towards the end did the Churchill oratory bite.

> The people should know the truth. They should know that there has been gross neglect and deficiency in our defences; they should know we have sustained a defeat without a war, the consequences of which will travel far with us along our road; they should know that we have passed an awful milestone in our history when the whole equilibrium of Europe has been deranged . . . And do not suppose this is the end. This is only the beginning of the reckoning. This is only the first sip – the first foretaste of a bitter cup that will be proffered to us year by year. Unless – by a supreme recovery of our moral health and martial vigour, we arise again and take our stand for freedom, as in olden time.

There had been shouts for peace. There were fewer by the time he finished. But a leader had spoken, and although it took several more months, it was inevitable from that moment forward, that Winston Churchill would be that leader.

The first step towards that eventuality came when Hitler invaded Poland on 1 September, ignoring Chamberlain's ultimatum and thus ensuring that Britain would declare war. Under the circumstances, Chamberlain needed the strongest men he could find to join the Cabinet and that meant sending Churchill back to his old First World War post at the Admiralty. Without needing to publicly admit it, Chamberlain knew that Churchill had been right all along and that the pair would now have to work in harmony.

Churchill adopting what Lord Beaverbrook had described as his finest character trait made this easier: magnanimity. There was no time for 'I told you so,' nor would Winston have wanted to utter such a phrase. There was no personal animosity and the two men, who would be treated so differently by history, would strive, in their vastly different ways over the coming months, to keep Hitler at bay.

It was not, of course, a simple task, and the tribulations that needed to be overcome were highlighted by the disastrous attempt to cut Hitler's supply of iron ore from Scandinavia by imposing a blockade down the western coast of Norway and landing troops at fishing ports near Narvik. For a variety of reasons, they had to be withdrawn in less than two weeks. This setback, coinciding with relentless German advances in France, put increasing pressure on Chamberlain's leadership which came under direct and ultimately fatal scrutiny on 7 and 8 May, during which time the House of Commons entered into what Roy Jenkins described as 'by a clear head both the most dramatic and most far-reaching in its consequences of any parliamentary debate of the twentieth century'.

Virtually everyone of any import on both sides of the House rose to have their say. Few contributions were more dramatic than that of Sir Roger Keyes, decked out in full regalia as Admiral of the Fleet, who, speaking of Churchill said, 'I have great admiration for my right honourable friend . . . I am longing to see proper use made of his great abilities.' Just to ram his point home, Sir Roger brought up the name of a great admiral of yore and added, 'One hundred and forty years ago, Nelson said, "I am of the opinion that the boldest measures are the safest," and that still holds good today.'

If that salvo shot holes in Chamberlain's sails, worse was to come for the Prime Minister who sat stone faced while opinions echoed around the hallowed chamber. Surprisingly, the most devastating shot was fired by Leo Amery, whose constituency in Birmingham neighboured Chamberlain's. It didn't matter. While admitting later that he had hesitated to use his favourite Cromwell quote which he felt might be considered 'too strong meat', he 'cast prudence to the winds and ended full out with my Cromwellian injunction to the Long Parliament [of April 1653] "You have sat too long here for any good you have been doing. Depart, I say, and let us have done with you. In the name of God, go!"'

Lloyd George, the former Prime Minister, told Amery later that it was the most dramatic climax to any speech he had ever heard and followed it himself by urging Chamberlain to 'sacrifice the seals of office'.

It was 10:11 p.m. on the second evening when Churchill himself rose to speak for 49 minutes in what was described as a tour de force. Harold Nicolson pinpointed the mastery with which Churchill had held the House in thrall so often over the years by writing:

> Winston has an almost impossible task. On the one hand he has to defend the Services, on the other, he has to be loyal to the Prime Minister. One felt it would be impossible for him to do this after the debate without losing some of his own prestige, but he manages with extraordinary force of personality to do

both these things with absolute loyalty and apparent sincerity, while demonstrating by his brilliance that he really has nothing to do with this confused and timid gang.

Some of the gang might have been timid but some were also drunk, an occurrence less frequent among Conservative members than their Scottish Labour colleagues. However, on this occasion, there were signs of intoxication on both sides of the aisle, not, is must be stressed, to the extent that they didn't know what they were voting for, but when the division was called, forty-one members who would normally have been expected to vote with Government went in to the Labour Lobby. Considering that only 486 out of 615 members of the House were present, it was inevitable that the Conservative majority of 213 would be cut. But not to the quick – and the final result of it being slashed to eighty-one was close to that.

This had been a moment when critics of Churchill might have expected this hugely ambitious politician to lunge for the prize that was so clearly within his grasp. But beneath the bluster there always lay a tenet of honour and decency. As Nicolson noted, this man who was so often accused of bold and irresponsible acts, of following paths that appeared foolhardy and even dangerous, had produced a speech of balanced brilliance and one that, astonishingly, had smothered his own ambitions in favour of the Prime Minister.

'At no time in the last war,' he began, 'were we in greater peril than we are now, and I urge the House strongly to deal with these matters, not in a precipitate vote, ill debated and on a widely discursive field but in grave time . . . and in due time . . . in accordance with the dignity of Parliament.'

This was the core of the man. All his life, propelled by some deep inner need to do justice to his father's memory and exceed his father's achievements, he had always wanted to be Prime Minister. But, even then, with that long held ambition at his fingertips, his first thoughts were of 'the dignity of Parliament'.

Even when Chamberlain called Churchill and Lord Halifax into his rooms after the debate, knowing that they represented the only two possible choices to succeed him and intimated that he could not go on, his would-be successor tried to talk him out of resignation. 'You have a good majority,' Churchill told Chamberlain. 'Do not take the matter grievously to heart.'

But Chamberlain was done. The burden had become too great, and his heart was faltering. And in the end the decision was made for him by the Opposition. Clement Atlee made it clear, speaking from the party's conference at Bournemouth, that Labour would not join in a coalition government under his leadership.

And so it came down to Halifax or Churchill? Chamberlain favoured Halifax, as did his good friend, King George VI. So did many Conservatives who still saw Churchill in his first incarnation as Lord of the Admiralty, a left-leaning Liberal whose hand had been on the tiller during the disaster of Gallipoli. But their hopes were dashed not by anything Churchill said, but by Halifax.

When the trio met at 4:30 p.m. on Thursday, 9 May – Churchill writing six years later seems to have, erroneously, placed it at 11:00 a.m. the following morning – Chamberlain tried to coax Halifax into accepting the job. But the thin, gaunt giant, who physically towered over his rival, explained that as a member of the House of Lords he would be too distanced from the everyday affairs of Government to do a proper job at such a critical time. That was certainly a valid reason. But there was another. Writing to his wife, Halifax said, 'Winston would still be Minister of Defence. I would be more or less an Honorary Prime Minister, living in a kind of twilight just outside the things that really matter.'

He was right, of course, and so Chamberlain turned to Churchill. History will never know whether His Lordship's intentions were as logical and as pure as he wanted to convey. Halifax was known as the 'Holy Fox' and may have had sneakier motives. As we have seen, Churchill still had many enemies and some of his critics forecast that a Cabinet under this controversial figure would be 'nasty, brutish and short'. If that turned out to be true, Halifax knew he would be well placed to step in amongst the wreckage and take charge. However, far from being short, the Churchill Cabinet survived for five years, becoming the most famous in Parliamentary history.

Although Churchill and Halifax were never as openly hostile to each other as is depicted in the otherwise excellent film *The Darkest Hour* in which Halifax is portrayed as the villain, the new Prime Minister did not want him peering over his shoulder. Later, in a masterly move, Churchill appointed Halifax as British Ambassador to Washington DC, where he served with great loyalty and skill for the rest of the war.

If Britain was indeed in greater peril than it had ever been in its history since the Norman invasion of 1066, the nation had fallen upon the one man whose pugnacity, courage and experience was capable of handling it. But the challenges that lay ahead were onerous beyond belief and there was no argument that a coalition government was required. Having made it plain that Chamberlain was not acceptable to Labour,

Atlee quickly agreed in a phone call from Bournemouth to serve under Churchill with an understanding that he would become Deputy Prime Minister in due course.

Writing of 1940 later in his life, Churchill had famously said that, on the night of his appointment as Prime Minister, he had felt as if he was walking with destiny and 'that all my past life had been but a preparation for this hour and this trial . . . I was sure I would not fail. Therefore, although impatient for morning, I slept soundly and had no need for cheering dreams.'

There was nothing cheering about the first few weeks of his Premiership. Within a fortnight, the nascent coalition government suffered a series of body blows that would have laid most governments and most Prime Ministers on the canvas. The German armour broke through at Sedan; Holland surrendered; Brussels was abandoned; Hitler's forces reached the Channel; the British and French forces were trapped, leaving Britain with the prospect of losing a quarter of a million men.

Churchill's response was to meet the disasters head-on, refusing to sugar-coat the situation for the House or the people. In a short speech that has passed in to folklore of a nation on the brink of collapse, Churchill said:

> I would say to the House, as I said to those who have joined this government, that I have nothing to offer but blood, toil, tears and sweat. We have before us an ordeal of the most grievous kind'... You ask, what is our policy? I will say: It is to wage war, by sea, land and air with all our might and with all the strength that God can give us: to wage war against a monstrous tyranny, never surpassed in the dark, lamentable catalogue of human crime. That is our policy. You ask: What is our aim? I can answer in one word: It is victory, victory at all costs, victory in spite of all terror, victory however long and hard the road may be; for without victory, there is no survival.

This Churchill felt in his bones, and it was why he paid little more than lip service to the entreaties of Lord Halifax – still Foreign Secretary before being dispatched to Washington – who was calling persistently for overtures to be made to Mussolini through his London Ambassador, Giuseppe Bastianini. Churchill agreed to let them talk, fearing that if he refused the notion entirely Halifax would resign from the Cabinet and take Chamberlain with him. That would leave the new Prime Minister hopelessly exposed to those Conservative members who still viewed him with suspicion.

So he allowed approaches to be made during the days prior to Mussolini formally joining Hitler in the war against the Allies on 10 June. But it was on 27 May, the darkest of days despite the endless sunny hours of that burning summer, that Churchill, striding towards Parliament from 10 Downing Street, resolved to make the kind of bold and, possibly reckless, move for which he had become famous. He decided to go beyond the seven ministers of his small War Cabinet and appeal to the twenty-five ministers not of Cabinet rank, using as an excuse the fact that he had 'not seen much of them' since forming his government.

His gamble was with numbers, searching for numerical, rather than hierarchal, support. So as he gathered them in his rooms in the Houses of Parliament, he talked of Britain not being better off if he were to make peace with Hitler right then than they would be fighting it out. Hitler would demand the Royal Navy – i.e. virtual disarmament – as well as our naval bases and much else. Britain would become a slave state. So with the immense resources and advantages the country still had at its disposal (a strident statement given that the vast majority of Britain's army was, that very day, still stranded on the beaches of Dunkirk), he suggested that 'every one of you would rise up and tear me down if I were, for one moment, to contemplate parley and surrender'. Pausing only to let that thought sink in, he continued with a devastating Churchillian flourish: 'So we shall go on and fight it out, here or elsewhere, and if this long story of ours is to end at last, let it end only when each of us lies choking in his own blood upon the ground.' The reaction surprised even Churchill himself. He wrote, 'Quite a number seemed to jump up from the table and come running to my chair, shouting and patting me on the back.'

The case was made. There would be no surrender, and when an exhausted Cabinet met again that evening at 7:00 p.m. for the ninth time in four days, news of what had occurred in the Commons had reached them. Halifax knew he was beaten. Events were moving at such a pace, with every hour bringing a new tidal wave of emotion as good news followed bad and vice versa, that there was no time to step back and evaluate, with every decision being taken by the minute and on the hoof.

Churchill did more than stride between Downing Street and Parliament. He flew to France no less than four times between 31 May, his last visit to Paris, and 13 June. He had wanted to return to the capital in early June, but it was too late. French government officials were preoccupied with burning documents and preparing to flee south-west, first to Briare, near Orleans where Churchill, Anthony Eden, General Sir John Dill and other officials met their French counterparts, including a newly-appointed Secretary for War called Brigadier General Charles de Gaulle. Paris was closing down and bracing itself for occupation. Price Waterhouse, whose offices on the Avenue de l'Opera were cleared and locked by a senior Partner, Harry Evans, the father of one of the authors of this book, on 10 June, was typical of foreign bureaus of overseas firms. It was time to get out. France was on the brink of collapse.

If this was catastrophic, it could have been so much worst but for the miracle of Dunkirk. Even Churchill had feared that less than half of the 350,000 troops stranded there could be rescued, but by the time of the Cabinet meeting on the morning of 28 May, he was able to report that 40,000 had been lifted off, and in the following few days practically the entire contingent, along with thousands of French troops, had been brought home, aided, of course, by the flotilla of 800 or so small craft, mostly sailed by their owners from English Channel ports. As a rescue operation, it was mythic.

The knowledge that he still had an army was sufficient to counter balance Churchill's mood as he began to come to terms with the fact that France was lost. As an insight as to how Britain's new leader was weathering these kaleidoscopic events, one can glean much from reading an extract from the diary of his personal private secretary, John Colville, who was present at a dinner at Chequers on Saturday, 15 June along with Professor J.A. Lindemann ('The Prof') and Duncan and Diana Sandys.

The meal began with Churchill in one of his grumpiest moods, but soon afterwards, he was walking in the rose garden with Sandys while Colville was busy making and taking phone calls. The young assistant wrote:

> It was still light and deliciously warm, but the sentries with tin helmets and fixed bayonets, who were placed all round the house, kept us fully alive to the horrors of reality. I spent most of the time searching for Winston among the roses, and listening to his comments on the war . . . He was now in high spirits, repeating poetry, dilating on the drama of the present situation, maintaining that he and Hitler only had one thing in common – a horror of whistling – offering everybody cigars and, spasmodically murmuring: 'Bang, bang, bang goes the farmer's gun, run rabbit, run rabbit, run, run, run.'
>
> [US Ambassador Joe] Kennedy rang and Winston, becoming serious for a minute, poured into his ears a flood of eloquence about the part America could and should play in saving civilization . . . At about 1:00 a.m. Winston came in

from the garden and we all stood in the central hall while the Great Man lay on the sofa, puffed his cigar, discoursed on the building up of our fighter strength and told one or two dirty stories. Finally, saying 'Goodnight, my children,' he went to bed at 1:30.

Thus was Britain being led in the most critical hour of its history. The word 'eccentric' surely must have been invented for Winston Churchill.

Another mood swing was not long in coming. Having met General de Gaulle – who had flown in from Bordeaux – for the first time the following day, Churchill was poised to fly to France again on Monday but at 9:00 p.m. there was a message from Prime Minister Reynaud cancelling the meeting. The next day he resigned, leaving France in the hands of Marshal Pétain, a hero in the First World War but now to be revealed as an ageing appeaser, bowing to the scurrilous might of the Nazi regime. Pétain took the new government to the Spa town of Vichy, where the waters better suited his taste but were poison to any Frenchman who championed freedom.

By then there was no question of Britain bowing to anyone. Earlier, on 4 June, Churchill had risen in the House of Commons to deliver a speech that will echo through the halls of time, a speech he had somehow been able to create and burnish through the days and nights of chaos that preceded them.

'Even though large tracts of Europe have fallen into the grip of the Gestapo, and all the odious apparatus of Nazi rule, we shall not flag or fail,' he began.

> We shall go on to the end. We shall fight in France. We shall fight on the seas and oceans. We shall fight with growing confidence in the air. We shall defend our Island, whatever the cost may be. We shall fight on the beaches. We shall fight on the landing grounds. We shall fight in the fields and the streets. We shall fight in the hills. We shall never surrender. And even if, which I do not for a moment believe, this Island or a large part of it, were subjugated and starving, then our Empire beyond the oceans, armed and guarded by the British fleet, will carry on the struggle until in God's good time the New World, with all its power and might sets forth to the rescue and liberation of the old.

These Churchillian orations might, as Roy Jenkins suggested, have sounded overblown in less dramatic times. 'Yet they matched the mood of the moment and were an inspiration to the nation and a catharsis for Churchill himself. They raised his spirits and thus generated even more energy than was consumed in their composition.'

Even though some Labour members were in tears, the reaction on the Conservative benches was still less than ecstatic even though supportive. It was left to an old cross-party ally, Colonel Josiah Wedgwood, to offer the most succinct accolade: 'That was worth 1,000 guns and was the speech of 1,000 years.'

One last desperate and extraordinary attempt had been made to keep France free as an existing state. First broached at a lunch attended by Halifax and the French Ambassador Charles Corbin at the Carlton Club, the astonishing idea was to merge Great Britain and France into one political entity. Churchill, occupied with finding a way to save the French fleet, disregarded the scheme as fantasy at first but when Sir Robert Vansittart, Leo Amery, Anthony Eden as well as Corbin, Jean Monnet (who, after the war, would become deeply involved in the formation of the European Union) and even General de Gaulle all began talking about it seriously, he took notice. They even got as far as having a declaration to unite Britain and France dictated to Kathleen Hill, one of the Prime Minister's most devoted private secretaries, who swiftly typed it up on her large black Remington.

On the night of 16 June, the proposal was still floating around Downing Street, but French Prime Minister Reynaud, who had agreed to carry on as a member of a newly-formed joint cabinet if the declaration was adopted, put an end to the fantasy with his sudden resignation.

Colville, in his diaries, felt that, given an extra 24 hours, the improbable could have become possible but, when the inevitable happened his mood became Shakespearian and he wrote: 'It is all too likely now that yesterday's "cloudcapped towers, the gorgeous palaces . . . shall dissolve . . . and leave not a rack behind" and that visions of a golden future which the Declaration held out are doomed to vanish. I feel like a deflated souffle.'

Tragically, the failure to formalize a binding relationship between Britain and France – phantasmagorical, to use a Winston word, as it might have seemed – led to the necessary destruction of several French warships at the hands of the Royal Navy. For a Francophile like Churchill, having to give such an order was odious to him, but with the Vichy government in place he could not run the risk of the French navy turning against Britain. From Gibraltar, Admiral Sommerville was ordered to blockade the Algerian port of Oran and offer his counterpart four ways out, including sailing to either a British or West Indies port or continue to fight against Germany. None were accepted. As a result a French battleship was blown up; the ironically-named *Dunkerque* ran aground and the badly damaged *Strasbourg* limped back to Toulon. In all 1,299 French sailors were killed. Churchill wept.

It was not the only sign that the Prime Minister was feeling the strain of shouldering a barely bearable burden. As the war progressed it was, perhaps, unsurprising that he became more difficult to deal with, changing his plans at will with scant regard for his staff and becoming, even to close associates, almost unapproachable. Clementine, knowing him as she did, picked up on increasing complaints from his colleagues and, after tearing up the first draft, finally took the plunge many months later, writing a remarkably courageous letter to her husband:

> My Darling, I hope you will forgive me if I tell you something I feel you ought to know. One of the men in your entourage (a devoted friend) has been to me and told me that there is a danger of your being generally disliked by your colleagues and subordinates because of your rough sarcastic and overbearing manner . . . I must confess I have noticed a deterioration in your manner and you are not so kind as you used to be . . .

The last line must have stung. Churchill knew he could be gruff, bombastic and overbearing with his staff, but there had always been an underlying kindness and concern which those working with him in the most taxing of circumstances fully recognized. Despite all his faults, he had always been lovable. If he were to lose that most precious element of his character his effectiveness would be diminished. Clementine's letter saved everyone from that frightening prospect and soon people noticed him making an effort to be more civil.

It was a vital factor in making life at 10 Downing Street tolerable through those historic and frequently terrifying early years of the war. For it was not just at No. 10 – a rickety old house not built to withstand bomb blasts – that Churchill and his team of ministers and secretaries worked – or slept. Colville never seemed quite sure where they would be spending the night. There were the heavily-entrenched War Rooms (now a tourist attraction), a government property at Dollis Hill in North London once used by Gladstone, a disused but refurbished Tube station on the Piccadilly Line called Down Street and, of course Chequers which, eventually was deemed too visible to the Luftwaffe on moonlit nights as it sat exposed in the Buckinghamshire countryside.

An alternative had to be found and Ronald Tree, an Anglo-American Conservative MP of considerable financial means, stepped forward to offer his spacious country mansion in Oxfordshire during weekends on an indefinite basis. Tree considered it a privilege when the offer was accepted and put up with the inconvenience of having the entire Prime Ministerial entourage dumped on him for a total of fifteen weekends until Churchill's final visit in March 1942.

All the while during the early summer months of 1940, Britain was living under the expectation of invasion. It seemed obvious that Hitler would attack once he had subdued France. Yet he was persuaded by Göring to let his Luftwaffe destroy the RAF before sending in land forces. And so, towards the end of July, the Battle of Britain began. Numbers varied hugely each day as to how many fighters on either side had been shot down, but for day after gorgeous summer's day in the skies above Kent, Sussex and Hampshire, Spitfires and Hurricanes pitted themselves against the Messerschmitt Me 109.

The dogfights never reached London for the simple reason that the Me 109 did not have the range to get that far, even from airfields in northern France, so the battles raged as people watched from their gardens and cricket grounds, as ready to untangle a pilot from his parachute as they were to catch a well-timed drive at long off.

It was an extraordinary way to battle for freedom – the very antithesis of being stuck for months on end knee deep in mud in a trench in Flanders. Now it was being free to fly like a bird, using split-second reflexes and acrobatic skills to stay alive – at least long enough for one more pint at the White Hart pub down the road from the RAF base at Biggin Hill in Kent. Visitors today can see the pictures of these brave young men on the walls of the pub, Canadians, Australians, New Zealanders and especially the daring Poles alongside British pilots, some of who were barely out of school.

At the outset it appeared that the number of aircraft ranged against each other made for a fairly even playing field in the sky – the RAF having 1,032 fighters at its disposal to the Luftwaffe's 1,011. But by 20 August it was clear that Göring could boast no longer about his Luftwaffe, brave as his pilots had been. They were being beaten and Churchill, addressing the House uttered another line that has been etched in history: 'Never in the field of human conflict has so much been owed by so many to so few.' Perhaps because memorable lines had become so commonplace working with a master orator, John Colville admitted that the line 'did not strike me very forcibly at the time. Later I saved the first draft from the waste-paper basket.'

Meanwhile, the Luftwaffe took to the skies at night and began a relentless bombardment of London and major manufacturing cities like Coventry and Birmingham (where 1,353 people died over a two-night period later in the autumn). From America, it seemed as if Britain must be on its knees, but President Roosevelt kept getting reports of a high morale, and C.P. Snow accurately reflected the public mood when he wrote, 'Oddly enough, most of us were very happy in those days. There was a kind of collective euphoria over the whole country. I don't know what we were thinking about. We were very busy. We had a purpose . . . We were sustained by a surge of national emotion of which Churchill was both the symbol and essence, evocator and voice.'

Ah, the voice! Decades later it may be difficult to grasp that essence, the growling inflections and literary mastery that fuelled the spirit of which Snow wrote. But throughout those early years, every setback was met with more defiance, unflinching in its honesty: 'Death and sorrow will be the companions on our journey,' Churchill told the House in October. 'Hardship our garment, constancy and valour our only shield . . . Our qualities and our deeds must burn and glow through the gloom of Europe till they become the veritable beacon of its salvation.'

During his constant travels around the country to visit armament factories and inspect bomb damage, working men and women, many standing in front of the rubble of their homes, waved and cheered him. 'Good old Winnie!' they cried as he replied with his famous V sign. There can have been few leaders like him.

In and around Whitehall, the business of directing and running a war continued even as the bombs rained down. Sleep was snatched between explosions. The Prime Minister was to be found dictating orders ranging from distribution of food rations to how many tanks to send to the Middle East, wearing his magnificent golden dragon dressing gown and tin hat – truly a sight to behold – while Colville, in a less splendid dressing gown, sometimes found himself tiptoeing in his slippers through broken glass in the dead of night as he tried to discover what latest damage had befallen Downing Street. The Carlton Club had gone, as had many other Regency houses in Pall Mall and Mayfair, but even as colonels, wing commanders, young majors and their ladies dined at the Ritz, a nightingale, surely, must still have been singing in Berkeley Square.

Throughout the closing months of 1940, Churchill's main preoccupation cantered on how to impress upon President Roosevelt Britain's dire need for aid. He knew full well that, given the isolationist feelings of large percentage of Americans, especially among Republican supporters, the chance of FDR suddenly throwing the United States into a full-scale war against Germany was remote, even after he had won election for a historic third term in November.

Churchill, however, never gave up and, at the end of the month, sent Roosevelt what he considered to be one of the most – if not the most – important letters of his career. For once, he took advice from close advisers, especially seeking guidance from Lord Lothian, Lord Halifax's predecessor as Ambassador in Washington. As ever the document was forthright, well argued but practical. He ended with this warning:

> The decision for 1941 lies upon the seas. Unless we can establish the ability to feed this Island, to import the munitions of all kinds which we need; unless we can move our armies to the various theatres where Hitler and Mussolini must be met . . . we may fall by the way, and the time needed by the United States to complete her defensive preparations may not be forthcoming.

Churchill did not play tennis, but as an example of how to put the ball back in your opponent's court, this was worthy of Wimbledon. The letter was forwarded to the President as he and his closest aide, Harry Hopkins, were enjoying a Caribbean cruise aboard the *Tuscaloosa* in early December. FDR brooded over it for two days before finally deciding that action was needed. As a result the Lend-Lease Act was born. Within its capacity, which was considerable, the United States would supply Britain with what it needed at knock down prices over a long period of time.

Addressing the nation on 29 December in another of his fireside chats on radio, Roosevelt spoke of Hitler, making it clear that he intended to enslave all of Europe and, in that, FDR said, 'there is no liberty, no religion, no hope'. He was bringing Americans to the accept of the inevitable and sought to rally them through Churchill's example. 'In a military sense Great Britain and the British Empire are today the spearhead of resistance to world conquest. And they are putting up a fight which will live forever in the story of human gallantry.' This was music to Churchill's ears, especially when Roosevelt spoke of America becoming 'the arsenal of democracy'.

With every passing day, Roosevelt knew that he must get to know Churchill better and, at some time in the future, arrange a means of meeting a man who was clearly extraordinary but of whom he was hearing differing opinions. Rather than wait, FDR decided to turn to his cruise companion who was soon to move into the White House to facilitate his daily interaction with the President. It seems to have been

Harry Hopkins himself who first proposed the idea of going over to London to find out exactly what 'this guy was like'.

Roosevelt, who felt the need was urgent, immediately approved the idea. 'Harry is the perfect Ambassador for my purpose,' he told his colleagues. 'He doesn't know the meaning of the word "protocol". When he sees a bit of red tape, he pulls out those old garden shears of his and just snips it.'

And so, accepting the role of go-between, Hopkins set off for London on a mission that we describe in detail in Chapter 9. Suffice to say that that Hopkins, who was not a healthy man, arrived feeling like death after a tediously long Atlantic crossing by air, but, to his surprise, he quickly became enveloped in the Churchill spell as the pair of them lunched in the Downing Street basement. By the time a certain number of glasses of brandy and port had been consumed, it was four o'clock, and Winston had found a new friend.

Hopkins, the son of an Iowan shopkeeper, had been expecting someone rather different, so confusing had been the stories he had heard about this member of the British aristocracy. He had been expecting an opinionated puffed-up autocrat who drank too much. He soon found himself asking 'What is too much?' They certainly drank but, as ever, Churchill showed no sign of being drunk. And as for opinions, Churchill offered many, but they were measured and balanced by wanting to know everything Hopkins could tell him about his boss back in the White House. The Prime Minister was acutely aware of the need to make a good impression on his visitor, and by one of those quirks of fate of which history is made, the unlikely pair almost instantly warmed to each other, became understanding of each other and completely relaxed in each other's company.

After Hopkins had been invited to extend his stay for several weeks and had been taken everywhere Churchill travelled throughout the country. One night he found himself at Claridge's Hotel and sat down to pen a note to the President on hotel stationery. Robert E. Sherwood, the American playwright and Pultizer Prize-winning author of *Roosevelt and Hopkins: An Intimate History*, includes the handwritten letter in his book:

Churchill IS the government in every sense of the word – he controls the grand strategy and often details – labor trusts him – the army, navy air force are behind him to a man. The politicians and upper crust pretend to like him. I cannot emphasize too strongly that he is the one and only person over here with whom you need to have a full meeting of minds.

Nor was Hopkins shy of making his feelings known to Churchill. When asked to speak at a function during their travels, Hopkins rose to say, 'I suppose you wish to know what I am going to say to President Roosevelt on my return. Well, I am going to quote you one verse from the Book of Ruth, "Whither thou goest, I will go; and where thou lodgest I will lodge; thy people shall be my people and thy God my God."' Then Hopkins added, 'Even to the end.'

By then, of course, Churchill was in tears. As we have seen, he cried easily and rarely had he been given a better excuse then now. These were the kind of sentiments he had been praying for since he had taken charge of his embattled nation. If FDR would accept Hopkins's evaluation of Britain and her leader, then Churchill knew he could rely on America and with America, he knew he could win the war.

It is not possible to exaggerate the importance of this new relationship. Had Roosevelt chosen a different emissary, one whose sensitivities might have recoiled at the sheer larger-than-life unorthodoxy of the man he would meet, relations between the two nations that would save the world, could have been very different. But Harry Hopkins was the right man, and by the time he died an early death at 55 in 1946, he had taken his place in history.

After Hopkins finally left for home on 10 February 1941, it became commonplace for Churchill to work closely with high-ranking American visitors. Wendell Wilkie, whose graciousness in defeat after the 1940 Presidential election, in addition to his pro-British feelings, had put him in Roosevelt's good books, had arrived towards the end of February, and he was followed by a new US Ambassador to the Court of St James, Gilbert Winant, a former Republican Governor of New Hampshire who bore a strange resemblance to Abraham Lincoln. Whatever his appearance, he proved to be a vast improvement over his predecessor, Joe Kennedy, the appeaser who might well have preferred Hitler to Churchill as a dinner companion. Happily for Anglo-American relations in later years, Kennedy's sons took a more balanced and progressive view towards Britain and the 'special relationship' lasted through numerous American presidencies.

No sooner had Winant been accepted into the Downing Street inner circle that Averell Harriman arrived to expedite the Lend-Lease Act. Tall, handsome and the son of the railroad magnate E.H. Harriman, Averell would not only go on to enjoy one of the longest diplomatic careers in American history but would also enjoy, less diplomatically, a not-so-discreet affair with Randolph Churchill's wife Pamela – the woman, amazingly, he would marry all of 40 years later. As we see in Chapter 14 this liaison caused huge tension and unpleasantness between Randolph and his father, who had chosen to turn a blind eye to the affair.

Needless to say, the Prime Minister was preoccupied with other matters and the following months were not easy. Crete had to be evacuated, the battlecruiser HMS *Hood* was sunk, and Rommel inflicted a heavy defeat on British forces in North Africa. The reverses struck Churchill hard, and for two days he retreated to Chartwell, and in his own words 'wandered about the valley disconsolately for some hours'. It would appear that Churchill's fits of depression have been exaggerated, but if ever his 'Black Dog' was to be found walking by his side it would have been at this moment.

There was better, and highly significant news on 22 June. Hitler, tearing up the Molotov-Ribbentrop Pact, invaded Russia. It was, of course, the fatal Napoleonic move that proved so disastrous to Hitler's ambitions. Forces that would have been needed to invade Britain were now required on the Russian front. Digesting the news over a well-attended Sunday lunch at Chequers, Churchill formulated the speech he was intending to give while taking in the opinions of Sir Stafford Cripps, his Ambassador in Moscow who happened to be visiting, Anthony Eden, Lord Beaverbrook, Gilbert Winant and Peter Fraser, the Prime Minister of New Zealand.

So much effort went into the dictation of what he intended to say that the final draft was not ready until 15 minutes before broadcast time. But, as Harold Nicolson observed afterwards, it turned out to be another masterpiece.

> We have but one aim and one irrevocable purpose. We are resolved to destroy Hitler and every vestige of the Nazi regime. From this nothing will turn us – nothing. Any man or state who fights against Nazidom will have our aid. Any man or state who marches with Hitler is our foe . . . It follows, therefore, that we shall give whatever help we can to Russia and the Russian people.

The words reflected his true sentiments, but in chatting to Colville late at night, he revealed the extent to which he was prepared to square his deeply anti-Communist feelings with the satisfaction of suddenly having Stalin as an ally. 'If Hitler invaded Hell, I would at least make a favourable reference to the Devil.'

Despite entreaties from Moscow to open up another front, Churchill stuck resolutely to his position that Britain, without American participation, was not ready, militarily, to mount the kind of offensive in France and the Low Countries that would draw Nazi troops away from the Eastern Front. Once Britain and Russia became 'co-belligerents', left-leaning organizations with Communist sympathies kept up a campaign to try and force Churchill's hand, but he stood fast. Even when America did come into the war, he was the restraining influence, which was ironic considering how his vocal critics had decried him as a man of impulse and poor judgement. D-Day was still a long way off.

What was imminent, however, was the all-important meeting between President Roosevelt and the man he only really knew as 'A Former Naval Person'. As far as was possible through cables and the occasional handwritten note, the two men had got to know each other a little but both knew that so much more urgent business could be achieved if they were to meet face to face.

No one was more cognizant of that than Harry Hopkins, and he set in motion all that needed to be done to get his old friend and his new friend to meet. The encounter, when it came, would be far from the fevered centres of activity from which both men worked, far, indeed, from the centres of civilization that both men were trying desperately to preserve. But the peaceful setting of Placentia Bay off a deserted stretch of Newfoundland coastline provided an appropriate backdrop for two great minds to meet, explore and produce a format by which the world's teeming masses could move forward and exist in peace. As Churchill might have said, it was a noble undertaking.

Chapter 9

Harry Hopkins

The *Cambridge Dictionary* defines the phrase 'go-between' as 'someone who helps to connect people who are unwilling or unable to meet'. Harry Hopkins may have been one of the most successful go-betweens of all time. Quite an achievement for a somewhat unassuming native of Sioux City, Iowa, especially given that the people he was asked to connect were the two men whose eventual collaboration and friendship were almost entirely responsible for winning the Second World War.

It was not that President Roosevelt and Prime Minister Churchill did not want to meet but, in 1940, they were situated on opposites sides of a dangerous ocean and hitherto had only communicated by letter, telegram or very occasionally by phone. Something needed to be done, and Hopkins found himself tasked as the man to do it.

Through an unlikely career path that we will follow later, in December 1940 Hopkins found himself sailing off the coast of Cuba near Guantanamo Bay on the President's yacht. Acknowledging the fact that a President of the United States can never switch off entirely, FDR was allowing the fishing tips he was getting from Ernest Hemingway to be interrupted by any messages deemed worthy of such disruption. A 4,000-word letter from Winston Churchill qualified.

The letter provided a very clear statement of the dire military and economic situation that the Prime Minister of Britain felt his country faced in its war against Nazi Germany. In the letter, Churchill stated that the British people were 'ready to suffer any sacrifice' and that the 'defeat of Nazi and Fascist tyranny is a matter of high consequence to the people of the United States'. Churchill emphasized that the letter was 'not an appeal for aid, but as a statement of the minimum action necessary to the achievement of our common purpose'.[1]

---

1. FDR Library Letter Churchill to FDR dated 7 December 1940.

As one of FDR's most trusted advisers, Harry Hopkins had been invited to accompany the President on his vacation and witnessed the impact of Churchill's missive. According to Hopkins, it was profound. Shortly after digesting the letter's implications, FDR was quoted as saying: 'We cannot escape danger, or the fear of danger, by crawling into bed and pulling covers over our head.'[2] And then in a 'fireside chat' radio address on 29 December – three weeks after receiving Churchill's letter – FDR stated for the first time that the only way to have peace with the Nazis was to have them totally surrender. Exactly one year later, the US would be at war with Nazi Germany and Japan after the bombing of Pearl Harbor. Shortly after returning to Washington from his vacation, Roosevelt had articulated his plan of action by stating, 'We must be the great arsenal of democracy'. In effect, the United States would avoid entering the war in Europe but would supply the aircraft, ships and other military hardware necessary for Britain and her allies to fight and defeat Hitler. Henceforth, FDR abandoned his approach of supplying Britain within the margins of what was politically acceptable. Instead he put forth the Lend-Lease Act, cleverly introduced as H.R. 1776 in the House of Representatives, on 10 January 1941. When approved and signed into law, Lend-Lease gave the President the authority to aid any nation whose defence he believed vital and would allow the United States to accept 'in kind or property, or any other direct or indirect benefit the President deems satisfactory' in exchange for that support. In effect, the bill gave the President a free hand to sell huge amounts of military goods and supplies to Britain and her allies while accepting unusual and delayed forms of payment. To a currency-constrained Britain, Lend-Lease was a much-needed safety valve. The Lend-Lease Act was overwhelmingly supported by the Democrats in Congress, but many of the Republicans who still favoured isolationism and expressed some distrust of the British were opposed to its passage. Lend-Lease was passed despite the debate and signed into law on 11 March 1941.

Some months before that, it had become clear that Britain's situation was dire to the point of desperation. The Blitz was severely hampering the production of ships and aircraft, and the Atlantic convoys, bringing vital supplies from America, were taking heavy losses from the marauding U-boats. FDR, still unwilling, or politically unable, to take the plunge and declare war, nevertheless wanted to help. Within the limits of cables and correspondence, he had established a good

2. Sherwood, p. 22.

relationship with Churchill. But he wanted more. Just a few days after the 29 December 'fireside chat', the President confided to Hopkins that he wished he could sit down with Churchill and meet him face to face. There was so much to discuss. Amongst the more obvious issues, the situation in Ireland had become of particular concern. Once again, Hitler had revealed his ruthless hand by invading Norway in April 1940, and Ireland, trying to remain neutral, was just as obvious a target. According to Hopkins, FDR said, 'You know – a lot of this could be settled if Churchill and I could just sit down together for a while', to which Hopkins asked what was stopping FDR from the meeting.[3] FDR turned that idea down immediately because of commitments like the upcoming State of the Union Address and the passage of the Lend-Lease Act. Hopkins offered, 'How about me going over, Mr. President?' Less than a week later, FDR announced at a press conference that Harry Hopkins would go 'as my personal representative for a very short trip, just a couple of weeks, just to maintain – I suppose that would be the word for it— personal relations between me and the British Government'.[4]

Given how little FDR really knew about the man behind the persona of the new British Prime Minister, his decision to send Hopkins to London was a master stroke. An air of pessimism had surrounded most of the reports and views FDR had received about Churchill up to that point. William C. Bullitt, the US Ambassador to Paris, speaking at a dinner given by Interior Minister Harold C. Ickes on a visit to Washington, was reported in Ickes's diaries to have said that he had no use for Neville Chamberlain and almost none for Churchill. Bullitt felt that the British government was in a bad way: 'There are no real leaders in all of England at this time of grave crisis.'

Ickes himself was even more scathing. 'I suppose Churchill is the best man for the job – even if he is drunk half the time,' he wrote. Even Under Secretary of State Sumner Welles, who had spent time with Churchill in London a month before, was concerned about Churchill's drinking, while admitting that 'his cascade of oratory was brilliant and always effective'.

So there was scepticism, to put it mildly, concerning Churchill's leadership qualities among those surrounding the President as he dispatched Harry Hopkins across the ocean and those sentiments might have lingered but for the almost instant rapport, developing into genuine

---

3. Sherwood, p. 230.
4. Ibid., p.231.

friendship, that Hopkins was able to strike up with the beleaguered Prime Minister. He would become the most effective of go-betweens – not a role he would have foreseen as we trace his earlier years.

Harry Hopkins was born in Sioux City, Iowa, in 1890, and his family moved to Grinnell, Iowa, when Harry was eleven. Harry attended public school in Grinnell, and, while he was in high school, he was active in student government affairs and excelled on the basketball team. In many ways his upbringing in Grinnell was typical for a young man growing up in the Midwest in the early 1900s. Home life was simple, and cash was always tight. His friends and neighbours were of English, Irish, Scottish and Scandinavian descent. As an adult, Harry commented that he never met a Jewish person until he attended college. Harry was one of six children, but one of his sisters died in infancy. His mother, Anna, was 'a devoted worker in the Methodist Church' and 'raised her children in stern rectitude, imbuing them with a sense of social responsibility and service to fellow human beings'.[5] His father originally worked as a harness maker but after moving to Grinnell opened a convenience store that was frequented by the students at Grinnell College. Harry's father claimed that he knew every student at Grinnell College by name by the time they graduated.

After graduating high school, Harry stayed in his hometown and attended Grinnell College. While Harry didn't excel academically or athletically while attending college, his time at Grinnell was transformative. In his senior year he was elected president of the senior class. He also formed lifelong friendships with Harry C. Dodge and Robert and Florence Kerr and came under the influence of several members of the faculty. Professor Edward Steiner had a particularly strong influence on Harry and his path in life. Steiner taught a course called Applied Christianity. Like all great teachers, Steiner gave his students more than the mere subject matter of his course.[6] Steiner was Jewish, had grown up in Czechoslovakia and obtained his doctorate from Heidelberg University. When Steiner moved to the United States, he became a Congregational minister. Steiner impressed upon his students a formula for life which combined humanity and compassion with a 'Jewish sense of man's responsibility to his God and the Christian ethic of love they neighbour'.[7] Upon Hopkins's graduation from Grinnell, Steiner referred him to a friend who worked for a settlement house on the Lower East Side of

---

5. Adams, p. 31.
6. Ibid., p.33.
7. Ibid.

Manhattan called Christadora House. The introduction changed the course of Hopkins' life. Harry had planned to open a newspaper in Bozeman, Montana, with a partner but, instead, went to work for Christadora's summer camp in Bound Brook, New Jersey. When summer ended Harry accepted a full time position with Christadora House in Manhattan. His salary was room and board plus $5 a month in spending money.

Christadora House was a different world for Harry. His job was to help the boys with their socialization and interaction and to help them adjust and succeed in America. Hopkins biographer Robert Sherwood writes that Hopkins 'had certainly known poverty in his own family and friendly neighbourhood in the middle west, but that kind of poverty involved the maintenance of a kind of dignity and self-respect and independence; it did not involve hunger, or squalor, or degradation . . . this was his birth as a real crusader of reform'.[8] Hopkins immersed himself in this community with total dedication and began to reveal the skills that would that would make him such an effective go-between. He organized games and activities, but he also lectured the boys on their civic duties.

He tried to instil in them the ideas of betterment, voting, service to community and helping neighbours. In the winter of 1913, Hopkins went to see Dr John Kingsbury, who ran the Association for Improving the Condition of the Poor (AICP) a well-funded charity supported by donations. Kingsbury took a liking to Hopkins and hired him on a 'training' basis at $40 per month with the idea that he would find a position for Hopkins after he had learned the workings of the organization and became more experienced as a social worker. During the day, Hopkins continued to work at Christadora House, and at night he was assigned to tougher districts along the waterfront where it was unsafe for female social workers.

The early years of the twentieth century have been marked as an age of reform and the birth of progressivism. During the 1890s, labourers and farmers in the Midwest, led by William Jennings Bryan, railed against the established leaders of the Democratic and Republican Parties and the 'moneyed' interests in the large Eastern cities, who Bryan and his followers claimed rigged the economy, the commercial markets and governmental laws and policies to advance themselves at the expense of the people. At the Democratic Convention in 1896, Bryan was nominated as candidate for President. While Bryan was never elected

---

8. Sherwood, p. 22.

President, his populism and critical view of society put the institutions of business and governance under the microscope. Many Americans began to be more reflective about their own ambitions and observant about the conditions of people around them who were less fortunate. Harry Hopkins was drawn to this movement, and it propelled him from his humble beginnings in Iowa to commit to career in social service at a young age in faraway New York City. FDR was also influenced by the progressive movement and measured himself in part by what he did from the perch of entitlement and comfort to improve the lot of others.

In 1913, while working for the AICP, Hopkins was asked to write a report on the causes of rising unemployment in New York and to make suggestions on how to reverse the trend. Hopkins's report stated 'that most of the jobless preferred an honest day's work to charity [what was then called 'the dole'] and that they were unemployed not because of moral shortcomings (e.g. laziness) but because of social and economic conditions beyond their control'.[9] Hopkins promoted this concept and pushed to see it implemented in social programmes. In 1915 Hopkins's idea was put to its first test when he and his partner at the AICP, William Matthews, organized a relief programme whereby 230 unemployed workers were paid a living wage to work on improvements to the Bronx Zoo. Matthews, who wrote about the programme more than a decade and a half later, stated that the Bronx Zoo undertaking was the first of its kind anywhere in the United States and that it would serve as a 'major form of aid for the casualties of the Great Depression'.[10] Eventually Hopkins would leave the AICP and undertake multi-year positions working with the Red Cross and Tuberculosis and Health Association.

In 1931 FDR began his second term as Governor of New York, and the Great Depression was devastating the country. There were an estimated 750,000 unemployed in New York State alone, and many were facing homelessness and hunger. Roosevelt established the Temporary Emergency Relief Administration (TERA) with an initial funding of $23 million. TERA provided chits for food, housing and health care jobs to work on infrastructure project. TERA was the first governmental backed relief agency anywhere in the United States, and Harry Hopkins was recruited to be its first administrator. In time TERA would provide direct aid to more than 1.2 million New Yorkers (10 per cent of the

9. Roll, p. 21.
10. Ibid.

population) and help create 80,000 jobs.[11] While Hopkins and FDR didn't socialize during this period they came in frequent contact as Administrator reporting to Governor. TERA was innovative in a time of great duress for millions of Americans, and it served as a beacon of progressive governmental support. Within a year of taking the leadership role at TERA, Hopkins was recruited by FDR to join him in Washington DC when the latter was elected President of the United States.

How a person could rise from obscurity in Iowa and a background in agency relief to serve as FDR's personal representative to meet with Winston Churchill in a time of great world crisis is a testament to Hopkins's talents and determination. Hopkins also developed an important personal relationship with Joseph Stalin, and during the Second World War served as FDR's personal representative to the government of the USSR. Along the way, Hopkins was married three times: divorced from his first wife Ethel Gross, whom he had married in 1913 and with whom he had three sons, he married his second wife, Barbara Duncan, in 1931 and with whom he had a daughter, Diana. Barbara tragically died of cancer in 1937. At the time of Barbara's death, Eleanor Roosevelt insisted that Diana, then five years old, come live in the White House, where the First Lady doted on her. Hopkins married for a third time to Louise Gill Macy in 1942, the wedding taking place in the White House.

But throughout the latter part of his life, Hopkins was battling ill health. Hopkins had a very serious bout of cancer, which required surgery to remove a significant part of his stomach in 1939, leaving him prone to bouts of serious illness. In fact, when Hopkins flew to Britain to meet with Churchill, he was so tired from his multi-leg trip that when his Pan Am Clipper landed off the coast of England at Poole, Dorset on 9 January 1941, he was unable to unbuckle himself from his seat belt and remained on the plane for some time until he felt strong enough to make the train journey into London. He was supposed to visit with Churchill for dinner upon arrival but elected to check into his room at Claridge's and get a good night's sleep before heading to 10 Downing Street for lunch the following day.[12]

He was met by Brendan Bracken, the Prime Minister's right-hand man. Bracken led him through the 10 Downing Street building to a stairway that opened onto a small dining room in the basement. Hopkins couldn't help but notice that the famous residence looked a bit down

---

11. Roll, p. 30.
12. Adams, p. 200.

at heel: 'most of the windows were out and workman were all over the place repairing the damage—Churchill told me it wouldn't stand a healthy bomb'.[13] Churchill might have noted that his visitor wouldn't have withstood a healthy push. Obviously fatigued, Hopkins looked far from robust and presented himself as 'ill dressed with a certain style' as Roy Jenkins puts it in his fine biography of Churchill.

Lunch was soup, cold beef, green salad and cheese. The Prime Minister insisted Hopkins take more mint jelly for his beef. After lunch they shared coffee and a light wine and port. The two seem to get on well from the start. After meeting with Hopkins the first time, Churchill was quoted as saying that he felt sure he had 'at last established a definite, heart-to-heart contact with the President'. That, of course, was Churchill's primary goal, but the intimacy he craved, even at long distance, might not have been conveyed by a personality less congenial than the American go-between. For the good fortune of all concerned, Hopkins was just the kind of man the Prime Minister instinctively warmed to, a sophisticated outsider with a touch of loucheness, as Jenkins put it. 'He had a mordant humour, he liked gambling and racetracks, and he was easily at home in any company where the tone was not too pious.' It would have been easy for Churchill to recognize a kindred spirit.

For his part, Hopkins came away impressed with Churchill in many ways, and as we have noted earlier, cabled FDR that 'Churchill is the gov't in every sense of the word—he controls the grand strategy and often the details—labor trusts him—the army, navy and Air Force are behind him to a man.'[14]

During the lunch Churchill explained why he thought Great Britain would defeat Germany if it tried to invade England. He also quoted facts which were designed to assure the American envoy that the United Kingdom had superiority over Germany in air power and that its relative air strength was increasing. At this first lunch, Churchill and Hopkins discussed the need for Churchill and Roosevelt to meet. Of course FDR had much to discuss but Churchill also relished the positive impact on morale the people of the British Empire would feel knowing that their Prime Minister was meeting with the President of the United States. During this first lunch, Churchill and Hopkins suggested that the two leaders could meet as early as April 1941 and Churchill lamented how nice it would be to meet in the waters near Bermuda.

---

13. Sherwood, p. 238.
14. Ibid., p 239

While the two didn't get specific about a date and location, the idea of a meeting between FDR and Churchill was put on the table.

Churchill invited Hopkins to join him for the weekend at Ditchley Park, a beautiful and grand country house owned by Ronald Tree, the grandson of the original Marshall Field from Chicago. The customary weekend retreat of British Prime Ministers was Chequers but at this time, it was considered too easy a target for the Luftwaffe when there was a full moon. Hopkins joined for the weekend and continued to travel with Churchill as he made stops throughout England, Scotland and Wales. The trip was originally anticipated to last two weeks but such was the camaraderie which struck up between the two men in such a short amount of time, it stretched more than twice that long. At one point Churchill took Hopkins to Scotland to tour naval bases and upon returning to London they made stops along the way including a formal dinner held in Glasgow. That night at dinner, Churchill introduced Hopkins as 'the personal representative of the President of the United States of America' and asked him to make a few remarks. As we noted in an earlier chapter, this is when Hopkins rose and quoted from the Book of Ruth and said, 'Whither thou goest, I will go . . . even to the end'. At which point legend has it that Churchill started to cry.

Throughout his visit to Britain, Hopkins was always very careful in what he said publicly in an effort to manage expectations of the British and avoid fuelling the isolationists' arguments back home. He gave several press conferences but always seemed to say, 'the Prime Minister and I just discussed areas of mutual interest'. However, one night towards the end of his visit to Britain, Lord Beaverbrook gave a dinner for Hopkins. Beaverbrook, the leading press lord of his time, had been brought into the government to take charge of the vital business of building as many Spitfires and Hurricanes as was possible. The Beaver's unorthodox methods, cutting through red tape in a manner that reflected his nickname, kept production whirring at a rate comparable to the presses of his newspapers. Eventually moving from Aircraft Production to the Ministry of Supply, Beaverbrook would prove to be one of Churchill's most inspired appointments.

Beaverbrook invited not only the editors and writers of his newspapers to the dinner for Hopkins, but also their counterparts from competing tabloids. After dinner was cleared and Harry was assured whatever he said would be kept confidential, Hopkins finally spoke. There are no notes of what he said because of the pledge of privacy. But Hopkins, speaking in an intimate way, said that the President and those around him were convinced that America's duty to the world could be successfully performed only in partnership with Britain. He talked of the anxiety and admiration that he and others felt as Britain waged its lonely fight. He had now travelled the country, side by side with the Prime Minister, for several weeks and seen the determination of the British people. Those in attendance left the dinner feeling that while America wasn't yet in the war, it was marching beside them and would see to it that Britain would not fall. Above all, Hopkins convinced his audience that the President and those around him had absolute faith in the future of democracy.

The go-between had done his job, and, through the long years of war that followed, he would continue to do so.

Chapter 10

General George Marshall

Serving as Churchill's emissary in North Africa at the height of the Second World War, Harold Macmillan, himself a future Prime Minister of Great Britain, would later write in his book *The Blast of War*, 'At this time (1943) General Marshall, the American Chief of Staff and the most powerful man in the United States after the President, was visiting Italy . . . '

It was almost a throwaway line. A statement of fact rather than opinion, and certainly one Macmillan would have expected no one to dispute. George Catlett Marshall Jr. was the second most powerful man in America. But this was not quite as apparent, or indeed as true, two years earlier when Harry Hopkins flew to London to confer with Churchill on which advisers should attend the forthcoming meeting between President Roosevelt and the British Prime Minister, scheduled to be held off the coast of Newfoundland on 9 August 1941.

Originally, FDR wanted to keep the number of attendees to a minimum. Churchill, in need of reinforcements to support the demands he would place on the President, was keen to bring a larger delegation in addition to military advisers. And so, a full list of names was discussed when Hopkins returned for another of his visits to 10 Downing Street, and the two men, who were becoming good personal friends, had no problem developing a roster to send back to Washington for approval.

The roster, of course, included American names, and when Hopkins sent off the telegraph cable, it began, 'The problems of supply and other matters so important that I earnestly hope you can bring Marshall with you'.

Hopkins pinpointed the right man. He had become well aware of General Marshall and the impact he made since being appointed Chief of Staff of the Army on 1 September 1939 – just a few hours before Hitler ordered his troops into Poland. A detailed military planner of exceptional strategic ability, the General, with his quietly imposing personality and calm, authoritative manner, already had a greater grasp of what would be required of the US military in the coming months and years than most of his colleagues at the Pentagon and the State Department. And he understood full well the enormity of his task.

At that moment in August 1941, the entire US Army, including the US Army Air Force, totalled less than 200,000 men. By the time Marshall left his post with victory achieved in 1945, he was in command of upwards of eight million men and women. It was the greatest fighting force the world had ever seen and remained so long after the General's remarkable career came to end – a career that saw him develop what became known as the Marshall Plan to rebuild the war-battered continent of Europe and included elite service in successive strategic positions: as President Truman's special envoy to China and the commanding position of US Secretary of State from 1947 to 1949; President of the American Red Cross from 1949 to 1950 and then Secretary of Defense under President Eisenhower, the very man whose military career he had helped to launch.

There were, of course, many American generals during the Second World War whose exploits in the field made them better known: the egocentric General Douglas MacArthur of Philippines fame, General Omar Bradley, General Mark Clark and the man who could be described as Marshall's antithesis, General George S. Patton. Marshall did not need to wear an ivory-handled pistol to make his point, but whenever the occasion demanded, he was never afraid to do so.

On the major strategic decisions of when and where to invade Nazi-occupied Europe, Marshall frequently argued with Churchill, a man with whom he shared few personality traits. But in one respect at least, he and Churchill shared a core value: both preferred to tell the unvarnished truth no matter how unpalatable it might be. Churchill did not try to diminish the enormity of the task Britain faced in the early years of the war and laid it out with his 'I have nothing to offer . . . ' speech. In private, Marshall was equally transparent with his boss.

At the height of the war, Marshall wrote: 'I am very careful to send President Roosevelt every few days a statement of our casualties. I try to keep before him all the time the casualty results because you get hardened to these things and you have to be very careful to keep them always in the forefront of your mind.'

The extent to which the President came to prize this outspokenly honest and level-headed man probably deprived Marshall of an even more famous role in history. Having become well-known to Churchill, who recognized his great strengths despite their differences, Marshall's name was first on the list of candidates to be appointed Supreme Allied

Commander as plans for D-Day progressed in 1943. But Roosevelt has been quoted as saying to Marshall 'I could not sleep at night if you were out of the country for any length of time'. So General Marshall stayed home, and it was General Dwight D. Eisenhower, whose career Marshall had nurtured, who got the job. By then, Marshall had become well known to Churchill and his staff, and despite disagreements had struck up a good relationship with Field Marshal Sir John Dill, who would later work in Washington as the British Military Advisor to the US Government.

In 1942, General Marshall was escorted to London for further talks by Hopkins who, by that time, knew his way around town. Nevertheless, it was a special moment even for Hopkins, for whom Churchill had opened every door, when he and Marshall were invited to lunch with the King and Queen at Buckingham Palace and then sat down with King George VI again later that evening when His Majesty paid a rare visit to 10 Downing Street for dinner.

According to Roy Jenkins, both occasions went well, but were perhaps a little less convivial than those Hopkins had enjoyed in Churchill's company on earlier visits. Although recording Marshall as a man of quiet charm, Jenkins wryly suggested the General might have been 'a less digestible social morsel than Hopkins'.

The Americans' mission was clear. General Marshall, backed by his President, wanted to convince the British that an assault on France directly across the Channel was the best and quickest way to placate Stalin, drawing Nazi troops away from the Russian front as well as creating a huge psychological advantage in the conduct of the war. Churchill, however, preferred the diversionary tactic of hitting Europe's softer underbelly through Italy and the South of France. The discussions – one could say arguments – continued through many meetings both in London and, later, in Washington when Churchill joined Sir John Dill in a verbal battle with FDR and Marshall.

Quoting George Elsey, a young naval reservist who was assigned to the White House Map Room where the exchange took place, historian Jon Meacham writes in *Franklin and Winston* that Churchill and Dill won the day because the American duo 'could not match the torrent of the voluble Brits, especially Churchill'. Not all battles are won on the front line.

And so, the man who had been born at Uniontown, Pennsylvania, on New Year's Day, 1880, was now a leading figure in the greatest global conflict mankind had ever known. He had become Roosevelt's planner-in-chief and, in conjunction with America's allies, was, with every decision made, responsible for the fate of tens of thousands of people from military personnel to innocent civilians in places as far flung as Nice and Naples or Singapore and Saipan. He did not shirk from the task. A life devoted to the technical aspects of warfare had prepared him for task ahead.

His family, solidly middle class, traced its roots to Virginia and had a distant relationship to Chief Justice John Marshall. After his early schooling, he attended the Virginia Military Institute (VMI) and, in 1902 at the age of 22, was commissioned as a second lieutenant. Marshall was immediately given a taste of life outside the United States when he was posted to the Philippines for several years. In stark contrast, he then found himself at Fort Reno, Wyoming, where, apart from there being considerably fewer people, there was nothing much to do. Fort Reno was established in the 1860s to protect settlers from hostile Indians but in the new century there was little hostility, and daily life was confined to the usual 'spit and polish' routine of army drills.

By 1906, Marshall had had enough of kit and barracks inspections and guard drills, so he contacted the VMI's Superintendent Scott Shipp for a more interesting posting. He did not get one from Shipp, but someone seems to have spotted his potential. He was assigned to a one-year course in the art of mobile warfare at Fort Leavenworth, Kansas, with an opportunity to continue if he excelled.

He excelled. After finishing first in his class, he was awarded a second year and promotion to first lieutenant. A summer posting to the Pennsylvania National Guard provided another stepping stone to a suddenly upwardly mobile career when he was noticed by General Franklin Bell. Quickly realizing Marshall's potential, General Bell, who became US Army Chief of Staff in 1907, served as Marshall's mentor and supporter throughout his early career, which included being put in charge of training 1,200 officers at Monterey, California. Salt Lake City and Plattsburgh, New York, followed, with Marshall acquitting himself so well that he was promoted to captain.

By the time the United States entered the First World War in April 1917, Captain Marshall had managed to get himself transferred from training officers to serving in the US Army's 1st Division, which sailed for France under the command of Major General William L. Sibert. The First Division was the advanced combat unit of the American Expeditionary Force led by the legendary General John 'Black Jack' Pershing.

The First World War gave Marshall the chance to distinguish himself, albeit as a planner rather than a front-line fighter. The opportunity came in March 1918 when Vladimir Lenin signed the Treaty of Brest-Litovsk with Germany, which took the new Bolshevik government out of the war. This released Germany troops for the Western Front and, going for a knockout blow after years of stagnation in the trenches, they staged a major offensive near the village of Cantigny on the Somme. The Allies staged a counter-attack led by the US 1st Division, with Marshall in charge of troop preparation, placement and planning. The counter-attack was successful and Marshall, deservedly, received notice and credit.

After Cantigny, Marshall was transferred to Pershing's headquarters where he eventually served as Chief of Operations. When the war ended a few months later, Pershing asked him 'to be one of his official aides, to serve as his adviser, and to take his place at times in routine matters'.[11]

During this time, Marshall had only obtained the permanent rank of major. Many others were promoted ahead of him because they led actual combat troops. But Marshall's experience training officers and soldiers set him apart. He understood the details of modern warfare better than most, and it was this vital skill that enabled him to rise so fast.

In their biography of Marshall, Debi and Irwin Unger write:

> General George Van Horn Mosley, a Pershing staff officer, would later explain that it has been Marshall's job to work out all the details of operations, putting them in clear and practical working order which could be understood by the commanders of all subordinate units. The order must be comprehensive, yet not involved. It must appear clear when read in poor light, in the mud and rain. It was Marshall's job and he performed it 100%. The troops which maneuvered under his plans always won.

That was some accolade, and it obviously fit with the opinion held by 'Black Jack' Pershing, then viewed by most Americans as the soldier who had won the Great War.

At the conclusion of the war, Pershing and his staff relocated to Washington, DC, where Marshall was reunited with his wife Lily, whom he had not seen for two years. They took an apartment in a hotel on Sixteenth Street, ate most nights in the dining room and tried to adjust to a humdrum life. It was a trying time for the ambitious soldier, who watched Congress vote to reduce America's standing army to a mere 280,000 – a drastic reduction that made opportunities for promotion scarce. But Pershing remained his lifeline. Marshall soon became a familiar

---

1. D. and I Unger, pp. 42–3.

face in the nation's capital as he accompanied the celebrated general to meetings with Congressional leaders and Cabinet Secretaries all the way up to the President.

When Pershing retired in 1924, Marshall satisfied his wanderlust by taking his wife on an extended tour of duty in Tientsin, China. Soon after they returned to Washington, DC, and Marshall took a post at the War Office in Washington DC, Lily Marshall passed away. Wanting to leave Washington, Marshall accepted the post of Assistant Commandant, Infantry School, Fort Benning, Georgia, where he trained officers in his approach to military training and tactics. He championed a 'war of movement' rather than the old doctrines of holding set positions. Many of these officers followed Marshall's principles and would put them to use during the Second World War. During his time at Fort Benning, Marshall made his mark on many officers, including Omar Bradley, later the first Chairman of the US Joint Chiefs of Staff, who served as a tactics instructor under Marshall. Bradley was quoted as saying that Marshall 'really established the standards of instruction as we know them today . . . a maximum of our training takes place on the ground, not in the class room'.

Despite his success at Fort Benning, Marshall grew tired of classroom teaching and welcomed the return to the field, which came when he was given command of a 400-man battalion at Fort Screven, Georgia. In March 1933 – shortly after Marshall's new appointment – Congress passed a law creating the Civilian Conservation Corps (CCC). It was originally designed to employ young men aged 18 to 25 in projects relating to forestry, prevention of soil erosion, flood control and other environmental issues. The US Army played a big role in the CCC, and in June it was decided to make use of Marshall's presence and give him the additional command of a CCC district that involved supervising nineteen CCC camps stretching 450 miles from Georgia to southern Florida.[2]

It was hardly surprising Marshall excelled in his new role. In a few months, he had overseen the building and staffing of camps in his district for 4,500 CCC workers. His experience training soldiers from rural and simple educational backgrounds proved valuable in this role and, after two and half years leading the Illinois National Guard in Chicago, he returned to CCC work supervising thirty-five camps in the Washington State and Oregon area.

---

2. George C. Marshall Foundation website.

By this time, it was 1938, and George Marshall had been promoted to brigadier general. And greater things beckoned. Even from the far side of the Atlantic, it was clear that Europe was being drawn into conflict, and when a position as Chief of War Plans opened up in Washington, Brigadier General Marshall was offered the post by the Chief of Staff of the Army Malin Craig. Craig made it clear that the appointment would quickly result in Marshall's elevation to Deputy Chief of Staff, but it seemed unlikely that a newly-promoted officer could thrust his way to the top job – which Marshall coveted – given the number of far more senior generals who would also be seeking it. However, after much thought, Marshall trusted Craig and accepted.

When Craig duly stepped down, Marshall discovered that he had more friends in high places than he had imagined. General 'Black Jack' Pershing was probably the most influential, and he wrote to the President to say that Marshall should be appointed Craig's successor. Harry Hopkins, who had come to know Marshall through his work with the CCC, a particular favourite of FDR's New Deal programme, also weighed in on Marshall's behalf. It was enough. On 23 April 1939, Brigadier General George C. Marshall was summoned to the White House where Roosevelt offered him the position of US Army Chief of Staff.

When Marshall took charge of the US Army, he faced numerous challenges and worries. But the real issues were how to enable a woefully under-sized and underprepared US military and find the resources to meet immediate commitments, let alone gearing up to defeat potential enemies on a worldwide scale. At the outset, Marshall had less than 200,000 personnel at his disposal. He knew that nothing less than a force of 2.8 million would put America in a position to competitively fight a global war, and he set about growing the ranks. He needed considerable help from military colleagues and members of Congress, but he had already attained sufficient stature to get people to listen to him.

Soon Marshall's influence was such that he was involved in all decisions appertaining to the war that broke out in Europe in the autumn of 1939. Like the Army, the US Navy was undermanned and there were differences of opinion as to where it should be deployed. The President was of the opinion that a significant portion of the fleet should remain in Hawaii to protect the West Coast, while others, Marshall among them, advocated sending a larger number of ships to the North Atlantic to help Britain combat the U-boat threat. Marshall felt that if the US helped relieve the British in the North Atlantic, it would free up British naval power to reinforce Singapore and keep Japan in check.

A full year before Pearl Harbor, the Army Chief of Staff clearly stated his position in a Joint Planning Committee report dated 21 December 1940. Marshall's idea was to avoid war with Japan and Germany until America was better resourced to wage war on a global basis. Until then, any equipment and supplies America could spare would be given to Britain so that Churchill had the wherewithal to continue his defiant stance against Hitler. The Lend-Lease Act helped bring this about, and the US Navy did offer assistance against the U-boats, but the bulk of the fleet remained in Hawaii.

With the hindsight of Pearl Harbor and the devastating Japanese aerial attack that brought the US into the war in December 1941, one can argue that it might have been better if more US Navy ships had been sent to the Atlantic. Nineteen were sunk by the Japanese, including eight battleships, and 2,403 American servicemen were killed in a few hours. Taken completely by surprise, 188 US aircraft were destroyed on the ground. The disaster would have been even worse had not the three US aircraft carriers been at sea and out of range.

However, Marshall's hope that the British would be able to stem any Japanese advance in Asia proved fruitless, too. The Royal Navy suffered a disastrous blow when, just three days after the attack on Pearl Harbor, the *Prince of Wales*, on which Churchill had sailed across the Atlantic just a few months before, was sunk along with the battlecruiser *Repulse* off Kuantan, just north of Singapore. Along with Captain Leach, a third of the *Prince of Wales* crew who had sung hymns with their American friends off Newfoundland perished.

These were blows of unimaginable proportions and it took strong men to keep a steady hand on the tiller. President Roosevelt and Prime Minister Churchill were such men but so, too, was the new US Army Chief of Staff. Marshall became an integral part of the Allied team for the remainder of the war.

But there was still work to do and, for George Marshall, no rest. Given his previous experience in China, he was asked by the new occupant of the Oval Office, President Truman, to return there as his special envoy immediately following the end of hostilities. Truman was lavish in his praise and allowed himself a little hyperbole:

> George Marshall is the greatest man of World War Two. He managed to get along with President Roosevelt, Winston Churchill, the Congress, the Navy and the Joint Chiefs of Staff and made a grand record in China. When I asked him to go to be my special envoy in China, he merely said, 'Yes, Mr. President. I'll go.' No

argument, only patriotic action. If any man was entitled to balk and ask for a rest, he was.

Even on his return from China, Marshall still had no time for rest. After being appointed Secretary of State in 1947, he went to work architecting nothing less than the reconstruction of Europe under what became known as the Marshall Plan. It entailed the United States donating $13 billion to the sixteen European nations who signed up to the plan. Most of them had seen their cities partially or, in some cases, wholly turned to rubble by the war. Their economies were, if anything, in worse shape. Without American dollars pumped into their exchequers, it was feared that they would become easy pickings for Stalin and his expansionist Soviet regime. Therein lay the prime reason for American largesse. By rebuilding Europe, the Americans kept Communism at bay. But that was not the only threat. William Clayton, the Under Secretary of State for Economic Affairs warned that 'millions of people in the cities are slowly starving. If nothing is done about it there will be a revolution.' Clayton's words added impetus to the grandiose scheme Marshall, aided by George Kennan, the historian who was his Director of Policy Planning was hatching. The task was daunting, to say the least, but General Marshall was in his element. Strategic planning was what he did and the Marshall Plan was his masterpiece.

Chapter 11

Freeman and Beaverbrook: A Turbulent Partnership

The Royal Flying Corps (RFC) was barely two years old. Air warfare was in its infancy. The First World War itself was only just beginning. But as France and her British allies dug in on a line from the Channel coast down to Reims, some 90 miles north-east of Paris, the advantage of being able to photograph enemy positions became immediately apparent.

Evidently ignoring orders that two pilots, presumably because of their scarcity, should not fly together in the RFC's rickety biplanes, Lieutenant Wilfrid Freeman and Lieutenant Dawes took off on 12 September 1914 on a photographic reconnaissance mission across the River Aisne where one of the first major battles of the war was just beginning.

Soon after Freeman and Dawes had spotted some German batteries just north of the river, their plane began to shake. The vibration soon became so bad that Freeman opted to crash land in a field before it fell apart. The two airmen then set off to try and walk back to the British lines, eight miles away. It took them two days, partially because a dense fog descended on the area just as they were locating the River Aisne, across which they had to swim. Their jubilation at finally making it back to base was short lived. Instead of congratulations, Freeman received a dressing down from the commanding officer for having taken another pilot with him instead of a navigator.

With hindsight, it was a good thing Freeman survived the incident for, had he not, the Battle of Britain, 26 years later, might not have been won, and Britain would have lost the Second World War. By then the young lieutenant had risen to the position of Air Vice Marshal of the Royal Air Force, which been formed by the merger of the RFC and the Royal Naval Air Service in 1918, and was the main instigator, along with Lord

Beaverbrook, of getting sufficient numbers of planes off the production line to challenge, and ultimately defeat, Reichsmarschall Hermann Göring's Luftwaffe.

Despite his faux pas at the Aisnes, Freeman emerged from the First World War with credit, having been awarded the Military Cross on 27 March 1915 when, with bullets perforating his propeller, he located some vital German battery sites and was able to pass on their location to the British artillery.

It was clear, from then on, that Wilfrid Freeman's star was on the rise and rapid promotion followed. He was appointed Commandant of the Central Flying School in 1925 and five years later took charge of RAF operations in Transjordan and Palestine.

But it was in 1936, the same year that an aeronautical engineer called R.J. Mitchell was getting his Supermarine Spitfire into the air, that Freeman started to make a real impact on Britain's ability to build an air force capable of challenging the Luftwaffe. He was appointed Director of Operations and Air Intelligence which soon turned out to be a pivotal job as the threat from Germany became clearer with every passing month. Incredibly, the RAF did not have a fighter squadron with monoplane aircraft when he took over.

Happily, there were senior RAF officers who were prepared to listen to the dire warnings of a sidelined backbencher called Winston Churchill and, after Hitler had bragged to the Foreign Secretary, Sir John Simon, that the Luftwaffe had gained numerical parity in the number of aircraft it had built and would soon also equal that of France, even members of Stanley Baldwin's National Government started to take notice. Freeman, soon to be joined in a somewhat unholy alliance with the tempestuous Canadian press magnate Lord Beaverbrook, was given the go-ahead to start producing aircraft at the required rate.

There were many choices to be made as to exactly what was required and, more than anyone, it was Wilfrid Freeman who made the right ones. Apart from the Spitfire, he authorized production of its stablemate, the Hawker Hurricane, the De Havilland Mosquito fighter-bomber and the Lancaster, the heavy bomber which was used to deliver terrible retribution on German cities in the later years of the war. In addition, Freeman played a leading role in replacing the original engine on the American P-51 Mustang fighter with the Rolls-Royce Merlin.

With his ability to work with designers and get things done at a faster rate than the normal bureaucratic machine would allow, one can only speculate what more could have been achieved had he been given the opportunity to work with R.J. Mitchell, who died of cancer in 1937.

An acerbic genius who spent most of his career designing flying boats from his base in Southampton, Mitchell was evidently a man who spoke his mind. Once the RAF had accepted his plans for the Supermarine fighter plane – the initial order in 1936 was for 310 to be built – he was told that it would be called the Spitfire. His reaction was curt: 'Just the sort of bloody silly name they would choose,' he said. Had Mitchell lived to hear the accolades his creation received from the pilots who flew it in the Battle of Britain he might, just possibly, have taken a gentler view.

Once Churchill was brought back into the government – initially as First Lord of the Admiralty on the declaration of war and then of course as Prime Minister in 1940 – the urgency increased and life in the engine room of war production became fraught as Lord Beaverbrook, bounced between the Ministry of Supply and Aircraft Production, clashed frequently with Freeman and Sir Charles Craven, the two experts given leadership of the Ministry of Aircraft Production (MAP) which Churchill had created as soon as he took control of the war effort. Craven, a well-known businessman, had been managing director of Vickers-Armstrongs, a huge manufacturer of ships, tanks and machine guns as well as aircraft. He and Freeman knew each other well, having worked together in the mid-1930s on the development of the medium-range Wellington bomber which would become the RAF's workhorse bomber and the only British plane manufactured continuously throughout the Second World War.

One of Freeman's early goals was to design a faster and longer-ranged bomber. Only a few years before the outbreak of war, the top two British bombers were the Hayford and the Hendon and their speed was no more than 130 to 150 miles per hour. Apart from design flaws which made them slow, they also carried bomb loads of only 2,500lbs compared with the 10,000lbs that the heavy bombers could manage. In effect Freeman focused on the concept of mass-producing planes that were holistically suited for the British military effort. A premium was put on planes which could be easily manufactured, with weight, speed, range and crew requirements all vital factors.

Freeman's technical eye for detail and personal flying experience ensured that the machines were designed with all the required expertise. But it was Lord Beaverbrook who reaped almost all the credit for getting them built at all.

Born Max Aitken, in New Brunswick, Canada, this short, pugnacious personality immigrated to Britain after making an early fortune and quickly thrust himself into local politics, getting elected to Parliament in 1910. He met Churchill a year later and the pair developed a tempestuous relationship which somehow survived their frequent and heated political arguments. But such was Churchill's admiration of Beaverbrook's ability to crash through bureaucratic barriers that he even overlooked the Canadian's short-lived alliance with Chamberlain over Munich when appointing him to the newly-created MAP within days of becoming Prime Minister.

Once installed, the Beaver's bite ensured that he made many enemies as he set seemingly unrealistic targets for aircraft manufacture. The fact that most of them were achieved was certainly to his credit, but it couldn't have been achieved without Freeman. Little is documented of their personal relationship, but it must have been fraught at best, and Beaverbrook was in the habit of resigning before being brought to heel when the Prime Minister simply ignored each resignation as just another of the Beaver's tantrums.

It is clear from the amount of time they spent together socially at No. 10 and Chequers in those early moments of the war that Churchill drew strength from Beaverbrook's grinning, upbeat and frequently devious personality. 'Some people take drugs,' Churchill was quoted as saying. 'I take Max.' Clementine couldn't stand the man. She found him loud and vulgar and was eventually given to writing to her husband in remarkably explicit terms. 'Try ridding yourself of this microbe which some people fear is in your blood.' Churchill had no intention of doing any such thing, and it was a very good that he didn't. Beaverbrook got things done.

And done with the required speed. Cracking the whip and cutting through much of the bureaucratic undergrowth that had made pro-duction so slow as the war had loomed in 1938–9, Beaverbrook and Freeman, in tandem with an ailing Craven, oversaw the production of 1,700 aircraft at the rate of approximately 400 per month during the summer of 1940, as Spitfires and Hurricanes were falling from the sky during the height of the Battle of Britain. Given the circumstances, this rate of production was nothing short of heroic. With so many men from companies like Vickers-Armstrongs called up into the armed forces, it was the moment Britain's female population rolled up their sleeves, donned their headscarves and proved their worth on the assembly lines.

Like the vast majority of the country, they were inspired by the words echoing from their wireless sets as Churchill's speeches galvanized a beleaguered nation. In the midst of some of the darkest hours, the Prime Minister was indomitable: 'We must thank God that we have been allowed, each of us according to our stations, to play a part in making these days memorable in the history of our race.'

So everyone played their part, and today historians view the achievements in aircraft production in the early months of the war as the key element in Britain's survival of the Nazi challenge. Lord Beaverbrook's robust energy and determination, coupled with the cool expertise of Freeman and Craven, ensured that the RAF pilots, navigators and gunners had enough machines at their disposal to meet that challenge and overcome it. Their availability was the difference between victory and defeat.

Craven's ill health did not allow him to witness the fruits of their labour, and he died in 1944. Freeman, in the meantime, had been singled out by Churchill as one of his most important advisers, and, after Harry Hopkins, in his go-between role, had worked out the final plans for the Newfoundland rendezvous for President Roosevelt, it was no surprise to see the name of Air Vice Marshal Wilfrid Freeman amongst the small coterie of senior military commanders who were to set sail with him on the *Prince of Wales*. Hopkins was instrumental in getting approval from both sides as to the make-up of the personnel attending to both FDR and Churchill. The initial idea was to have only a small number of individuals meet at Newfoundland but Winston, wanting to be as well prepared as possible for what he saw as a crucial 'getting to know you' meeting with the President of the United States, argued for a larger attendance. As a result the First Sea Lord, Admiral Dudley Pound, Chief of the Imperial General Staff, General Sir John Dill, Under Secretary of State for Foreign Affairs, Sir Alexander Cadogan, and two War Cabinet secretaries, Colonel L.C. Hollis and Lieutenant Colonel E.I.C Jacob as well as Freeman were included in the party. There were others, including Churchill's trusted personal bodyguard, Inspector W.H. Thompson.

Lord Beaverbrook, who was already in the States at Churchill's behest, joined in the discussions once they got under way aboard the *Augusta* (which are detailed elsewhere) and was then sent back to Washington DC to further investigate what the United States was actually able to come up with in terms of aircraft and munitions. It transpired that the Americans had underestimated Britain's need and that Britain had overestimated America's capacity to produce the goods. Members of FDR's entourage were staggered when Freeman requested 6,000 more heavy bombers and 4,000 other aircraft. The Air Vice Marshal had been led to believe American hangars were bulging with new planes which was something of an exaggeration.[1]

---

1. Davis, *FDR – The War President*.

However, it is clear that Freeman's experience and expertise made him a valuable member of Churchill's inner circle. He may have remained in the shadows compared to Lord Beaverbrook, but there is little doubt that Freeman was the pivotal figure in ensuring that the RAF were sufficiently well equipped in the early years of the war. He was, as Ken Meyers wrote in the *Daily Telegraph* in 2000, 'The Hero that Time Forgot'.

Chapter 12

Sumner Welles

The US Secretary of State, Cordell Hull, was not among the fourteen officials invited to join President Roosevelt on the voyage to a secret meeting with the British Prime Minister at Placentia Bay. But his deputy, Sumner Welles, was.

Why? The question was contentious and logical. It was posed by Ensign Franklin D. Roosevelt, like his brother Elliott, who was at his father's side throughout the four days of historic meetings. FDR's reply was typically pragmatic. 'One, I trust him. Two, he doesn't argue with me. Three, he gets things done.'[1]

But there was a bit more to it than that. Firstly there was the family history between Welles and the Roosevelts. As a 12-year-old, Welles had been a pageboy at FDR's wedding to Eleanor in New York in 1905. They did not, however, develop any kind of friendship until 1923 by which time Welles had started his diplomatic career.

Secondly, one must take into account the relationship between Welles and his boss, Cordell Hull, once they both took up the senior positions at the State Department. Hull, whose father was a sharecropper in Tennessee, was born in a log cabin. Welles was raised in the high society of New York's Upper East Side and his family lived just a few blocks from the Roosevelts.

As they assumed their duties at State, it soon became clear who was going to do the bulk of the work. It is true that Hull's absences were often as a result of ill health but, as the *New York Times* wrote, 'Hull, never an expert at paper-shuffling, has long left the actual administration of the Department to his chief aide'.

Add to the mix the fact that FDR simply preferred Welles's company and it becomes even clearer why it was the No. 2 who got the No. 1 job

---

1. Benjamin Welles, p. 301.

as far as the Newfoundland meeting was concerned. As we have noted, FDR never shied away from befriending somewhat scabrous characters. Louis Howe was an obvious example and, although a very different personality in many ways, Welles became another. He was a heavy drinker whose career was ended in 1943 when he was forced to resign after allegations of an inappropriate sexual approach to two black Pullman Car porters while returning from Huntsville, Alabama. The President, who had been attending a funeral, was in the next carriage during the incident which Welles tried to dismiss as 'a couple of words when I'd had too much to drink'. But rumours of Welles's bisexual tendencies lingered.

Born in 1892, Welles was ten years younger than FDR but the first family connection came as a result of his wife, Eleanor, having a younger brother, Hall, who was one of Sumner Welles's closest friends. Also at the age of 12 Sumner was sent to attend Groton where he excelled academically in his first year, finishing at the top of his class. But as Sumner reached his teenage years his academic performance became skewed. One of his classmates noted that Sumner in course work was 'an extremist, at the top or bottom, seldom in between'.[2] Sumner was tall and lean but not much of an athlete nor was he well-liked by his classmates at Groton. He tended to keep to himself and was seen as distant and aloof. Welles in his final years at Groton developed only one meaningful friendship, Ives Gammel, who was from Rhode Island and one year younger. While most boys at Groton were focused on sports and adolescent camaraderie, Welles's interests were more cerebral and included all things French and a budding interest in opera. In June 1910 he graduated from Groton and, like fellow Grotonian FDR who had preceded him a decade earlier, was admitted to Harvard the subsequent autumn. Welles took advantage of the lifestyle freedoms and partying afforded a wealthy young man attending Harvard in the second decade of the twentieth century but otherwise his time at university was similar to his time at Groton. He was unpopular and ostracized by the athletes who he referred to as the 'Kings'. He wasn't asked to join a Club and was turned down when he applied for a position at the Harvard 'Crimson'. His grades in 1913 still reflected his academic 'extremist' tendencies; A in French, B in English and C or worse in all other courses including a D in his major, Fine Arts.[3] Despite this mediocre academic record, Welles was told at the end of the school year that he had completed the necessary academic requirements for a degree,

2. Benjamin Welles, pp. 11–12.
3. Ibid., p.24.

in part, because he was given credit for class work done while at Groton, and would graduate with his class in Harvard in 1914 without further requirements. This left Welles free to spend nine months travelling first to Paris and then to sail from Italy through the Suez Canal and explore Africa before committing to return to Paris in July 1914 to study and obtain a degree in architecture. But the outbreak of the First World War intervened. The assassination of Archduke Franz Ferdinand in Sarajevo in June 1914 which sparked the bloodiest conflict the world had seen to that date occurred midway through Welles's European sojourn and caused him to return to Boston.

Welles, now past the age of 21, had access to enough of his trust funds to establish a relatively opulent lifestyle for a young man living in Boston at this time. He took a flat at the intersection of Commonwealth Avenue and Berkeley Street and hired both a valet and a chauffeur. He also began to spend time with Esther Slater who in April 1915 would become his first wife. Upon his return from abroad Welles began to reflect on his career choice. Architecture attracted him but Paris even more so. He wished that combining the two would become an option but would his socially prominent New York family approve of him trying to establish himself in a demanding profession amid the temptations of such a seductive city towards the end of La Belle Epoch?

The reluctance of his family to approve of such a venture coupled with the imminent outbreak of the First World War scuppered any such notion and, more in keeping with what was expected of him, young Sumner turned to diplomacy. He was offered the chance to take the diplomatic exam which he did in June 1914 and passed with the very high score of 93. This impressive result led to him receiving a coveted posting to Tokyo where, accompanied by Esther, he served for two years. After Japan, Welles began to specialize in Latin American affairs. He became fluent in Spanish and was posted to Buenos Aires in 1919 and subsequently had assignments to monitor Cuban elections in 1920 and after that to review the situation in Haiti. The assignment in Haiti was focused on whether the United States should end its occupation of that country.[4] His third diplomatic assignment occurred when then Secretary of State Charles Even Hughes appointed Welles as a Special Commissioner to the Dominican Republic in 1923.

Despite his reserved personality, Welles was obviously blessed with the ability to make the most of his language skills and deal with a range

---

4. Michael J. Devine, American National Biography, Feb. 2000.

of different societies. Reserved or not, Welles did not seem to have any trouble striking up a friendship with President Roosevelt when FDR eventually began seeing his former pageboy socially during the time he was Assistant Secretary to the Navy and Welles was learning the diplomatic ropes in Washington before being sent to Japan. The two became friends and spent time together. According to Welles, 'I had just passed my examinations . . . was living in Washington and saw a great deal of him'. Years later Welles further reported, that at that time when he met with FDR he 'was enthusiastic, enjoyed dinners at the Chevy Chase Club and . . . a good time'.[5] The relationship between the two didn't really take a more serious hold until 1923 when Welles was serving as Special Commissioner to the Dominican Republic and offered to visit FDR. Unsurprisingly, Welles found that his friend had changed. Two years earlier FDR had suffered his attack of polio and was noticeably different, according to Welles. He reported:

> It was exactly as if all the trivialities in life had been burned [out] of him. A steel had entered his soul; he never made any reference to his tragedy. He was tremendously interested in Santo Domingo and reminded me that he had been there in 1918. We talked a lot about the country. He told me how absorbed he was by what was going on in the world . . . asking me to give him ideas. From then on, our contact was never broken.[6]

Welles's Latin America assignments continued and in 1923 he spent three whirlwind weeks in Honduras.[7] Of course each of these assignments was different but several themes could be generalized. Typically, when a diplomatic crisis occurred, the immediate concern was the safety of Americans and their interests in that nation. Welles's task was to protect and stabilize which he did with great skill and commitment as well as, in some cases, putting himself in harm's way to negotiate and interact with the local players at the centre of the crisis. In each of his assignments he was successful and received recognition and complements from the highest levels of the US Government including the State Department and members of Congress. In March 1924, elections were held in the Dominican Republic with high voter turnout. Most importantly the atmosphere, for which Welles could take some credit, was such that

---

5. Benjamin Welles, p. 123.
6. Ibid.
7. Ibid., p. 102.

the loser congratulated the winner and promised to support the new government. Welles received a cable from Secretary of State Charles Even Hughes citing 'the splendid work you have performed, not only in bringing about . . . elections in Santo Domingo, but in having [them] conducted in a thoroughly satisfactory manner'.[8]

Much to Welles surprise, less than 18 months later in July 1925 Frank Billings Kellogg, then Secretary of State, called Welles to tell him that President Coolidge had asked him to resign from his post and from the diplomatic service. At the time there were no reasons given and, for the most part, Coolidge's sudden decision remained a mystery. One likely explanation is that in October 1923, Welles's wife Esther filed for divorce on the grounds of desertion.[9] Since 1921 Welles had been involved with another woman, Mathilde Townsend Gerry who was unhappily married to Senator Peter Goelet Gerry. Mathilde was a very wealthy women in her own right whose father had been President of the Erie Railroad. She was also eight years older than Welles and a very flamboyant personality with a large social footprint. In June 1924 she asked Welles to attended the Democratic Convention to be held in New York City. President Coolidge was a Republican and the couple's attendance surely caught his and other Senate Republicans' attention. Mathilde was divorced in the early in 1925 and she and Sumner were married in June 1925. Welles's phone call with Kellogg was in July. In short, Welles marriage to an older, wealthy, socially prominent divorcee may have proved too much for the socially conservative Republican Coolidge or Senator Gerry's friends in the US Senate.

Still in his early thirties Welles found himself with time on his hands. He decided to write a book called *Naboth's Vineyard* which referred to the biblical story of King Ahab who had Naboth stoned to death because he wouldn't sell the King his vineyard. It was an allegorical story for his namesake and historical family relation, Charles Sumner, blocking President Grant's desire to acquire the Dominican Republic as a naval base.[10] After that he joined the Council on Foreign Relations, the Academy of Political Science and Foreign Policy Association. He continued to stay current with friends and leaders in Latin America and when possible to spend time with FDR and join his inner circle. Welles befriended FDR's somewhat eccentric aide, Louis Howe, and worked hard to become one of FDR's confidants with respect to setting foreign policy. The relationship

---

8. Benjamin Welles, p. 101.

9. Ibid., p. 97.

10. Ibid., p. 121.

strengthened over the ensuing years and when FDR gave his acceptance speech at the 1932 Democratic Convention in Chicago, Welles and his wife Maltilde were invited to sit in the box with Eleanor.

Upon FDR's election to the Presidency, Welles was appointed Assistant Secretary of State for Latin American Affairs. In the ensuing years Welles worked closely with FDR and his inner team on many matters relating to Latin America while Cordell Hull was Secretary of State. Hull was a Senator from Tennessee who was known, for among other things being a proponent of the 'Good Neighbor Policy,' first proposed during Woodrow Wilson's Presidency but implemented during FDR's term in office. The policy promised that the United States would not interfere in the affairs of Latin American countries and would be a good neighbour. Hull shared this idea and was supportive of its implementation as was Welles but that did not prevent a personality clash. While Hull and Welles served the same President and shared common values, Hull was seen as a poor manager of the State Department and was away from work for extended periods of time because of lifelong struggle with sarcoidosis, often mistaken for a form of tuberculous. Hull was also wary of Welles relationship and friendship with FDR. Despite Hull's reluctance, FDR saw to it that in 1937 Welles was promoted to Under Secretary of State which at that time was the second in command at the State Department, a position, as we have seen, he continued to hold at the time of the Atlantic Conference in August 1941. Coincidently, Hull had just returned to work after a period of absence for medical reasons only several days before the Atlantic Conference was to begin. As we have mentioned at the start of this chapter, FDR had his reasons for inviting Welles but Hull was offered no explanation. In fact, to his great discontent, he was not even let in on the secret voyage until it was well under way.

From the moment FDR and Churchill set the Atlantic Conference in motion by greeting each other on the deck of the *Augusta* on 9 August, Welles became an integral part of the meetings that followed even though there were times when he did not make the top table. When FDR, Churchill and Harry Hopkins withdrew to the President's quarters for lunch, other members of the British and American delegations were served a US Navy cold-plate meal in the wardroom of the *Augusta*. Sir Alexander Cadogan, Under Secretary at the Foreign office and Welles's British counterpart to the Atlantic Conference, recorded in his diary how 'very unsatisfactory' he found the lunch offered. After this less-than-hospitable beginning Welles and Cadogan left the *Augusta* and boarded Welles's ship the *Tuscaloosa* where they could organize the agenda for the upcoming conference in the privacy of Welles's quarters. One of the first things Welles asked Cadogan when they were alone concerned whether the British had any secret agreements that the United States needed to know about. There was a concern on the American side over agreements they suspected Britain might have entered into at the conclusion of the First World War had led to much of the bitterness, hardship and confusion, leading eventually to the creation of Nazi Germany. The terms of the Versailles Treat in 1919 had certainly been harsh on Germany and, without doubt, led to the rise of Hitler. But Welles was happy to be assured by Cadogan that Britain had not taken any further punitive action against the defeated nation.

A major topic of conversation between Welles and Cadogan in their first meeting aboard the *Tuscaloosa* was what message to send the Japanese. Just weeks prior to the Atlantic Conference, Japan had occupied French Indochina which was seen as a direct threat to US interests in the Philippines and British interests in the Far East and Dutch East Indies. Cadogan and Welles both indicated that their respective leaders saw the need for a strongly worded message of displeasure delivered to Japan for its imperialist actions and the drafting of that message would be included in the agenda of the Conference.[11] Their concern about the imperialistic actions of the Japanese was taken from both FDR and Churchill who saw the issue of what to do about Japan as one of the most important reasons for their meeting at sea. When the two leaders and their attendees met for dinner the first night of the Conference on 9 August the conversation initially cantered on the Japan issue. But after the Japanese problems were discussed, Prime Minister Churchill brought up the need for a joint communication on a broader topic to be issued at the end of the Conference. The next morning Sir Alexander handed Sumner a copy of the joint communication which has hence forth been referred to as the first draft of the Atlantic Charter.

Welles has reported that before leaving Washington for the meeting with Churchill, FDR

> had told me some detail how he thought the approaching meeting with the British Prime Minister should be utilized to hold hope out to the enslaved peoples of the world. The English-speaking democracies both stood for the principles of freedom and justice. They should bind themselves now to establish at

---

11. Sumner Welles, p. 6.

the conclusion of the was a new world order based upon these principles.[12]

Welles took the draft that Sir Alexander had given him and prepared a second draft that he then shared with FDR. The President and Welles considered and discussed every word. According to Welles, FDR then instructed Welles to prepare a third draft 'containing the changes and amendments he [FDR] had indicated as well as any further provisions, along the general lines we had been discussing, which might seem desirable to me'.[13] When FDR, Churchill, Hopkins, Cadogan and Welles met at 11.00 a.m. on the *Augusta* on 11 August they worked from Welles's third draft. Cadogan and Welles jointly prepared the fourth draft which, with minor changes to phraseology, became the final version. It was the final item agreed to by FDR and Churchill at their last meeting of the Conference on 12 August and issued as a joint declaration after being telegraphed to London. Soon after it became known as the Atlantic Charter.

---

12. Sumner Welles, p. 6.
13. Ibid., p. 10.

Chapter 13

Sir Alexander Cadogan

Interrupting an Englishman in the middle of his breakfast is generally considered an imprudent move, not least when the meal is being enjoyed in the admiral's cabin on one of His Majesty's warships. However, there was never a second's doubt that the eggs and bacon would have to wait – congeal if necessary – when Sir Alexander Cadogan realized that the raised voice on deck of the *Prince of Wales* was that of the Prime Minister demanding his attention.

Since their arrival at Placentia Bay the previous day (Saturday, 9 August 1941) it had become clear from their initial meetings that President Roosevelt was set on agreeing to some form of joint declaration with the British Prime Minister and that an initial draft to that effect needed to be worked on immediately. The immediacy was not lost on Cadogan who later wrote of the incident thus: 'I hadn't quite finished my eggs and bacon, but I pulled a sheet of notepaper out of the stationary rack before me and began to write.' And so, from these initials scratchings, copied probably from the scraps of paper on which FDR and Churchill had already laid down some thoughts, what became known as the Atlantic Charter was born.

Cadogan went on to describe his observations, interactions and contributions to the drafting of the Atlantic Charter in his diaries which have been expertly edited by David Dilks. Cadogan provides a description of the early stages of drafting the Atlantic Charter:

> As regards to the 'joint declaration' which was to become the Atlantic Charter, the preamble and the first three articles stand now as I drafted them (actually the first two and a half). I had a skeleton of some of the remaining five articles, but these subsequently came in for a good deal of discussion (they were not easy to formulate) and were consequently modified, expanded and re-written.

Cadogan had to work fast because the Church Service of which we have written in an earlier chapter was due to start at 11.00 a.m. and Churchill had made it clear he wanted something in his hand to give to the President when he boarded the *Prince of Wales* for the Service. So Cadogan's notes were hurriedly typed out by the stenographer Patrick Kinna and handed to Churchill who apparently expressed 'general but not very enthusiastic approval'. Cadogan describes how, when they went up on deck, 'The PM thrust my little drafts into a side pocket of his jacket, and in the course of their conversation after the Service I saw the PM draw them out and pass them rather tentatively to the President'.

For the next 48 hours the document was discussed, argued over, nit-picked and generally knocked into shape by Cadogan and his co-author for this historic task, Sumner Welles. As personalities, the pair were well suited to the demands of the job, both emanating from upper class backgrounds, albeit on opposite sides of the Atlantic, and both each other's equal intellectually. Neither would ever be known as the life and soul of the party (at least not when Welles was sober) but both, dedicated as they were to their countries' cause, knew how to tackle at speed a difficult assignment at the behest of demanding masters. Neither was lacking in practice.

Cadogan's impressive family history suggested that some form of public service was always on the cards. The first Earl Cadogan won his spurs at the Battle of Blenheim in 1704 and from then on his descendants became active members of the nation's upper class establishment. Buying land in what was then a suburb of London seemed like a good idea and it turned out to be spectacularly so. Anyone leaving the back entrance to Harrods will walk through the red-brick buildings that make Pont Street so distinctive and on down Sloane Street to Sloane Square, passing Cadogan Square.

The 93-acre Cadogan Estate came into being around 1712 as a result of the 2nd Earl Cadogan marrying Elizabeth Sloane, the daughter of the explorer and physician Sir Hans Sloane, who began the process by buying the Manor of Chelsea. So the Estate not only encompasses the iconic King's Road but also stretches down to the Embankment. In size the Estate is second only to the Duke of Westminster's.

For historians the Cadogan Estate is a treasure trove. The blue plaques on the side of buildings denoting the former residency of famous artists, actors and politicians abound. Jane Austen wrote *Pride and Prejudice* while living on Sloane Street while Oscar Wilde was arrested while staying at the Cadogan Hotel in April 1895 although he had mostly resided in Tite Street. For two years Mark Twain had a house down the road at Tedworth Square.

Alexander Cadogan was the last of nine children when he was born nearby on 25 November 1884. The family's prominence was advanced when his father, George Cadogan, became the first Mayor of Chelsea in 1900 – a position which no longer exists. Given the carnage that followed, the Cadogans were, perhaps, fortunate to lose only one of seven male members of that generation, William, in the First World War.

By then the baby of the family was growing up. Alexander followed a familiar educational path – Eton and Balliol College, Oxford where he read History; the perfect preparation for a career in diplomacy. Despite a reserved demeanour, Alexander was not above instigating the occasional college prank and turned out for a less than first-class cricket team which called itself The Erratics. The name may have fitted Cadogan as a cricketer but he was far from that professionally as he set forth on a career that was marked by a fastidious attention to detail. By the time he joined the Foreign Service in 1908, the young Cadogan had become known as a terse and taciturn character, making few friends but impressing all with his work ethic and intelligence.

His first diplomatic postings took him to Constantinople (now Istanbul) and Vienna and he was also present in a junior capacity with Lloyd George's British delegation at the Paris Peace Conference in 1919. His work behind the scenes obviously caught the eye because he was selected to head up the League of Nations section as President Wilson's brainchild started to come into existence. Disarmament eventually became the major topic of conversation among those assigned to make the League of Nations a viable reality and Cadogan, in a paper he wrote in 1927, made the logical point that nations would never give up their arms unless they felt secure. Most didn't, so a Disarmament Conference was called in Geneva in 1932.

It did not start well as far as the British delegation was concerned. The Prime Minister, Ramsay MacDonald, was unwell and the Foreign Secretary Sir John Simon could not leave London as Japan's attack on Shanghai had created a Far East crisis at that precise moment. So J.H. Thomas, a Labour member in McDonald's Coalition Government of the early 1930s who was Colonial Secretary, was sent out to Geneva where he was met by Cadogan at the station. On being told that he needed to attend a Service of Dedication and listen to Archbishop Temple preach, Thomas' immediate reaction was: 'Oh, 'ell. Do I 'ave to go?'

It was clear from this opening remark that Thomas, who began life as a cleaner on the railways, did not speak in the sonorous tones used by the vast majority of Cadogan's acquaintances at Westminster. Given his outward persona one might have expected the aristocrat to recoil. Far from it. Proving himself to be anything but a snob, Cadogan developed a liking for 'Jimmy', as he was known to his trade union colleagues, and enjoyed his refreshingly honest company.

Even with Sir John Simon and Anthony Eden arriving as reinforcements, Britain, despite persistent American support, could not mount enough impetus to push the Conference forward. In retrospect, Simon's pessimism over the chances of nations giving up their arms was fully justified. Germany, having withdrawn from the proceedings early on, was lured back but inevitably walked out again in 1933. Why should anyone have been surprised? Disarmament? Hitler must have been sniggering throughout the entire proceedings. It was the French who ended the farce in June 1934 by refusing to continue in view of the continued rise in German spending on armaments. France, of all countries, was never going to cut back on military hardware without reciprocity from her aggressive neighbour.

Cadogan had tried to remain as optimistic as possible and received praise from Eden, who would eventually become his boss at the Foreign Office. 'Alexander carried out his thankless task with a rare blend of intelligence, sensibility and patience,' Eden was quoted as saying.

As we learn from Cadogan's diaries, Alexander tried for as long as he felt able to maintain some hope that Hitler could be contained and reasoned with. Later in the decade he was very much with Neville Chamberlain as the Conservative Prime Minister favoured a policy of appeasement with the Nazi Dictator. But Cadogan was nothing if not a realist and, as his constant cries for getting Hitler to reveal his true plans went unanswered, his belief in a peaceful outcome to the crisis that was engulfing Europe began to fade.

For a while Cadogan had to concentrate on another theatre of concern. Having enhanced his reputation in Geneva despite the overall lack of success, Cadogan was sent to Peking, as it was known in that era, as the British Minister in charge of the Legation. It was a major promotion and it was with some pride that he took his wife – Theodosia whom he had married in 1912 – and their three daughters off to Asia in 1934. He knew he would be arriving in China at a critical moment of that nation's long history as Japan had been sabre-rattling for years and invasion seemed imminent. But for the two years Cadogan remained in Peking, nothing happened.

At the time he wrote: 'It is rather like the situation in Europe for the decade before the [First World] War. Everyone knew that it MUST come: No one could tell WHEN. Germany would, we knew, choose her own time. Japan must explode in one way or another one of these days: no one knows when . . . it will be Japan who will pull the trigger.'

Five years later, he would be proved tragically correct when Japan attacked Pearl Harbor but, in the meantime, Cadogan was charged with keeping close watch on China's complicated political landscape. His task was not eased by the fact that Chiang Kai-Shek was having to deal with the threat within his own borders – that of the murderous Communist leader Mao Zedong who was beginning to gather considerable support. Chiang, no less ruthless, put down various rebellions, killing hundreds of thousands in the process.

Cadogan's task was not made any easier by the fact that China's government at the time preferred Nanking to Peking while Chiang refused to move his own headquarters from Nanchang. Cadogan travelled there to meet him and had to convey the delicate message that, while Britain supported China, Chiang should not expect material or military support. No fool, Chiang realized he needed all the friends he could get and received the British minister cordially.

With his family settling into their luxurious house in Peking with all the trappings of colonial comfort, the sudden invitation from Anthony Eden, newly appointed Secretary of State at the Foreign Office, to return to London in 1936 was only partially welcome. Cadogan felt he had more to offer in China but he knew it would be foolish to turn down a position as joint Deputy Under Secretary that he felt, rightly, could lead to Permanent Under Secretary, effectively Britain's No. 2 diplomat.

So he returned to Whitehall and began the main work of his life – counselling, shepherding and often consoling two of Britain's most important political figures of the next ten years – Eden and the man who came close to succeeding Neville Chamberlain in 1940, Lord Halifax. Both had long spells as Foreign Secretary during that tumultuous and often desperate time and Cadogan was never far their side. The position, inevitably, led to almost daily contact with Chamberlain, whom he continued to admire, and, later, Winston Churchill.

Happily for anyone who likes to know what goes on behind the mask of an expressionless and seemingly imperturbable British civil servant, Cadogan revealed what he was really like in his Diaries. On duty, the mask never slipped. If one needed a stiff upper lip, Cadogan was your man.

But almost every night, Cadogan found time to scrawl down a few lines that revealed the emotions of a much less rigid character. His writings were less detailed & descriptive than those, for instance, of John Colville, but did not lack opinion. On an almost weekly basis he railed against Sir Robert Vansittart, the man he would replace as Permanent Under Secretary in 1937 ('much too emotional') and for most members of the House of Commons he had little but contempt.

The popular television series *Yes, Minister* offered humorous insight into the way civil servants viewed (and tried to control) the elected ministers they worked for but not many politicians would see the humour in one exasperated entry of Cadogan's Diaries. 'Silly Bladders!', he wrote. 'Self advertising, irresponsible nincompoops. How I hate Members of Parliament! They embody everything that my training has taught me to eschew – ambition, prejudice, dishonesty, self-seeking, light hearted irresponsibility, black hearted mendacity.' If that constituted getting something off one's chest, Cadogan admitted it in a subsequent paragraph. 'Feeling better tonight, after dinner and after the above outburst.'

Cadogan retained the ability to turn away from the affairs of the Foreign Office, even at the most difficult of times, and change the subject on the golf course if anyone tried to talk 'shop'. To quote David Dilks, 'Though unclubbable, he was by no means unsociable.' One could add, also, that his observations were not without a certain humour. While enjoying small dinner parties, he found cocktail party small talk tested his patience to its limits. Describing one, he wrote, 'The atmosphere was terrible: one lady fainted full length on the floor and, seeing her lying there, I envied her and wished I had thought of the same thing myself.'

On deck he was forever upright, trying to guide his superiors through the choppy waters and not so infrequent storms that blew up in those fraught years leading to Hitler's war. Thus the entry of 21 September 1938, at the time the Nazi machine was overrunning Czechoslovakia.

> As I left the house to pick up Halifax [then Foreign Secretary] had telegram saying Benes [Czech Prime Minister] had capitulated. Further discussion as to how PM [Chamberlain] should conduct conversation. He seems agreed that he can't go further than he has done and he can't champion Poles and Hungarians. This is ESSENTIAL. Lunched at home. Cabinet at 3.00 p.m. Joe Kennedy [US Ambassador] at 3.30 and I did what I could. Press campaign is developing now here and in the US against 'Betrayal of Czechoslovakia'. That inevitable and must be faced. HOW much courage is needed to be a coward . . . How I realise these scrappy notes give no idea of what I feel. We must go on being cowards

up to our limit, but NOT BEYOND. I have tried to impress this. But what of the future?

This passage of the Diaries reflects accurately the stresses Cadogan was under during the build-up to war and how he managed to keep himself sane by describing in detail on his way home what kind of flowers the gardeners were planting in St James' Park. Later, when he moved his wife and children to a cottage in Sussex, he wrote with relief of the gardening chores he undertook and the long country walks around Rye that he enjoyed with Theodosia to whom he remained devoted.

But the events immediately after the fall of Czechoslovakia only got worse as he relates on Saturday, 24 September.

> Hitler's memo now in. It's awful. A week ago when we moved (or were pushed) from autonomy to cession, many of us found great difficulty in the idea of ceding people to Nazi Germany. We salved our consciences (at least I did) by stipulating that it must be an 'orderly' cession – ie under international supervision. Now Hitler says he must march into the whole area AT ONCE (to keep order!) . . .This is throwing away every last safeguard we had. PM is transmitting this 'proposal' to Prague. . . . Meeting of 'Inner Cabinet' at 3.30 and PM made his report to us. I was completely horrified – he was quite calmly for total surrender. More horrified still to find that Hitler has evidently hypnotized him to a point.

If Cadogan had been an appeaser till then, Chamberlain caving into Hitler over Czechoslovakia seemed to be a turning point. Appalled at the attitude of the Prime Minister and Lord Halifax he allowed the mask to slip as he drove his boss home, and gave his Lordship a piece of his mind.

Resuming the Diary, he wrote

> I KNOW there is a shattering telegraph from Eric Phipps [Britain's Ambassador in Paris]; I KNOW we and they are in no condition to fight; but I'd rather be beat than dishonoured. How can we look any foreigner in the face after this? How can we hold Egypt, India and the rest? Above all, IF we have to capitulate, let's be honest. Let's say we're caught napping; that we can't fight now but that we remain true to our principles, put ourselves straight in war conditions and REARM. DON'T, above all, let us pretend that Hitler's plan is a GOOD one! I've never had such a shattering day, or been so depressed and dispirited. I can only hope for a revolt in the Cabinet and Parliament.

His closing thought that night was a question: 'What WILL be written on the remaining pages of this Diary?'

The answer came from the man who, 18 months later, would replace the faltering Chamberlain. 'Blood, toil, tears and sweat' was what Winston Churchill had to offer the British people and Cadogan was not alone in respecting his honesty. Churchill had not been Cadogan's choice to lead the country in its hour of greatest peril, not least because Halifax was the only alternative and he had grown to like the giant aristocrat who towered over him by almost a foot.

As we have noted in the Churchill chapters, Winston could be the most maddening taskmaster and it took Cadogan a while to come to terms not merely with his eccentricities but with the fact that his energy and spirit set him apart from any other statesman he had ever served. Heeding Halifax's advice, Cadogan never allowed Churchill to bully him and through the long months and years they spent in each other's company, the mutual respect only grew.

It was no surprise when the Prime Minister chose his Permanent Under Secretary at the Foreign Office to be one of the favoured few picked for the journey to Newfoundland in 1941, nor that Cadogan was able to work in tandem with Sumner Welles to produce the required document under such demanding conditions. It did not go unnoticed. In his Diary, Cadogan related an incident which occurred on the final day at Placentia Bay when he took the draft telegrams of the Atlantic Charter to Churchill for his approval.

'As I entered the Admiral's cabin he lowered the paper in his hand, took off his spectacles and said, "Thank God I brought you with me." The simplicity of the seven-word tribute and his manner of saying it were proof of its sincerity and I was deeply moved and puffed up with great pride.'

It was a succinct and telling accolade delivered by a great man to one of Britain's greatest Civil Servants and, on Churchill's death in 1965, Cadogan was able to reciprocate. 'What a privilege it has been,' he recorded when asked for a tribute, 'to have served him during his grandest period and to have won, as I dare to think that I did, some regard and even affection from him.'.[1]

---

1. Alexander Cadogan had been knighted in 1941 and became known as Sir Alec. Having served at the Foreign Office throughout the war, Sir Alec was appointed by Clement Atlee, the new Labour Prime Minister, to be Britain's first Permanent Representative at the United Nations in New York. He and his wife entertained fulsomely at their Connecticut home from 1946 to 1950

Chapter 14

Randolph Churchill

Temper is a terrible thing. It can ruin a man's reputation. It certainly ruined Randolph Churchill's. He carried it like a hand grenade, concealed deep inside his soul, the pin all too ready to be pulled at the slightest provocation, curses and accusations exploding across a room or a dinner table like shrapnel, leaving friendships in shreds.

Tragically, it was what defined him. The savagery of his behaviour lingers longer than the brilliance of his mind, the talent of his pen or his brave, uncompromising determination to seek out and state the truth.

'Lies are so dull,' he told Michael Foot, his dear friend and political arch enemy. Maybe it was his relentless pursuit of the truth, a frequently hapless task when surrounded by politicians, and his refusal to sugar-coat his opinions which led him into a seemingly endless series of rows and confrontations.

At the time of Anthony Eden's premiership, of which Randolph was hugely critical, a profile commented, 'Randolph Churchill's personality seems fuelled by an apparently endless flow of truculence . . . Compulsive pugnacity has been the quickest escape route from Sir Winston's giant shadow.'

Ah, the father. It would be ridiculous to think that any son could make his way easily in the world with a father like Winston Churchill. Psychologists will tell you that sons of powerful men – be they prime ministers, business tycoons or sporting champions – will be faced with two unenviable choices. One would be to seek quiet pastures, devoid of ambition, far from the high-powered world inhabited by their father. The other, so filled with peril, would be to try and emulate him. This latter path is almost always doomed to failure. The son is not as big or strong or experienced as the father and will be crushed by the huge ego towering over him.

There are always exceptions, but successful men are much more likely to be driven by the tough, demanding love of a mother. It is easier because he is not trying to emulate her. All he wants is her approval and a comforting hug. Daddy's approval is so much more difficult to attain. Franklin Roosevelt's relationship with his ever-present mother, Sara, offers an example.

Yet, because of his exceptional talents, Randolph did frequently earn praise from Winston. When the pair of them toured the United States and Canada in 1929, Winston wrote this of his 17-year-old son, 'Randolph has taken a most intelligent interest in everything and is a remarkable critic and appreciator of the speeches I make and the people we meet.'

Perhaps Winston's effusive praise of his teenage son was prompted by the memory of his own father's refusal to acknowledge him as little more than a wastrel, incapable of doing anything constructive other than playing with toy soldiers. It was obvious that Winston was going to ensure that young Randolph suffered no such humiliation and, perhaps swinging the pendulum too far, he was accused by friends of being too soft on his rambunctious offspring.

Nevertheless, all seemed set fair for an excellent father-son relationship until, tragically, Winston failed to offer him even a hint of the affair his wife Pamela had embarked upon with the American advisor Averell Harriman while Randolph was serving in the Middle East during the Second World War. For reasons that were not adequately explained, the Prime Minister turned a blind eye to the embarrassing situation, which he must have known about because it was the talk of the town. On returning home, Randolph was, unsurprisingly, incensed, and the rows that followed between himself and his father led to his mother banning him from 10 Downing Street. Clementine felt, with good reason, that Winston had more than enough on his plate conducting the war without expending emotional energy on a cantankerous and hurtful family dispute.

Yet somehow the deep love the two men felt for each other prevented any permanent separation and, strangely, it was the father who proved the greater beneficiary of a willingness to keep their battered relationship intact.

As becomes clear on reading *His Father's Son*, a brilliant biography of his father by Winston Jr., Randolph was able to offer pertinent advice to his father prior to the rift and for many years afterwards. The catalogue of ways in which Britain's great war leader benefited from what his son had to offer is surprisingly long and, because of this, we have included him in this Actors section of the book despite him being the only one not have been present at the writing of the Atlantic Charter off Newfoundland.

It was, for instance, Randolph who first rang the alarm bells over Hitler when, already operating as a foreign correspondent for *The Sunday Graphic* at the age of 21 in 1932, he made this shrewd observation: 'Nearly all of Hitler's lieutenants fought in the last war. They burn for revenge. They are determined that Germany once more should have an army. I am sure once they have achieved it, they will not hesitate to use it.'

As the world knows, it was very soon afterwards that the House of Commons was bombarded with warnings of German rearmament and the threat posed by its charismatic Nazi leader from a largely disregarded backbencher called Winston S. Churchill. He had listened to his son and read his dispatches while also taking note of what was happening across the Channel when he had visited Germany himself during research for his biography of Marlborough. It was soon after this that his son had managed to get himself invited onto Hitler's plane as the yet-to-be-elected leader campaigned from city to city before descending on Berlin for a final rally attended by 120,000 people.

Randolph described the scene as a 'a mixture between an American football game and a boy-scout's jamboree, animated with the spirit of a revivalist meeting and conducted with the discipline of the Brigade of Guards'.

But the 21-year-old was not just content to present a factual account of what he saw. He also offered this sage assessment:

> Nothing is more foolish than to underestimate the intensely vital spirit that animates the Nazi movement. Hitler has no detailed policy. He has promised all things to all men. Many Germans say that he no longer wants power – that he is frightened of all the forces he has called into being. They say he does not want a majority and merely wishes to be part of a coalition. I do not believe this to be true.
>
> He is surrounded by a group of resolute, tough and vehement men who would never tolerate any backsliding from their leader. Nothing can long delay their arrival in power. Hitler will not betray them. But let us make no mistake about it. The success of the Nazi party sooner or later means war.

Obviously, Randolph was proved right, but it is interesting that he should have pinpointed Hitler's hesitancy; a hidden weakness in his character; a fear. All that has been forgotten, but one example of it came to light when, during Churchill's visit to Germany before the Nazi leader had been shored up by the legitimacy of an election, he ran scared from meeting the man who would prove to be his fatal enemy.

On arriving in Germany, Randolph had become friends with Ernst Hanfstaengl, a Harvard graduate who was a confidant of Hitler. When he became Hitler's press secretary, Hanfstaengl arranged for the young Englishman to join the Nazi campaign. Now another opportunity opened up. Winston, deep into his research of Marlborough and the battle of Blenheim, was staying overnight in Munich, accompanied by Clementine, Randolph and Sarah. Realizing what a great opportunity lay at hand, Randolph contacted Hanfstaengl to suggest a meeting. Putzi, as the Nazi press officer was known, needed no second bidding and, quoting from his own account from his memoirs, *Hitler: The Missing Years*, immediately tried to make it happen.

'I caught up with Hitler at the Brown House and burst into his room,' Putzi wrote. '"Herr Hitler," I said, "Mr. Churchill is in Munich and wants to meet you. This is a tremendous opportunity. They want me to bring you along to dinner at the Hotel Continental tonight." I could almost see the asbestos curtain drop down. "Um Gotteswillen, Hanfstaengl, don't they realize how busy I am? What on earth would I talk to him about?"'

Putzi did his best, citing all the subjects that might interest them both, but it was no use. 'My heart sank. Hitler produced a thousand excuses, as he always did when he was afraid of meeting someone, the uncertain bourgeois re-emerging.' What a damning insight into the man who would wreak such cruel havoc in the world. Poor Hanfstaengl tried one last time, catching Hitler saying goodbye to a friend in lobby of the very hotel where the Churchills were dining. 'What are you doing here?' Putzi almost screamed at his boss. 'Don't you realize they may well have seen you come and go? They will certainly learn from the hotel servants that you have been here! They are expecting you for coffee and will think this is a deliberate insult.'

But Hitler was unshaven and used that, as well as having to get up early in the morning, as another excuse and quickly walked out. It would be stretching the imagination to believe that a meeting between Churchill and Hitler over coffee in a Munich hotel in 1932 would have changed the history of the world – Winston, remember, did not even have a Cabinet post at the time – but the fact that it never came to pass was no fault of Randolph's and Putzi's. They tried.

With a prescience that has stood the test of hindsight and history, the writings of this fledgling international observer offer impressive evidence of Randolph's acute mind. On 19 September 1932, he wrote this in *The Daily Dispatch*:

There is a dynamic force in Germany today which will grow stronger the more it is repressed. The clash between the French desire for security and the German refusal to accept terms of a second class power – THERE is the peril of the next war. European statesmanship must concern itself with this topic above all others if we are to avoid universal annihilation . . . We are virtually committed to take one side or the other in the next war between France and Germany.

Both Winston and Randolph could, in the words of Winston Jnr in his book *His Father's Son*, be termed 'appeasers' at this stage as Hitler chafed at the bit, Mussolini watched like a hawk to see where Italy's best advantages lay and Russia and Japan brooded on the sidelines. Both father and son strongly opposed the continuing disarmament of France and Britain while, and at the same time wanted to see Germany's grievances addressed so as to avoid another conflict. Randolph favoured revising the Treaty of Versailles which, in the opinion of many perfectly sane Germans, had stripped the nation of its manhood, while his father was open to the idea of an actual alliance between Germany, France and England. That dream would only be realized more than a decade later after 20 million people had lost their lives.

None of these dangers were foreseen by the leading political figures of the day in Britain where anti-war sentiment was deeply embedded in the nation's psyche after the human catastrophe of the First World War. If Winston's speeches in Parliament or Randolph's warnings in his newspaper articles had been given anything but the shortest thrift, maybe, just maybe, the disasters that lay ahead could have been avoided or softened in their impact.

On 3 October 1932, Randolph had this to say in the *Sunday Dispatch*:

The world is tired of war. Despite this general and, I believe, increasing abhorrence of war there is a widespread realization today that if the world continues along anything like its present economic and political path war will be inevitable sooner or later . . .

Armaments today are the defence of civilization. That is a terrible but incontrovertible fact. Despite this, however, we are constantly told that it is countries such as Britain and the United States who should lead the world in disarmament and set an example to others. I pray that we shall not be deluded by these absurdities

Prayers were not enough, and it was only a few short years before Winston Churchill, brought into Neville Chamberlain's government in his old role of First Lord of the Admiralty, was finally listened to and, as Hitler's voracious appetite and intentions became clear, was installed as the wartime Prime Minister Britain so desperately needed.

But, prior to that, there had been the wilderness years during which time Churchill could count his political friends on one hand – his own Conservative Party scorned his warnings even more so than the Labour opposition – and he would have felt lonelier still had it not been for the burgeoning journalistic career of his bombastic, outspoken but always loyal son. Randolph might still only have been in his mid-twenties, but his voice, either through his pen or through his speeches on the stump as he tried, and failed, on numerous occasions to be elected to Parliament, was becoming impossible to ignore.

Public speaking came naturally to him, as became clear when he undertook a speaking tour of the United States and, on another visit in 1936, when he was asked, within a week of arrival, to address the nation through the medium of a CBS Radio broadcast. It was an opportunity Randolph grabbed with relish.

Opening with the question 'Will there be war in Europe?' the young Churchill went on to outline the devilish ambitions of Nazi Germany:

> The whole brain and manpower of this gifted and scientific race has been ceaselessly employed during the last four years in the most gigantic armament production the world has ever seen. Last year the United States spend $800 million upon national defence. Great Britain spent about $600 million. $4000 million was the amount expended by the German government. I wish I could accept the suave assurances of those who, visiting Germany for the Olympic Games and noticing trivial facts such as the absence of litter on the streets of Berlin, return to praise the demeanour and intentions of the Nazi Government. What is the point of trying to blind oneself to real facts?'

Explaining why England's hours of weakness was Europe's hour of danger, Randolph went on:

> Where will this process end? If the few remaining democracies in the world are unable to show a little more common sense and resolution in the face of impending disaster, they will assuredly be assailed from without or engulfed from within, one after

the other, by the hydra-headed Communist, Fascist or Nazi dictatorships which man has contrived for his own degradation and enslavement.

Reading the speech many years later, Randolph's own son could not help but be impressed and called it a tour de force, which it surely was. When Hitler began engulfing Europe from within and without in a matter of months, one wonders how many CBS listeners remembered the warning they had been given with such eloquence by their 27-year-old visitor.

Randolph's natural ability to coherently voice his thoughts off the cuff had not gone unnoticed by his father. It may come as a surprise to many that Winston Churchill was not a naturally fluent speaker. During his early days in the House of Commons, he used to work and fret over his speeches, and, when called upon to deliver, he read from his longhand script or memorized large passages. It was only after listening to his son that Winston gathered up the courage to trust his tongue.

In April 1935, Winston wrote to Clemmie, who was in Marseille on her way back from a trip to the Far East, primarily to reassure her that Randolph was recovering well from a severe attack of jaundice. However, he also added this piece of information. 'At sixty, I am altering my method of speaking, largely under Randolph's tuition, and now talk to the House of Commons with garrulous, unpremeditated flow. They seem delighted. But what a mystery the art of public speaking is!' Thankfully for the future of the world, Churchill mastered 'the mystery' in time to galvanize his nation in its greatest hour of need. And for that, to some extent at least, Randolph should claim a slice of the credit.

Having failed to secure a seat in the House of Commons on two occasions, Randolph was virtually handed free passage when a seat at Preston in Lancashire became vacant and was unopposed by Labour. There followed another of those Churchillian days when the chamber, putting its political prejudices to one side, rose to acclaim the sight of the Prime Minister introducing his own son to Parliament.

It was, by then, November 1940; the nation was at war, and Randolph had taken a commission in the 4th Hussars. A year before, he had also met and instantly fallen in love with the beautiful 19-year-old Pamela Digby. Within a month they were married. Both parties were reprimanded by their friends for being so foolhardy. Pamela recalled being told by Lord Stanley after the couple had been spotted at a restaurant, 'He's a very bad man and you shouldn't go out with people like that.'

Pamela protested, 'But he's one of your best friends!'

Ed Stanley replied, 'Yes, he is one of my best friends, but he shouldn't be one of YOUR best friends.'

Pamela, quoted by her son Winston, recalled how everyone was against them getting married, except the Prime Minister. 'Clemmie, my mother and father all said it was ridiculous . . . But old Winston was splendid. He brushed all the arguments aside and declared, "Nonsense! All you need to be married is champagne, a double bed and a box of cigars!"'

As we have seen, the marriage needed rather more than that to survive the hopeless test of separation that put paid to so many unions during the war. Much as he loved Pamela, there was no way Randolph was going to sit at home, kicking his heels with the 4th Hussars while the regiment remained in England rather than being posted to some glamorous theatre of war. Just like his father, action was what he craved, and he found it, of all places, at the White's Club bar. For years, this private establishment on St James', just a few steps from Piccadilly, had been his watering hole and, one evening, he heard talk of his friend Lieutenant Colonel Robert Laycock forming a Commando unit to be trained for special operations. That was more like it!

Having managed to pull the required strings and get himself transferred from the 4th Hussars to No. 8 Commando, Randolph found himself billeted in no great discomfort at the Marine Hotel, Largs, which lies on the Ayrshire coast, just south-west of Glasgow. No. 8 Commando consisted of ten troops of fifty men, each commanded by a captain and two subalterns. The men were hardened professional soldiers, handpicked from crack Guards regiments such as the Coldstream, Grenadiers and Household Cavalry. The officers, less so. By and large they consisted of the best drinkers from the White's Club bar. Evelyn Waugh, the acerbic author of *Scoop*, the bestselling novel about journalism, was to be found among their number.

Pamela visited Largs, and her assessment was telling. 'Bob Laycock's biggest problem was to find functions for this White's Club group because they were absolutely unemployable, while the men were excellent.'

It is a funny thing about the British upper classes – no matter how louche and lazy they may appear in repose, the boarding school upbringing through which all of them suffer, and most survive, tends to instil a hidden fibre of bloody-minded courage when called up to perform. They soon found themselves asked to provide proof of this behind the lines in North Africa. Randolph, barely able to contain his glee, went with them.

Tales of his exploits, hair-raising and occasionally hilarious, could fill chapters. But the attempt to blow up German ships with limpet mines so as to block Benghazi harbour in May 1942 does perhaps stand out. Led by Fitzroy Maclean, a linguist who was fluent in Italian, the raiding party infiltrated Rommel's lines and, inflating a rubber dinghy in which they intended to row out into the harbour so that they could attach the mines to side of ships, got as far as the quayside which was being guarded by an Italian unit.

However, their activities had, unsurprisingly, started to attract attention, so Maclean, a Scottish aristocrat whose laconic attitude towards adventure would inspire Ian Fleming's James Bond, went on the offensive before any suspicion could set in. As Randolph recounted in a letter to his father, Maclean demanded, in his perfect Italian, to know who was in charge. When a corporal emerged from a tent, Maclean ordered him to call out his guard and proceeded to give them all a terrific dressing down.

'We are German officers,' Randolph reported Maclean as saying, 'and we have come here to test your security arrangements. They are appalling. We have been past this sentry four or five times. He has not asked us once for our identity cards. For all he knows, we might be English saboteurs. We have brought great bags into the dock. How do you know they are not full of explosives? It is a very bad show indeed.'

It must have been difficult to stifle laughter. The Italian corporal offered a sheepish salute as the raiding party withdrew with their equipment, having ascertained that there was no way they could get far enough out into the harbour to carry out their mission without causing genuine suspicion.

They made it back to Alexandria, but on the last lap to Cairo, disaster struck. David Sterling, who later went on to captain England at rugby, was driving when an oncoming truck swung out of line and just touched their rear wheel, swinging their vehicle broadside across the road. Sterling was the only one who survived unscathed. Maclean, Randolph and a Sergeant Rose all suffered quite serious injuries, but Arthur Merton of *The Daily Telegraph*, who had hitched a ride in Alexandria, was crushed under the vehicle and died before they could get him to hospital.

Randolph suffered badly crushed vertebrae and spent several weeks in a Cairo hospital before being invalided back to England. He was to return soon enough, however, and went on to become involved fighting with Tito's partisans in Yugoslavia. As these stories suggest, the White's Club crowd had acquitted themselves well enough, and Randolph was no exception. For all his character faults, lack of courage could not be counted among them. He had his father's lust for danger and, despite being a trying companion on occasion, his superiors were never blind to the qualities he brought to any operation.

Maclean spelt this out in his book *Eastern Approaches* when discussing whom he should take with him for the parachute drop into Yugoslavia to join Tito's forces:

> Randolph, it occurred to me, would make a useful addition to my mission. There were some jobs – work, for instance, of a sedentary description at a large Headquarters full of touchy or sensitive staff officers – for which I would not have chosen him. But for my present purposes he seemed just the man. On operations I knew him to be thoroughly dependable, possessing both endurance and determination. He was also gifted with an acute intelligence and a very considerable background of general politics, neither of which would come amiss in Yugoslavia. I felt, too – rightly as it turned out – that he would get on well with the Yugoslavs, for his enthusiastic and at times explosive approach to life was not unlike their own. I knew him to be a stimulating companion, an important consideration in the circumstances under which we lived.

As predicted, Randolph succeeded as British Liaison Officer with the Partisans, who were impressed that the British Prime Minister had seen fit to allow his own son to join them in their fight. During numerous visits, Randolph acquitted himself with distinction in Yugoslavia, surviving various skirmishes with German troops until, on a trip back aboard a Dakota transport from Bari in Italy, the plane crashed while trying to land in bad weather near the Croatian village of Topusko. Evelyn Waugh, who was on the flight, was badly burned as the plane caught fire, and Randolph injured both legs as he tried to extract himself from the wrecked fuselage. Waugh found him, a short while later sitting in tears in a cornfield. Twice, he had tried to get back into the plane to try and rescue his batman, Corporal Sowman, but had been beaten back by the flames. The corporal, who had tended to Randolph's needs for the previous eighteen months, was burned to death.

It is interesting that Maclean cited Randolph's political acumen and 'acute intelligence' as reasons he wanted him in Yugoslavia, as Randolph had already revealed those qualities not long after his arrival in Cairo. Taking the bull by the horns in typical style, Randolph had telegraphed his father suggesting a major shake-up in the command of British Forces in the Middle East. Suggesting that the commanding officer, Field Marshal Archibald Wavell, be relieved of some of his duties, Randolph's cable began: 'Do not see how we can start winning the war here until we have competent civilian on spot to provide day to day political and strategic direction.'

He went on to suggest sending a member of the Cabinet and, after offering some names, signed off by saying, 'Please forgive me troubling you but consider present situation deplorable and urgent action vital to any prospects of success.'

The Prime Minister wasted no time in replying and acting. 'I have been thinking a good deal for some time on lines of your helpful and well-conceived telegram.' Randolph was delighted by the tone of his father's reply and even more so by the swift result. Wavell was soon replaced by General Sir Claude Auchinleck and, soon after, Oliver Lyttelton, a member of the War Cabinet, was appointed as Middle East Supremo so as to give political direction to the war effort in North Africa.

It was not Randolph's last imprint on that complicated theatre of war. As late as 1945, he was writing to Harold Macmillan, the future Prime Minister, whom Churchill had appointed as his political strategist in the Middle East, showing once again that his explosive temperament rarely interfered with his sober judgment. The issue on this occasion was the fate of Trieste, the Italian port that sits just a few miles from the border of what used to be Yugoslavia.

Speaking with Tito in Belgrade, Randolph realized that Trieste's sovereignty was at stake. His top-secret memo to Macmillan read in part:

> While talks continue and telegrams pass, Tito is rapidly infiltrating Trieste. His people will not, repeat not, go underground and will assert an ever growing political tyranny as the price for giving us military facilities . . . Under the terms of Italian capitulation our case is as overwhelming as the forces at our disposal and there is no legal reason why Trieste should be treated differently than Milan. But if we argue the matter with Tito, we are bound to lose in the long run if not sooner. If we act decisively Tito is bound to acquiesce. Force is the only thing which he respects. Please repeat this telegram to Prime Minister is you think it helpful.

Obviously, Macmillan did because Randolph's recommendation was heeded. Had it not been, the citizens of Trieste might have found themselves living under a different flag these past several decades.

What to make of the man? A conflicted personality only scratches at the surface. At moments like this one was left surmising that there were two complete, contrary human beings in one body. Robert Louis Stevenson, apparently, saw him coming, but Randolph Churchill would have given Dr Jekyll and Mr Hyde a run for their money.

Examples of Randolph's intuitive judgment continued in the post-war years when, having lost his Preston seat in Parliament, he made journalism his full-time career. Covering the visit of the new British Prime Minister, Anthony Eden, to see President Eisenhower in 1956 as the Suez Canal crisis erupted, Randolph was scathing in his condemnation of what he described as a 'pompous declaration and uninformative communique' and added, 'when statesmen and politicians cannot think of anything else to say, they always drag in God. Last night's declaration did it twice over . . . It was obvious from the start of the conference that, as no planning had been done by either side, no joint plan could be produced.'

The result, of course, was ultimate humiliation for Britain and its new leader as Eden, having failed to secure American backing for the invasion of the Suez Canal, was forced to withdraw. Continuing his merciless attack on Eden in *The Evening Standard*, Randolph wrote: 'Three months ago I wrote in this column that British foreign policy in the Middle East lay in ruins. I was rebuked by many friends who said this was an exaggerated and alarmist view. I doubt if these friends would rebuke me today.'

But rebuke him they did, especially those who were offended on behalf of the likeable but ineffectual Eden, who, largely as a result of ill health, was forced to tender his resignation to the Queen in January 1957. So who would succeed him? All the national newspapers opted for Rab Butler, who had been among the Conservative 'appeasers' in 1939. Only a lone voice, writing from the depths of Suffolk at his new country home at East Bergholt, proffered a different opinion. Having spent the night on the phone, rousing politicians and pundits of every stripe from their slumbers, Randolph felt confident enough to file this for *The Evening Standard*'s early morning edition: 'By tea time today, Mr. Harold Macmillan, Chancellor of the Exchequer in Sir Anthony Eden's former Government, will have been invited by the Queen to form a new administration.'

Once again, Randolph was right. It was an old-fashioned scoop, and Lord Beaverbrook, who owned *The Evening Standard* at the time, was quick to cable 'Congratulations on today's article. It is brilliant journalism.'

Even political foes, like the Labour MP Tom Driberg, joined in the plaudits. 'So Randolph Churchill's much-talked-of-scoop in *The Evening Standard* really was the result of intelligent guesswork, and of frequenting the right clubs and not, as some supposed, of a "leak" from his father . . .'

It said so much of the power of Randolph's personality and the respect in which he was held even by those who thoroughly disliked him, that he could use his vast array of 'contacts' in the true journalistic sense and get them to talk. The combination of that stentorian voice and the withering effect of his pen elicited information that few could call upon and he undoubtedly deserved the accolade afforded him by the eminent historian Hugh Trevor-Roper who wrote, 'Randolph Churchill is incomparably the best political journalist writing in England today'.

Considering the frequency of his whisky-fuelled outbursts of abusive temper, it was somewhat surprising that there were always those who could see past the bombast. One such man was John Betjeman, who credited Randolph with giving him the confidence to persevere with his poetry while at Oxford. At dinner parties, Randolph would encourage the embarrassed young poet to recite his latest poems. As Betjeman recounted to Winston Jr., 'Randolph used to ask for special favourites and then listen with eyes wide open, and laughter in his face, and lead the applause at the end. It was through him that I gained self-confidence.'

In 1961, by which time Randolph had set up a company called Country Bumpkins Ltd, so enamoured had he become of the Suffolk pastures surrounding East Bergholt, Betjeman replied to a request for a signature on one of his latest works, like this: 'Of course I'll sign it, old top . . . I look forward to a return to Country Bumpkin Ltd and to see how your landscape garden progresses. I go to Belfast quite soon so it will have to be when the primroses send their shy blossoms through the Suffolk earth.'

Unhappily, there was nothing poetic about the letter Randolph was to receive from one of his oldest friends, Pam Berry, the daughter of his godfather F.E. Smith. Something he had written in *The Evening Standard* had offended her, and no wonder. He made reference to the fact that she had 'omitted to shave her upper lip,' a gratuitously unpleasant comment about someone he had known and liked for decades. Why? What possessed him to be so insulting, not merely to political foes, which was one thing, but to respected female friends? What triggered this behaviour? Alcohol was frequently the answer in free-wheeling social occasions, but this was written about a charity function that Ms. Berry had organized. If he valued his friendships, it cost him dear because he lost this one.

In an attempt to apologize, Randolph took her a Christmas present, presumably as a peace offering. The door was slammed in his face. A letter followed.

I understand you think it unreasonable of me not to want to
see you. As you know, I used to be very fond of you. But the

simple fact is that after a sufficient number of wounds and injuries have been inflicted, indeed repeated, with monotonous regularity, over the years scars are produced which cannot be assuaged by a few words at a wedding reception or by a personal visit at Christmas . . . Believe me I feel no ill will to you and hope you will prosper in anything you do. On our old days of companionship and fun I look back with regret and sadness. But it wasn't I that put an end to them.

His tantrums and rudeness put paid to his second marriage, too. Randolph had married June Osborne, the 26-year-old daughter of an Army colonel, in November 1948, and their daughter, Arabella, was born just over a year later. When they moved into their new home in East Bergholt, Suffolk, June set about decorating the lovely house with enthusiasm, but she, too, had a temper, and soon the place rocked with the sound of their shouting matches.

Worse, it spilled over into the public domain. Arriving late for a dinner at a Sloane Square restaurant one evening, Randolph, already fuelled with alcohol, starting abusing June, calling her, according to witnesses, 'a paltry little middle class bitch'. The insults grew in ferocity, and his voice filled the room. Anita Leslie, a cousin of Winston Jr., eventually felt she had to intervene and told him he really should not be so rude to his wife.

'What the hell do you mean by butting into to a private conversation?' he roared, rattling he glassware on the tables. Anita, trying to be witty, replied, 'I am sorry, but I thought you were having a public conversation!'

Many of his friends felt that Randolph never properly understood how dreadful he could be, but he kept being reminded. Less than a year later, June left him.

Yet for every bullying and unforgivable act, there were counter-weights of bravery and courage, in both the physical and moral sense that allowed him to keep some friends, many under sufferance. One friend was Iain Macleod, who was Colonial Secretary in Ted Heath's Cabinet when the pair set off on an official visit to East Africa. Friend or not, Macleod was rather apprehensive at the thought of having to travel a long distance with such an opinionated companion, and his hopes rose when it appeared that Randolph had missed the plane.

Macleod related the scene. 'We waited and waited. Finally, after a small commotion, Randolph appeared and, brushing aside my papers and my civil servants, seated himself beside me. "Ho!" he said. "I suppose you thought I'd missed it!" "No," I said. "I just hoped."'

It would be wrong to suggest that Randolph went to bat for the coloured members of the Commonwealth, but apartheid regimes like that in South Africa, which he visited in 1960, offended his sense of decency. His friend Stephen Barber of *The Telegraph* recalled flying with him to Johannesburg as he wrestled with the immigration form.

There was a question about Race. 'Damned cheek!' Randolph exploded and began writing furiously all over the form and into the margins. Barber recalled it read like this:

> Race: human. But if, as I imagine, the object of this inquiry is to determine whether I have coloured blood in my veins, I am happy to be able to inform you that I do, indeed, so have. This is derived from one of my most revered ancestors, the Indian Princess Pocohontas, of whom you may not have heard but who was married to a settler named John Rolfe . . .

And so it continued. To a question demanding the purpose of his visit, he put 'Fun'. At the bottom of the form, where there was a choice of giving a signature or a mark, he chose the latter option, covering his thumb with ink from his ballpoint pen and imprinting it on the form.

Unsurprisingly, his passport was seized on arrival. Bellowing about entering a police state, he was allowed to proceed to his hotel. He had been asked to return to pick up his passport the following day, but that wasn't going to happen. 'They can damn well send it round to me,' was his response. Amazingly, the authorities did just that. As Randolph reported in the *News of the World*, 'Next morning, the Chief Immigration Officer waited upon me in my hotel. He offered profuse apologies, admitted I was fully entitled under South African law to put my mark instead of my signature and returned me my passport. This small incident was settled in a manner wholly satisfactory to me – unconditional surrender by the Union authorities.'

With his dreams of following his father's footsteps into 10 Downing Street long forgotten, Randolph still harboured ambitions of emulating Winston's biographical abilities. Winston's epic tome about his own father, Lord Randolph, had set the standard, and it was the younger man's dearest wish that he would be called upon to write the life of Winston S. Churchill.

However, he realized that writing reports in various newspapers, no matter how perceptive and brilliant, offered no proof of being able to produce a scholarly biographical work. So he set about writing the life of Lord Derby, a political figure and noted racehorse owner during the early part of the twentieth century. Edward Stanley, to use his birth name, was Secretary of State for War three times between 1916 and 1924 and also spent a period as British Ambassador to Paris.

Lord Derby might have been an unlikely choice as a proving ground for Randolph's biographical skills, but it worked. Praise flooded in from the likes of Michael Foot and Roy Jenkins, as well as this reaction from the then-Prime Minister Harold Macmillan, which Randolph treasured: 'Your book constitutes in my opinion an absolutely first class account of the politics of some thirty or forty years. You have used very skilfully the figure of Lord Derby on which to hang this admirably written and very well documented work.'

But there was, of course, one person whose approval he desired more than any other. In May 1960, Winston Churchill wrote this to his son: 'I think that your biography of Derby is a remarkable work and I should be happy that you should write my official biography when the time comes . . .'

Knowing how his emotions could spring to the surface, it is hard not to imagine Randolph's eyes filling with tears of unbounded joy as he read those words. It was what he desired more than anything in life, not only just the great task that was being offered, but the fact that he had earned, to some significant degree, his father's trust in him.

Randolph concluded his return letter thus: 'Thank you again from the bottom of my heart for a decision which, apart from what I have already said, adds a good deal to my self-esteem and will, I trust, enable me to do honour in filial fashion, to your extraordinarily noble and wonderful life . . .'

Back in 1947, Winston had urged his son to give life his purpose and 'to try and build yourself a castle'. In his book *A Father's Son*, young Winston picked up on this theme when he wrote:

> By turning his back on the shallowness of a life that cantered around the bar and gambling tables of White's Club, putting down deep roots in the countryside and producing a serious political biography, he had made his landfall. Aged forty nine, he now set about building his castle, which was to be a monument to the father he loved so dearly and admired so intensely . . .

However, Winston Jr., did not – indeed could not – shy away from the great sorrow of their relationship. He added, 'It was a tragedy that these two human beings, so deeply devoted to each other, sharing many characteristics and espousing all the same causes, should have such an antagonistic relationship.'

Gaining the approval of his father to write his life story was not the only joy that came to Randolph relatively late in life. A couple of years earlier, he had fallen in love at first sight. Natalie Bevan, who lived with her ex-naval officer husband, Bobby Bevan, in Boxted, just a few miles from Bergholt, had come round to see a friend, Lord Kinross, who had happened to be staying with Randolph. Anita Leslie described what happened:

'Patrick Kinross opened the front door and Randolph had walked across the hall to greet her. He stopped in his tracks and stood looking at Natalie for a long time in the strangest way. She looked back at him silently. The rapport was instantly established. After a moment of what one might almost call extraordinary recognition, Randolph stepped forward and took her by the hand. 'Come out onto the terrace and smell the roses,' he said. Then he addressed her almost tearfully. 'I have been waiting for you for so long. I love you.'

Incredibly, Randolph's feelings was reciprocated and, almost imme-diately, they became lovers. Equally amazing was the manner in which the relationship developed. Despite Randolph's entreaties, Natalie refused to leave her husband but also refused to stop seeing Randolph. Until his death, she paid regular visits for afternoon trysts with her lover at Bergholt, a state of affairs that Bobby Bevan seemed to accept with equanimity. Not the least extraordinary aspect of this unusual situation was the fact that Randolph, realizing no doubt that he was on delicate ground, was always exceptionally cordial to Bobby whenever social activities threw them together, and there was never a hint of a row.

Nor, indeed, were there any explosions between Randolph and Natalie, as there had been when he was married to June. Asked if she had ever found Randolph troublesome, Natalie replied, 'Certainly not! He knew I would not have stood for it!' Refusing to accept any kind of bullying was, indeed, the basis of Randolph's few lasting friendships. As his son sadly noted, to anyone revealing a sign of weakness, Randolph 'could behave insufferably'.

He was, however, mostly quite reasonable with the group of young men who took on the onerous job of becoming one of his researchers, both on the Lord Derby book and, later, when Randolph finally started work on the greatest project of his life, the biography of Winston Churchill.

By then, of course, the great man had died. As we have noted in an earlier chapter, the entire family, save for Winston's daughter Diana,

189

who had died the previous year, gathered at his home at Hyde Park Gate to celebrate his 90th birthday on 30 November 1964. Randolph concluded the candlelit evening with a toast to 'the author of our being'.

The end was not long in coming. On the night of 9 January 1965, Winston Churchill suffered a massive stroke and never regained consciousness. But even then he fought on and did not succumb until the 24th, which, one can only presume, was exactly what he wanted because it was the day of his own father's death 70 years earlier.

For Randolph the day of the funeral was a physical as well as an emotional ordeal. It had become clear in the previous months that his body was feeling the effects of smoking 80 to 100 cigarettes and consuming well over a bottle of whisky a day. His son Winston describes the difficulties he faced in walking the entire funeral route, refusing, as he would, the comfort of a ride in one of the Queen's carriages.

> As we climbed Ludgate Hill on the final lap to St Paul's, the naval gun carriage crew strained at their heavy load and the horses pulling the carriages were slipping. I glanced anxiously at my father by my side who, by now, was very out of breath. It was an ordeal for him but, determined as always to be 'steady on parade,' he gritted his teeth, stuck out his jaw and soldiered on.

He would soldier on through the first two volumes of his father's life, driving his team of researchers hard, knowing that he might not have all the time he needed. One of his chief helpers was a young man from Oxford called Martin Gilbert who was destined to play a pivotal role in the 'Great Biography'. However, there was a crisis when, soon after the team's workload had risen to absurd heights when Randolph offered to help his son to write a 'quickie' book on the Six-Day War in the Middle East. Gilbert wrote Randolph a letter beginning: 'I'm afraid I have bad news. The doctors say I cannot continue as I am without SERIOUS danger to my health.'

Randolph, himself in increasingly poor health, was devastated. However, contrary to what some people might have expected, the pair remained good friends, a situation which had much to do with the fact that Gilbert, having recovered his own health, would accept the onerous and humbling task of finishing the 'Great Biography' after Randolph's death.

Given that Randolph had a large slice of a nicotine-stained lung removed and never reduced his alcohol intake as much as he should, it was perhaps surprising that he survived the last years of his life as well as he did. He had Natalie for support, of course, and for much of the time life at Bergholt, though busy, trundled along in a manner that Randolph had come to love – much work on the garden which had become his pride and joy and numerous visits from friends, relatives and neighbours.

One such neighbour, Penny Corke, later to become the wife of the show business lawyer Keith Turner, remembers happy afternoons playing with Arabella as a child. 'My grandmother lived directly opposite the Churchill house,' Penny recalls.

> We used to rush over during school holidays to ride ponies and play with Arabella who was much less of a wild young thing at that age than she became in her hippie days. She was probably afraid of her father although, mostly, I remember him being very kind to us and only shouting at us to keep quiet occasionally because he was trying to work.

Penny remembers meeting both Winstons. Firstly, she was the beneficiary of a five-pound note – a big sum of money in those days – which the former Prime Minister gave to the kids to spend at the local sweet shop. The second occasion was when young Winston arrived at the controls of a helicopter that landed on the croquet lawn before he drove them all into Ipswich to see *Lawrence of Arabia*.

'They were good times,' she says. 'My cousin Zoe Saunders who was older than me recalls Randolph being especially kind to my grandmother at local functions when she needed help.'

Although spending more time tending to his roses and bluebells, Randolph didn't stop travelling entirely. He went off to Barbados to spend some time writing in the sun and, on the way, stopped in Washington DC to see Robert and Ethel Kennedy, who had become good friends.

Towards the end of a family dinner at the Kennedy home at Hickory Hill in Virginia, Bobby had started to talk about his brother and the book being written by William Manchester on the assassination. Clearly, it was painful for Bobby to talk about it, and he suddenly changed the subject, bringing up Randolph's second volume on Winston. He had only read the reviews and asked when Randolph expected the project to be finished. 'In 1970,' Randolph replied. 'By then we will have all President Kennedy's papers sorted,' Bobby went on. 'Would you like to edit them?'

Randolph was stunned. 'Yes, of course, I would,' he replied, adding, 'and should I write his Life too?'

'Certainly,' Bobby replied, saying that he would like it done in the same objective manner as his book on his father.'

Writing to Natalie Bevan back in Suffolk, Randolph said, 'It was like being given three Nobel Prizes for Literature piled on top of each other. It was the greatest compliment ever paid to me in my life. After all, I had a natural right to do my father's Life. This is something so extraordinary that I could hardly believe it. I shall now have to plan to live an extra five years till 1976. You must look after me.'

Natalie tried, but the task proved beyond her. On the morning of 6 June 1968 – the anniversary of D-Day, Winston Jr. noted – he received a phone call from one of the chief researchers at Bergholt, to say that Randolph had died in his sleep. We shall never know to what extent the news that had arrived from Los Angeles just two days earlier, had affected him. June 4th was the day Robert Kennedy was assassinated.

So the plans talked of that evening at Hickory Hill were torn asunder, destined never to be fulfilled because of an assassin's bullet and, in Randolph's case, a lifetime of self-inflicted wounds. One man, in the opinion of many observers, had been on the verge of gaining the nomination of the Democratic Party for President and would probably have entered the White House. The other could have cemented his place as one of the great journalists and biographers of the twentieth century.

Both men had been vilified by their enemies while drawing deep affection and loyalty from those who could see past tough exteriors and appreciate the finer points of their complicated natures. Both still had so much to do, and Randolph, certainly, would have benefited greatly from Bobby's friendship. Two great families could have been drawn closer than they already were. But it was not to be.

Robert Kennedy was in the process of changing people's perception of him because Jack's death had allowed him to shed the image of the tough little brother and seek solace in Camus and Aeschylus.

It would have been too late for Randolph to change to a similar degree but at least some of the shrewder observers of the British literary and political scene were beginning to realize that there was much more to the man than an explosive and wounding temper.

That, in itself, was a tragedy because Randolph Churchill had served his country, and not least his father at critical hours of need, with skilful fervour and devotion. Perverse and contrary to the last, he had just done his best to conceal it.

Epilogue

On 11 August 1991 a conference was held to celebrate the 50th anniversary of FDR's and Churchill's risky meeting at sea. Appropriately, it was held at Placentia Bay where the destroyer USS *Valdez* had been positioned off as a backdrop to commemorate the story that we have written here; the story of the Atlantic Charter whose creation had done so much to bring two great leaders and their two great nations closer together at a moment of extreme peril in the history of the world.

The words outlining the Eight Points of the Charter were not written naively. Neither Franklin Roosevelt nor Winston Churchill regarded them as laws never to be broken. Both men had seen too much of life to expect that. In a speech he made to the House of Commons near the end of the war, Churchill made it clear that horizons were limited. 'We are now entering a world of imponderables, and at every stage occasions for self-questioning arise. It is a mistake to look too far ahead. Only one link in the chain of destiny can be handled at a time . . . No one can guarantee the future of the world.'

However, in an attempt to lead it towards more civilized pastures than were apparent during the early years of the fraught and bedevilled 1940s, FDR and Churchill had laid out guidelines that were intended to form the groundwork for a better world.

As early as New Year's Day 1942, the Charter was being used as a template for a 'Declaration by United Nations' signed by twenty-six nations at a meeting in Washington DC. It would be more than three years before the United Nations came into existence as an entity – fifty-one nations signing up as members in San Francisco on 24 October 1945.

Given that both FDR and Churchill were starkly aware of the disaster that followed the First World War, when the rambling arguments of the Paris Peace Conference patched together by the United States, Britain, France and Italy in 1919 had created more problems than they solved, it was inevitable that they would be highly sensitive to the need for something better. The Atlantic Charter sowed the seeds for that and its full intentions eventually saw fruition in the formation of the United Nations.

In the view of the Columbia University Professor Volker Berghahn, who was born in Berlin in 1938, the urgency felt by both leaders when they met at Placentia Bay needs to be contextualized by the failure of the League of Nations and the rise of fascism. Even as they discussed the crisis at hand, Roosevelt and Churchill were thinking ahead. 'It was clear that, presuming Hitler could be defeated, the aftermath would have to be very different from the failures emanating from 1919,' said Professor Berghahn in a recent conversation: 'This accelerated their thinking in terms of a Western Alliance as was demonstrated with the emergence of The Atlantic Charter.'

As we have demonstrated in the preceding chapters, the existence of the free world was teetering on a precipice. 'The year of 1941 proved to be the turning point,' says Berghahn. 'Britain was desperately hanging on alone; the Nazis had seized Western Europe and were camped outside Moscow ready to win the battle for east,' Berghahn says. 'Only the icy winter and the surprising gallantry of Stalin's troops stopped them.'

Hitler's forces ended up losing 900,000 men – a catastrophe for the Nazis that changed the course of the war. Until America's entry into the conflict following Pearl Harbor in December 1941, the outcome of the war was far from clear, which made the list of aims laid out by FDR and Churchill in August that year all the more pertinent. The Eight Points of the Charter came, as a United Nations document states, as a message of hope to occupied countries, and the fact that it had little legal validity did not detract from its value. 'The value of any treaty lies in the sincerity of its spirit,' said the UN correspondent, and it was the spirit of cooperation and friendship that grew so quickly between Franklin Roosevelt and Winston Churchill that added impetus to the turning of the tide. They were the leaders, without whom, western democracy would not have survived.

It is poignant, looking back to 1991, to realize that the Remembrance Ceremonies, carried out partially on land at Placentia Bay while the USS *Valdez* rode at anchor, were suffused with an optimism that is difficult recreate today. Brian Fall, the British High Commissioner, who was one of three speakers that day, captured that mood when he spoke of Britain, Canada, France and the United States as well as Germany, Italy and Japan working together with the Soviet Union following the London summit with Mikhail Gorbachev.

Referring back to 1941, Fall, as documented by Douglas Brinkley and David Facey-Crowther, said, 'More often than not in the course of history, it has been the guns of fighting ships that have reverberated around the world. In the case of the *Augusta* and the *Prince of Wales*, the real power lay in ideas; ideas that, over the last 50 years, have not ceased to reverberate around a world that they continue to challenge.'

The optimistic mood was backed by fact. Gorbachev was in the process of allowing the Soviet Union to transform itself as it gave way to Boris Yeltsin's liberalism; the Berlin Wall had come down, allowing freedom to flood East Germany; South Africa was no longer an apartheid nation, and Nelson Mandela had walked out of prison to become an inspiration on the world stage. There was every reason to believe that the twentieth century would hand over the world to the twenty-first in much better shape than most people could have imagined after the horrors that preceded it.

Yet now, as we near the end of the second decade of that twenty-first century in a world that social media has made almost impossible to control, it is difficult to believe that two leaders of such stature, vision and determination as Franklin Roosevelt and Winston Churchill can step forward to ward off the pockets of populism that are springing up, promoting ideas that endanger the tenets of decency, understanding and fair play that lie at the heart of what the Atlantic Charter intended.

Let us pray that the guns remain silent and that the words, ideas and judgments profiled in this book continue to be at the forefront of free peoples as they hold their nations accountable.

Bibliography

Adams, Henry, *Harry Hopkins: A Biography*, Putnam, 1977.

Brands, H.W., *Traitor to His Class*, Anchor Book/Random House, 2009.

Brinkley, Douglas, and David R. Facey-Crowther, *The Atlantic Charter*, St Martin's Press, 1994.

Cadogan, Sir Alexander, *The Diaries of Sir Alexander Cadogan*, edited by David Dilks, Putnam, 1972.

Carew, Michael, *The Power to Persuade*, University Press of America, 2005.

Churchill, Winston S., *His Father's Son*, Weidenfeld & Nicholson, 1996.

Cimino, Al, *Roosevelt & Churchill – A Friendship That Saved the World*, Chartwell Books an imprint of The Quarto Group, N.D.

Colville, John, *The Fringes of Power – Downing Street Diaries 1939–45*, Hodder & Stoughton, 1985.

Davis, Kenneth S., *FDR – The War President*, Random House. 2000.

Demont, John, 'A Meeting of Giants', *Maclean's Magazine*, Canada, 1991.

Felzenberg, Alan, *The Leaders We Deserved*, BasicBooks, 2008.

Freidel, Frank, *Franklin D. Roosevelt – A Rendezvous with Destiny*, Little Brown, 1990

Furse, Anthony, *Wilfrid Freeman*, Spellmount Ltd, 2000.

Groom, Winston, *The Allies*, National Geographic, 2018.

Jenkins, Roy, *Churchill*, Macmillan, 2001.

Kimball, Warren F., *Churchill & Roosevelt*, Princeton University Press, 1984.

Lukacs, John, *Five Days in London – May 1940*, Yale University Press, 1999.

Manchester, William, *The Last Lion: Winston Spencer Churchill, 1874–1922*, Delta Books, 1983.

Manchester, William, *The Last Lion: Winston Spencer Churchill, 1922–1940*, Delta Books, 1988.

Manchester, William and Paul Reid, *The Last Lion: Winston Spencer Churchill, 1940-1965*, Bantam Books, 2012.

Meacham, Jon, *Franklin & Winston*, Random House, 2003.

Morton, H.V., *The Atlantic Meeting*, Methuen/Reg Saunders, 1943.

Pogue, Forrest C., *George Marshall*, Viking Press, 1966.
Roberts, Andrew, *Churchill – Walking with Destiny*, Viking, 2018.
Roll, David L., *The Hopkins Touch: Harry Hopkins and the Forging of the Alliance to Defeat Hitler*, Oxford University Press, 2013.
Roosevelt, Curtis, *Too Close to the Sun*, Public Affairs, 2008.
Sandys, Celia, *Chasing Churchill*, Tauck, 2003.
Shermwood, Robert E., *Roosevelt & Hopkins*, Harper & Brothers, 1948.
Smith, Jean Edward, *FDR*, Random House, 2007.
Stafford, David, *Roosevelt & Churchill – Men of Secrets*, Overlook Press, 2000.
Unger, Debi & Irwin, *George Marshall*, Harper Collins, 2014.
Welles, Benjamin, *Sumner Welles*, St Martin's Press, 1997.
Welles, Sumner, *Where Are We Heading*, Harper and Brothers, 1946.
Wilson, Theodore A., *The First Summit*, Houghton Miflin, 1969.

Index